THE CHRISTIAN R
TO
INDUSTRIAL CAP

To Denzil Jenkins
with best wishes
from Anne & Willie Charlton

The Christian Response to Industrial Capitalism

William Charlton
Tatiana Mallinson
Robert Oakeshott

Sheed & Ward
London

ISBN 0–7220–1975–0

Published in Great Britain in 1986 by
Sheed & Ward Limited,
2, Creechurch Lane,
London, EC3A 5AQ

Book production Bill Ireson

Filmset by Waveney Typesetters, Norwich, Norfolk
Printed and bound by
A. Wheaton & Co. Ltd., Exeter, Devon

Contents

Preface

In July 1982 a conference was held at Plater College, Oxford. Its theme was Catholic Social Teaching and Worker Ownership, and it had three sponsors: Plater College itself, the Christian Association of Business Executives, and Job Ownership Limited. Cardinal Basil Hume, Archbishop of Westminster, and the Rt Hon David Steel MP were the conference's joint patrons. Among those who attended it were the three present writers.

One thing which emerged very clearly from the conference was the need for a simple, introductory book which would outline not only the development of Catholic thinking about the social problems which have followed industrialisation, but the thinking of other Christian bodies and individuals, and which would, if possible, place the Christian response as a whole in relation to the response of progressive reformers outside the Christian tradition. This book is an attempt to meet that need. The field is an enormous one, and we are vividly aware that there are important areas we have not been able to cover at all, and others we have covered only superficially. It has seemed worthwhile, however, to present our findings to the public rudimentary as they are. We hope that others will be stimulated to go deeper into the subject and that meanwhile young people in particular will be enabled to get to grips with these issues at an earlier age than we ourselves did.

We are glad to be able to acknowledge help of various kinds from the following: J. A. E. de Bauw, Rev John Breen, Rev Paul Brett, Guy and Molly Clutton-Brock, James Cornford, Princess Djordjadze, Rev J. R. Frese SJ, Dr and Mrs A. Hellen, Linda Henry, Walter Kendall, Rev P. Laurent SJ, Mrs M. Melotte, Gemma Nesbitt, Rev Robert Nind, Alphonse Ramilet, Prof Rezsohazy, and the Librarian of Ushaw College.

CHAPTER ONE

The Social Problem

In the second half of the eighteenth century a process began in England which was to spread to other countries and which in some parts of the world is still going on. It was the French who found for it the name 'the Industrial Revolution'. It comprises three elements: (i) There is mechanisation, or the introduction of machines and techniques by which one man can do the work formerly done by several; (ii) The population grows – in England and Wales between 1780 and 1910 it grew from 8,000,000 to 36,000,000 persons; (iii) The growth is concentrated in expanding towns, while country districts stagnate or are depopulated. A key feature, part cause and part effect, of these processes, is that work is no longer put out to people in their homes, but workers are concentrated in factories where strict rules of discipline are enforced by overseers.

It is obvious that in itself, labour-saving machinery is desirable. It shortens the hours of work needed to keep a population in being, and brings within the reach of everyone things that otherwise could be afforded only by the rich. Industrialisation would naturally be expected to produce leisure and luxury, and in fact it has almost always in the long run caused a rise in living standards throughout society. Nevertheless it has also generated problems which collectively are sometimes called, especially by Continental writers, 'the social problem'.

In the first place, it is inevitable that industrialisation should cause a profound dislocation of people's lives. If the skills traditional in a society cease to be useful, if the balance of ages is altered and population outstrips the accommodation available, if people are forced – on this account and to obtain food and work – to move into unfamiliar environments it is obvious that connections with the past and the known will be broken, and lives thrown into confusion.

There is intense resentment at the discipline imposed on the new factory labour by the factory owners and their overseer henchmen. There is resentment at the loss of freedom embodied in the shift away from the partly self-controlled situation of the former outworkers. There is resentment too at the exploitation embodied in the grossly unequal wage 'bargain' between the new factory owners and their workforces. And it is widely remarked and regretted that all or almost all customary interpersonal relationships and responsibilities as between master and men have been swept away by the hated new wage bargain, by what Marx called the cash nexus.

Some of the worst effects of industrialisation are transitional; once the shift from agriculture and handicraft to industry has been effected they diminish and may even disappear. But their disappearance cannot be counted on. Mechanisation is not a process that occurs once and for all. It continues, and in advanced societies today under the influence of the electronics industry it is accelerating. In many countries long-term unemployment has been increasing, and with it unhappiness, demoralisation and violence. What wonder, if people are leaving school with no prospect of ever doing anything except casual, unskilled labour?

Even where the problems of transition have been smoothed out, other problems remain. In Western Europe where it began, industrialisation established itself in the form of industrial capitalism. By 'industrial capitalism' we mean a system in which there are in principle two parties to an undertaking: a proprietor who owns the assets and decides how they are to be used, and workers who contract to labour under the proprietor's direction.

The first proprietors were often individuals who themselves worked in the enterprise. As time went on, these were replaced by persons who had less and less connection with it. In the private sector of modern industry the assets belong to shareholders who mostly have no knowledge of the business and no say in it whatever; and an intermediate class of managers has arisen who run the business, often on more or less bureaucratic lines. At the same time there has developed, most conspicuously in the Communist bloc, a public sector in which the electorate as a whole, or their representatives or rulers, may be regarded as the proprietors, and the management merges into the bureaucracy proper. Despite obvious and important differences, both these systems, the private and the State, can be viewed as varieties of the same thing, industrial capitalism in the broad sense.

Industrial capitalism is not a product of the Industrial Revolution. In essence it existed in the fifth century BC. The Athenian statesman Nicias had a thousand slaves in the silver mines, and it was with brilliant irony that Plato chose as the setting for his great dialogue on justice, *The Republic*, the house of Cephalus, a man who employed 120 slaves in an armaments factory. By the beginning of the fifteenth century the silk and woollen industries were organised in Italy on capitalist lines. The Industrial Revolution was not the inception of the system but its expansion to a state of dominating the economic scene.

It is prone to two defects. It tends, especially in the private form, to deprive the worker of his just share in the value generated by his labour, and gives this to the proprietor. The result has often been a flagrantly unfair distribution of income and wealth. It also tends to deny the worker any real control over the conduct of the enterprise. The democratic principle asserts that people have a right to choose who will govern them, and to a say in the decisions about government policy. As Seebohm Rowntree observed, 'democracy often stops at the factory gate'.

Christianity has always professed a concern with human well-being in this world as well as in the next. Did Christians perceive the social problems to which the Industrial Revolution gave rise? Were they able to implement or propose any solutions to them? Or did they exacerbate them?

In 1904–5 Max Weber put forward (in *The Protestant Ethic and the Spirit of Capitalism*[1]) a thesis about the relationship between Christianity and modern capitalism which has attracted much discussion. He defined capitalism in general as the systematic pursuit of profit, an activity the purpose of which is to end up with assets more valuable than those with which you started. Capitalism in this sense, he observed, has existed in many ages and societies; but in the modern West it is distinguished by three further features of which the first is the most striking and important: the organisation of free labour under imposed rules of factory discipline, the removal of work from the home, and systematic book-keeping. This development, Weber reasoned, could not have occurred unless a fair number of employers and employees had accepted that work in profit-making business is a good thing for its own sake; and it did not occur before the seventeenth century or outside Europe and North America because this is a difficult and surprising thing to accept. What, then, led to its acceptance? Weber finds the answer in Protestantism. In the Middle Ages, if you wanted to lead a specially holy life, you joined a religious order. Luther rejected this course and, looking for something to put in its place, introduced the idea of a 'calling' (*Beruf*). According to this idea, one's job, one's ordinary economic activity in the world, is a way of serving God. Weber thought this was the extent of Luther's contribution; for the rest, Luther was a traditionalist, suspicious of commerce and wordly riches. The Calvinists, however, oppressed by the frightening doctrine of Predestination, were encouraged to immerse themselves in capitalist activity in order to banish doubts about whether or not they were saved; and to Puritans of an ascetic turn, Pietists, Quakers and others to whom monastic life was closed, idleness seemed a sin, and hard work, either as an entrepreneur or as an employee, a legitimate form of asceticism.

R. H. Tawney, in his foreword to Talcott Parsons's English translation of Weber and again in his own book *Religion and the Rise of Capitalism*, has criticised this thesis. The accusation that Weber places 'too exclusive an emphasis upon intellectual and ethical forces' Weber himself in some measure anticipates in his Chapter II; but it may be questioned whether Protestantism really did have a monopoly of the work ethic. Some historians[2] detect the spirit of capitalism in the free economy of the twelfth century. It is already robust in fifteenth-century Italy, and the great expansion of Dutch capitalism preceded the capitalists' conversion to Calvinism in the 1560s. Our concern is not with capitalism in general but with industrial capitalism. We may concede that an esteem of hard work for its own sake was more marked among Protestants than among Catholics. Weber himself, however, lays emphasis on the organisation, in modern capitalism, of free labour. Why was there this labour to organise? To answer that we must look, in Tawney's words, to 'economic organisation and social structure'. In the eighteenth century, England had a large population of persons with nothing but their labour to sell.

Weber and those for whom he wrote probably thought that to have given rise to capitalism was a feather (if it could be shown to belong there) in religion's cap. Another school of thought has viewed religion with less friendly eyes. Bakunin speaks for it when he says:

> We are convinced that the most harmful of all things, for humanity and for truth and progress, is the Church. Could it be otherwise? Does it not fall on the Church to pervert the younger generations and especially the women? Is it not She who, by her dogmas, her lies, her stupidity and her ignominy, seeks to destroy logical thinking and science? . . . Does she not turn what is living into a corpse, cast aside freedom, and preach the eternal slavery of the masses for the benefit of tyrants and exploiters?[3]

These are strong words, but they are not uttered without excuse. In 1788 Louis XVI's minister Necker published *The Importance of Religious Opinions*[4], which was translated into English the same year by Mary Wollstonecraft, later the wife of William Godwin. In this book Necker maintains that 'it belongs to the essence of the laws of property to introduce and maintain constantly immense disparities'[5]. The arguments of orthodox economists are wholly incapable of persuading the poor that it is to their interest to take part in a system 'in which one could say that one part of society had been formed solely for the convenience of the other', and only religion will suffice to keep them acquiescent.

On a careful reading, however, even Necker seems rather ingenuous than cynical, and it is difficult to argue that Christianity in itself favours exploitation and repression. The Industrial Revolution occurred in countries which were, in name at least, Christian. Those who caused the social problems and who exploited the poor and weak usually professed Christianity and tried to obtain the support, or at least the neutrality, of the Christian authorities. They often succeeded. But then those who grappled with the problems and sided with the exploited, even when like Proudhon they were bitterly anti-clerical, had their preconceptions and outlook influenced or even shaped by Christianity. Many of them were motivated directly by what they thought were Christian principles, and in thinking this, it will be argued, they were right. More plausible than Bakunin's accusations are those of indolence, weakness and cowardice, of failure to proclaim Christian principles and to denounce injustice through fear of losing privilege and wealth.

> The bloodiest persecutions have done less harm to the Church than the courtly servility of bishops.

The author of those words was no anti-clerical but himself a bishop, W. von Ketteler[6], one of the leading Catholic social reformers of the nineteenth century.

This book is not intended either as an indictment of the Church or as a piece of white-washing or panegyric. We shall consider the Christian response to industrial capitalism not in order to reach a moral judgement on our Christian ancestors, not to decide whether they did as well as could reasonably be expected, but to obtain light from the past on problems which are still with us.

Our field of enquiry is vast and rich; it has been necessary to impose limits of time and space, and to apply further principles of selection within them. We start with the mid-eighteenth century, though there is, of course, no exact date at which the Industrial Revolution began. It was made possible by earlier events, and it hardly became noticeable until later. Industrialisation is still occurring in some parts of the world, and has not yet reached others. We shall concentrate, however, on the areas where it occurred first: Britain and that adjacent part of Europe which comprises north-eastern France, Belgium and West Germany.

It was in Britain and France (one might say it was through a fertile interaction between Paris and Edinburgh) that the economic theories were developed which sanctioned the rise of industrial capitalism; and it was in those countries too that the first attempts were made to devise solutions to the problems which ensued. During the nineteenth century Germany gave birth to a distinct and fresh approach to these problems from which the communist regimes, which govern half the world today, are descended. In the interests of brevity and simplicity we say less in this book about Belgium than about Germany or France; but it may be stated here that the space we give to them is no index either of the independence of Christians in Belgium, or of their practical achievements. We have not included Belgium in our survey of the non-Christians as their contribution in that country was of practical rather than ideological significance and warrants another kind of study. There was extensive industrial development in North America in the nineteenth century, and we shall see American Christians from an early date proposing alternatives to conventional capitalism. But North America had other social problems[7] besides those stemming from industrialisation, and it has seemed to us that on issues connected specifically with industry, Christian social thought formed mainly in Europe.

We shall try to follow Christian thinking in the technically advanced countries down to the present, but we have given more attention to the formation of Christian social thought and hence to the period before 1939, than to its most recent developments, the significance of which it is too early to assess. Thought and action in the less developed countries we have regretfully but largely ignored. Our excuse is that insofar as the problems in these countries are the same as those which appeared in Europe, it is enough to say what the first Christian response was; everyone now recognises these problems, and all parties join in discussing them. Insofar, on the other hand, as the difficulties of developing countries are new – and the shanty towns of Latin America are not, in fact, exactly the same as the slums of industrial England – they call for a separate study.

Industrial capitalism raises a number of major issues of principle which must be covered by any theory which is to be an adequate theoretical basis for tackling social problems. It may be useful to formulate some of these issues here.

1. What is the moral basis of the private ownership of productive property? How are ownership rights legitimately acquired? Are they absolute? If not, to what conditions are they subject?

2. What are the relative rights and responsibilities of capital and labour? What rights have those who work in an enterprise to direct it? To what proportion are they entitled of the fruit of their labour?
3. What is a just wage?
4. What rights have workers to combine to get higher wages, better working conditions, etc.? What kinds of association are most desirable? Should owners, managers and workers belong to the same associations? What goals should an association have? What means can it use, and in particular what rights, under what conditions, has it to effect a strike?
5. What should be the relationship between industrial enterprises and the State? How far should the State direct industrial activity?
6. What principles should govern competition, combination and the scale of enterprises?
7. What is the relative contribution of individuals and societies to the creation of wealth and to economic activity generally?
8. What is the purpose of economic activity? What part has work to play in the best life for man?

In the chapters which follow we hope to show how Christian answers to these questions emerged. We shall give prominence to the official pronouncements and initiatives of churches and other organised religious bodies. But we shall also consider the writings and projects of private individuals when they are inspired by Christian religious principles and belief. If some of these individuals are little known to fame, we should reflect that the value of a suggestion or a model of action is not to be measured by the quantity of support or imitation it receives.

There are two matters which fall outside our enquiry but which should be mentioned here. The first is slavery. We can better understand the way in which the Industrial Revolution proceeded in England and France if we remember that those countries accounted between them for more that three-quarters of the slave trade. Cobbett complained that the most prominent campaigners against slavery were themselves responsible for acute misery among workers in England. But however the material conditions of life in English manufacturing towns may have compared with those on American plantations, that status of the slave was a more blatant injustice, and a society could hardly be expected to feel troubled in conscience about its free working population at home while it still permitted slavery in its colonies, as England did until 1833 and France until 1848.

The second matter is land reform. This is relevant in two ways. Social thinking for a long time took place against the background of a sometimes unrecognised assumption that agriculture dominates economic life. This was believed both by the authors of laissez-faire economics, the French physiocrats and the youthful Adam Smith, and by its first critics, Mably and Morelly in France, Wallace, Spence and Ogilvie in Britain. With some notable exceptions, later ideas about reform in an industrial society are the offspring of projects for land reform. But more important, it has been held by some Christian writers, not without reason, that industrialisation generated the problems it did chiefly because it occurred in a society in which monstrous inequalities already existed and were generally accepted. Writing in 1883 Bateman reports that out of a population in England and Wales of 25,000,000, only one person in a hundred owned as much as one acre of land, and nine persons out of ten owned no land whatever.[8] The situation had, no doubt, been deteriorating throughout the nineteenth century, but it is safe to say that in the mid-eighteenth century the great majority of the English were landless, and only a tiny minority had more than the smallest of small holdings. When the Industrial Revolution started, then, most people had no means of support apart from their labour, and a small number of proprietors owned all the means of production from which this majority would have to be supported. These proprietors had virtually no legal responsibilities except a local poor rate. This situation, it may be thought, must inevitably generate problems as soon as the processes described at the beginning of this chapter got under way; especially as workers were prevented by the Combination Acts from joining together in trade unions.

As industrial capitalism dug itself in as the dominant power in the land it clearly did so at the expense of working people. The latter were politically disenfranchised: they had no votes. They were, for practical purposes, economically disenfranchised as well. They had no property; and social welfare provisions were minimal. They were prevented by the then laws of the land from using their collective power through combination and the forming of trade unions. Today the most glaring of these injustices have been removed in the Western democracies on which we are largely focusing. But the distribution of wealth and property remains very unequal. And the great mass of working people, although free to form and join trade unions, have very little in the way of a positive say in the affairs of their offices, shops or factories.

Against that background it is easy to summarise the two questions with which we shall be concerned in what follows. The first is: what has been the record of Christians in remedying the grave injustices of industrial capitalism in its original version? The second is: how far are they willing or able to help remedy the most important injustices which still remain?

CHAPTER TWO

The Eighteenth Century Church and Laissez-Faire

In the middle of the eighteenth century the position of the Church in society looked as strong and as lofty as ever. In England, the bishops sat in the House of Lords; in France, the clergy formed the First Estate; and throughout Europe the higher clergy, at least, enjoyed revenues vast in comparison with what they receive now. But despite this healthy appearance, the real hold of the Church on the minds of men, and its ability to influence events, had declined steadily since the Middle Ages and were in some respects less than they are today.

In the Middle Ages canon law, the law of the Church, was the best kind of law available throughout much of Europe, and was administered through ecclesiastical courts separate from those of civil authorities like kings and barons. Bishops – the title comes from a word meaning 'overseer' – regularly discharged governmental functions in towns. Just as the concept of a father or husband varies from society to society because, although the biological facts of procreation are the same everywhere, the duties and privileges associated with biological roles vary, so the medieval concept of a bishop or an abbot (or abbess) was different from ours, even though the purely religious or sacramental powers were the same. To an able young man in the Middle Ages a career was open which he might call a career in the Church, but to which there is now no exact equivalent, either in the Church or out of it.

Between the fifteenth and the seventeenth centuries the functions which are today discharged by lay authorities were removed from the Church, and even its religious activities came increasingly under civil control. In Protestant countries like England and Prussia the political ruler was thereby head of the Church, a position that until recently carried real power. It is impossible to think of the German Lutherans or the Anglicans in the eighteenth century as an organised body capable of acting independently of the government. But we sometimes forget that the Church in Catholic countries was similarly placed.

The Catholic Church is ruled by bishops, and indirectly controlled, therefore, by whoever appoints the bishops. In theory a bishop could be chosen by the clergy and laity of his diocese themselves; but (except in parts of Holland and Switzerland) there has been no approach to that in modern times. In countries with a Protestant government, Roman Catholic bishops have generally been appointed by the Pope. It is this system of Papal control (favoured by canon law) which led Adam Smith in *The Wealth of Nations* (1776)[1] to describe the Church of Rome as 'the most formidable combination that ever was formed against the authority and security of civil government, as well as against the liberty, reason and happiness of mankind, which can flourish only where civil government is able to protect them'.

Governments in Catholic countries partly agreed. In Spain the right of presentation to bishoprics belonged to the king from 1523 onwards. This right, known as the *patronato real*, was confirmed by concordats (agreements with Rome) in 1753 and 1851, and the State was not deprived of all say in appointments until 1967. In France the concordat of 1516 gave the Crown the right of presentation to the principal benefices, and in the eighteenth century it was regulating all ecclesiastic affairs. This system, known as Gallicanism, was restored after the French Revolution by the concordat of 1801, and came to an end only with the separation of Church and State in 1904. The Catholic bishops on the Rhine, the bishops of Cologne, Mainz and Trier, were elected by their clergy, and as sovereign princes in some measure perpetuated the medieval fusion of religious and civil life. Their sees, however, were backwaters, and in the late-eighteenth century, in the last generation before they were suppressed, they evolved their own form of Gallicanism, called 'Febronianism' after a pseudonymous work (1763) by the bishop of Trier. If it had succeeded, this would have effectively caused a schism between German Catholics and Rome. In Austria the place of Gallicanism and Febronianism was taken by

Josephinism. To many Catholics of a reforming turn of mind this subordination of national churches to the State seemed an abuse, and they connected religious freedom with Ultramontanism, the policy of looking across to the far side of the Alps.

While the State kept the clergy on a pretty tight rein, the hold of the clergy on the people was less sure than critical writers sometimes pretended. Doubtless the influence of priests in countries like Spain has been much greater than anything which the Anglican clergy have enjoyed. But a striking example of Spanish clerical impotence is also worth quoting; the case of Bishop Bartolemé de Las Casas in the sixteenth century. Casas went to his diocese of Chiapa in Central America with the backing of Charles V, bearing with him the famous New Laws for the Indies which included provisions for liberating slaves and preventing further slave-raids. The outlying parts of his diocese refused to recognise him as bishop (he was known to have the chief responsibility for the laws) or pay tithes. Arriving at his cathedral town he took advantage of the rule that Catholics must go to Confession and Communion at Easter, to refuse absolution to persons who would not free their slaves. The townspeople objected that they had appealed against the New Laws, blockaded the bishop's house, and threatened his life. Casas called on the local authorities to enforce the laws, and threatened to excommunicate them if they did not comply. They replied by denying that he had any authority to carry on in this fashion, and sent complaints about him to the Emperor and the Pope. In the end Casas found he could achieve nothing, and went back to Spain.[2]

Politically and practically, at the start of the Industrial Revolution, the Christian churches were everywhere weak. Intellectually, at the same time, they were reeling from the onslaught of Hume and Kant. Until the eighteenth century it had been supposed that there were good rational grounds for believing in the existence of God and the divinity of Christ. Hume and Kant showed, or the leading intellectuals of the time believed them to have showed, that there are no such grounds. In academically sleepy Catholic countries like Italy and Spain, Hume's *Dialogues* (1779)[3] and Kant's *Critique* may have gone unnoticed. In France (where Hume spent the years 1734–7 and 1763–6, and was much admired) many educated men became atheists or deists. In Protestant Germany Christianity received a blow which paralysed it for 50 years, and from which it recovered only by entirely rethinking the relationship between faith and reason.

Nature abhors a mental no less than a physical void. With Christianity silenced, something else was needed to fill men's minds. It was provided by philosophers and economists. The Industrial Revolution took place against an intellectual background, not of Christian ethics, but of laissez-faire economics supported by empiricist philosophy. The views of these philosophers and economists are often called 'liberal', but it is important to recognise that that word has been applied to opinions and systems of at least three different kinds.

In the first place, there is economic liberalism. This is the doctrine of laissez-faire, which in theory, at least, favours unlimited competition and excludes any State intervention whatever in economic processes. In practice it has often winked at monopolies and encouraged the State to intervene on the side of capital against labour, by forbidding trade unions or strikes.

Next, political liberalism is a tradition in politics which goes back at least to Locke and receives a classic exposition in Rousseau. Rousseau held (1762)[4] that the general will can be properly formulated only if each individual expresses his own personal opinion, and he therefore sees the ideal political structure as approximating to a mere aggregate of individuals. There should be no 'partial associations' between the individual and the State itself. The French Revolution in its early stages is an attempt to put political liberalism into practice, and the abolition in 1791 by the Chapelier law of the old craft guilds and all other private associations was in line with Rousseau's thought. This apart, political liberalism lays great emphasis on the freedoms of thought, speech and association.

In Continental countries, political liberals have tended to favour laissez-faire economics and to oppose legislation, often including widening the franchise, which is aimed at social reform. Continental liberal parties, then, have by English and American standards been rather conservative than liberal. England, however, and America have seen a third variety of liberalism, which combines the more attractive features of laissez-faire economics and political liberalism with an acceptance of the need for some legislation to regulate conditions of work and provide social security. Whereas political liberals on the Continent have tended to be anti-clerical or even anti-religious, the English-speaking social liberals, as they may be called, have drawn much of their strength from committed Christians and even ministers, at least of non-conformist churches.

Continental Christians have often said that liberalism is to blame for the evils which attended the Industrial Revolution. It is against laissez-faire economics that this charge is most plausible. No doubt other factors, such as avarice, stupidity, and the bad distribution of property contributed; but there is a group of ideas comprised in or associated with laissez-faire economics which provided a theoretical basis for industrial capitalism in its most inhuman manifestations, and which the reformers we shall be considering in later chapters had to challenge and replace.

The chief minds responsible for these ideas were those of Quesnay (1694–1774) and Turgot (1727–81) in France, and Hume (1711–76) and Adam Smith (1723–90) in Britain. The actual words 'laissez-faire, laissez-passer, le monde va de lui meme' are sometimes attributed to Quesnay, though sometimes to his friend Gournay, and Quesnay advised Louis XV's government against intervention in economic processes. Turgot professed himself his pupil. Hume was a friend both of Turgot and of Adam Smith, and Smith spent three years in France before writing *The Wealth of Nations*.

The central idea of laissez-faire is that economic processes left to themselves will automatically promote the general good. To believe this requires optimism, and the optimism which prevailed among laissez-faire thinkers can be gauged from Hume's essay 'On Refinement in the Arts' (1742–3).[5] Hume says that progress in commerce and the arts has already conferred amazing benefits on the nations of Europe: Louis XIV was able to put into the field twenty times as many soldiers as Charles VIII. At the same this progress has a humanising effect:

> Even foreign wars abate their cruelty:.... treachery and cruelty seem peculiar to uncivilised ages.[6]

And no wonder; for

> Can we expect that a government will be well modelled by a
> people who know not how to make a spinning wheel, or to
> employ a loom to advantage?[7]

The first formulation of laissez-faire philosophy comes a
generation earlier, in Bernard Mandeville's *The Fable of the
Bees* (1714):

> The root of evil, Avarice,
> That damned, ill-natured, baneful vice,
> Was slave to Prodigality,
> That noble sin; while Luxury
> Employed a million of the poor,
> And odious Pride a million more . . .
> Thus Vice nursed Ingenuity,
> Which, joined with time and industry,
> Has carried life's conveniences,
> Its real pleasures, comforts, ease,
> To such a height, the very poor
> Live better than the rich before.[8]

Mandeville wrote with a cynicism which brought him into
disrepute. Hume and Adam Smith were careful to disown or
even to denounce him. But Adam Smith is only clothing his
thesis in respectable garments in this celebrated passage from
his *Theory of Moral Sentiments* (1759):

> It is to no purpose that the proud and unfeeling landlord views
> his extensive fields, and without a thought for the wants of his
> brethren, in imagination himself consumes the whole harvest
> that grows upon them . . . The produce of the soil maintains at
> all times nearly that number of inhabitants which it is capable of
> maintaining. The rich . . . consume little more than the poor,
> and in spite of their natural selfishness and rapacity, though they
> mean only their own conveniency, though the sole end which
> they propose from the labours of all the thousands whom they
> employ, be the gratification of their own vain and insatiable
> desires, they divide with the poor the produce of all their
> improvements. They are led by an invisible hand to make nearly
> the same distribution of the necessaries of life, which would
> have been made, had the earth been divided into equal portions

among all its inhabitants . . . When providence divided the earth among a few lordly masters, it neither forgot nor abandoned those who seemed to have been left out in the partition. These last too enjoy their share of all it produces. In what constitutes the real happiness of human life, they are in no way inferior to those who would seem so much above them. In ease of body and peace of mind, all the different ranks of life are nearly upon a level, and the beggar, who suns himself by the side of the highway, possesses that security which kings are fighting for.[9]

It will be noticed that Adam Smith speaks of landlords with extensive fields, and beggars sunning themselves on the highway, not of entrepreneurs with factories or paupers in smog-shrouded urban slums. In 1759 the process of industrialisation had hardly begun, and laissez-faire economists faced it with a theory which was devised under a quite different economic order. When the invisible hand is sighted again 17 years later in *The Wealth of Nations*,[10] Smith is more muted about its distributive powers; but neither he nor his successors are able to suggest anything to replace it.

In the 1790s Bentham (1748-1832) began his *Manual of Political Economy*[11] by saying that the sole aim of political economy is to increase the total wealth of the nation, and summed up the role of government in the precepts 'Be quiet' and 'Stand out of my sunshine'. His advocacy of social reform by means of legislation makes Bentham a social liberal, but it is noteworthy that in his *Defence of Usury* (1787) he seems honestly unable to see any reason for the traditional Christian opposition to usury except the, to him, obnoxious principle that we should abstain from pleasure: he could not imagine any objection to usury except that it is enjoyable.

In 1803 the British economic philosophy was presented to French readers by J. B. Say (1767-1832) and J. C. L. Simonde de Sismondi (1773-1842). In his *Treatise on Political Economy*,[12] Say insists that 'the poor man, who can call nothing his own, is equally interested with the rich in upholding the inviolability of property'. Sismondi's *On Commercial Wealth* takes a similar line. In 1818, it is true, Sismondi changes his mind. His *New Principles of Political Economy*[13] contains a sombre indictment of the English system.[14] Political economy, Sismondi argues, is concerned with the distribution as well as the creation of wealth;

industrial progress 'tends to increase inequality',[15] and the State should intervene to protect the proletariat, a word the meaning of which, in 1818, he finds it necessary to explain.[16] The alternative to laissez-faire which Sismondi favours is not collectivism of the Robert Owen type but rather a kind of distributism in which large landed estates are broken up, there are many independent workshops, and responsibility for welfare is placed on the proprietors and masters in the various sectors and trades. In the short term, however, he proposes only legislation to favour the division of inheritances, the hiring of labour on long contracts, and profit sharing, proposals which suggest that we should perhaps classify him with the English-speaking social liberals.

These ideas were taken up by some of the thinkers we shall meet in later chapters, such as Villeneuve Bargemont, but on the whole Sismondi's apostasy went unheeded by orthodox economists. At the end of his life Frederick Bastiat (1801-50) could say, with the tide of revolutionary socialism rising around him:

> Study, then, the social mechanism as it comes from the hand of the great Mechanician, and you will find that it testifies to a universal solicitude which far outstrips your dreams and chimeras. You will then, I hope, instead of presumptuously pretending to reconstruct the divine workmanship, be content to admire and bless it.[17]

Where Bastiat saw divine providence, Herbert Spencer (1820-1903) preferred to see natural laws, but even in the 1890s the practical conclusions were the same: the State ought to protect citizens against violence to their persons and property, and it ought to do nothing else.[18]

When it became plain that under the laissez-faire system the poorer members of society were miserable, the orthodox laissez-faire solution was that they should exist in fewer numbers. In 1798 Malthus (1766–1834) published his *Essay on the Principle of Population*.[19] This work was partly a reply to Godwin's *Enquiry concerning Political Justice* (1793).[20] Godwin's 'great error', Malthus declares, was the 'attributing of almost all the vices and misery that prevail in civil society to human institutions', when in fact they 'result from the laws of nature and the passions of mankind'. Godwin had proposed an anarchistic form of Communism which he and Malthus called 'a system of equality'. Following a less well known Scottish writer, Robert Wallace (1697–1771), Malthus maintains that the great Principle of Population (that population naturally increases faster than food) is the rock on which all such schemes must founder. Once the population exceeds the food available, private property and inheritance will have to be reintroduced, and inequality will necessarily follow.[21]

The only real solution, says Malthus, is that the poor refrain from marriage: 'The means of redress are in their own hands, and in the hands of no other persons whatever.'[22] Legislators can help them, however, by abolishing poor relief. The first step is 'formally to disclaim the *right* of the poor to support'. Then, after fair notice has been given, there should be no more public relief for children. Those who marry or have illegitimate children must look for help to private charity. A national insurance scheme would simply remove the incentive to work, and 'the principal difficulty would be to restrain the hand of benevolence from assisting those in distress in so indiscriminate a manner as to encourage indolence and want of foresight in others'. Malthus concludes:

> If the parents desert their child, they ought to be made answerable for the crime. The infant is, comparatively speaking, of little value to society, as others will immediately supply its place . . . [if the parents will not care for it] the society cannot be called to put itself in their place; and it has no further business in its protection than to punish the crime of desertion or intentional ill treatment in the persons whose duty it is to provide for it.[23]

The doctrine that the cause of the sufferings of the poor is their having too many children is connected with a theory about wages. In *Reflections on the Origin and Distribution of Riches* (1766)[24] Turgot says that those who have nothing to sell but their toil, 'sa peine', are inevitably forced by competition among one another for employment to accept a bare subsistence. In a letter (25 March 1767) to Hume, indeed, he qualifies this: workmen need, besides subsistence, 'un certain profit' in order to provide for accidents and bring

up a family; Hume with his usual optimism stands on the
view (September 1767) that there is no one who could not
work a few hours longer or consume a little less. Adam
Smith too thinks that, in general, labourers cannot earn more
than the minimum necessary to stay alive and keep the
number of labourers available up to that required by
employers. He continues:

> The demand for men, like that for any other commodity,
> necessarily regulates the production of men . . . Every species of
> animals naturally multiplies in proportion to their means of
> subsistence, and no species can ever multiply beyond it. But in
> civilized society it is only among the inferior ranks of people that
> the scantiness of subsistence can set limits to the further
> multiplication of the human species.[25]

Of liberal economists, John Stuart Mill (1806–73) is the
least insensitive to the sufferings of the poor and the least
averse to government intervention. Indeed, as we shall see in
Chapter Seven, he came to think of himself later in life as in
some sense a socialist. And there are grounds for thinking
that he modified in old age the views about wage determina-
tion with which he was identified as a young man. But he is
adamant that it is only by limiting births that conditions can
be improved. It is also true that for Mill in his younger, more
laissez-faire days, wages are determined by competition and
the laws of supply and demand, and the level to which they
gravitate is the total wage fund available, divided by the total
number of persons seeking employment. The government
may use tax-payers' money to increase the wage fund, but it
will be useless to do that without also imposing restrictions
on marriage and 'severe penalties on those who have children
when unable to support them'. Mill does not, like Malthus,
deny absolutely that the poor have a right to support. But he
says (1848) :

> Everyone has a right to live. We will suppose this granted. But
> no one has a right to bring creatures into life, to be supported by
> other people . . . Yet there are abundance of writers and public
> speakers, including many of the most ostentatious pretensions to
> high feeling, whose views of life are so truly brutish, that they
> see hardship in preventing paupers from breeding hereditary

paupers in the workhouse itself. Posterity will one day ask with astonishment, what sort of people it could be among whom such preachers could find proselytes.[26]

In a similar spirit Bastiat protests against asking the rich to nourish 'the children of those who had abandoned themselves to the brutishness of their instincts'.

There were not lacking books to dispute the factual basis of Malthusianism, for instance Henry George's *Progress and Poverty* (1881),[27] Charles Devas's *Groundwork of Economics* (1883).[28] Nevertheless in 1896 Spencer could still write:

> In the cause of social progress, parts, more or less large, of society are sacrificed for the benefit of society as a whole . . . Men are used up for the benefit of posterity; and so long as they go on multiplying in excess of the means of subsistence, there appears no remedy.[29]

In the mid-nineteenth century, the philosophy of laissez-faire drew new strength from Darwin's theory of evolution. That theory was itself inspired by laissez-faire economics. Darwin acknowledges his debt to Malthus, and it was doubtless because he was convinced that competition is a good thing in the economic sphere that he casts it as a major agent of progress in biology. Spencer was among the first to welcome the principle back with Darwin's blessing on it. In 1850 he writes:

> The poverty of the incapable . . . and those shoulderings aside of the weak by the strong which leave so many 'in shallows and miseries' are the decrees of a large, far-seeing benevolence . . . the same beneficence which brings to early graves the children of diseased parents.[30]

Forty years later he comments on our attempts to intervene in the struggle for survival:

> Having by unwise institutions brought into existence large numbers who are unadapted to the requirements of social life, and are consequently sources of misery to themselves and others, we cannot repress and gradually diminish this body of relatively worthless people without inflicting much pain. Evil has been done, and the penalty must be paid [apparently by those *to* whom, not *by* whom it was done].[31]

The ideas of Darwin and Spencer were particularly welcomed[32] in the United States, not only by economists like William Graham Sumner, but also by militarists like Homer Lea and millionaires like Andrew Carnegie. Applied to human society, Darwinism seemed to sanctify unlimited ruthlessness in business and aggressive racism in international affairs.

The philosophy of laissez-faire is not, of course, to be judged by the North American social Darwinists. Its founders and leaders were men of a quite different stamp; Turgot, Adam Smith, John Stuart Mill must be counted among the finest products of eighteenth- and nineteenth-century secular culture. But that being so we may wonder how they could accept that it was not unjust for the great majority of the population to have no property and no security, and that it was impossible for workers to receive more of the produce of their labour than was needed to keep their numbers up to the level desired by the rich. How could such men believe that the State should take no action to correct this state of affairs, but confine itself to trying to minimise births and maximise the total wealth of the nation?

Part of the explanation lies in their assumptions about the origins of society and property. They seem to have assumed that the human race began with a handful of individuals who were intellectually just like themselves. These individuals first mated and at a later era came together into political societies; and they gradually spread out enclosing and cultivating a hitherto uninhabited earth like seventeenth-century colonists establishing themselves in America. This is the picture painted by Locke in his *Second Treatise of Civil Government*,[33] and we find it preserved in Turgot's *Reflections* and Mill's *Principles of Political Economy*.[34]

Locke starts from the traditional Christian doctrine that God gave the world to men in common. A man's labour, he reasons, is that man's private property, and he appropriates land and the produce of nature by mixing his labour with it – unless he has sold his labour for wages, in which case it is his employer who appropriates.[35]

Locke does not mention any restrictions on the ownership rights so acquired, and he did not foresee any problems arising from shortage of land or produce to appropriate. In

his day not only were there vast areas of North America
awaiting colonisation, but even in England there were
extensive commons still unenclosed. But Turgot's *Reflections*
mirror a more disturbing state of things. By now, land has all
been appropriated. There has appeared a class of entrepreneurs who pay skilled artisans subsistence wages. It is
convenient to suppose that in some past age, a large
proportion of the population chose not to make any land
their own; and whether that is true or not, we have now to
recognise a large class of people who seem to have no chance
of ever acquiring any kind of capital.

Today all these ideas seem profoundly questionable. If
men evolved from some sub-human species, the first men
must have been very different from seventeenth-century
Europeans. Instead of setting up societies by means of a
voluntary social contract they may well, like some of the
higher non-human species now, have been socially organised
from the start. In any case they could hardly have developed
agricultural techniques and appropriated land without a high
degree of social organisation. So far, then, from society's
being called into being to protect property, appropriation
would be introduced by society, and introduced, presumably, for the common good.

To dubious ideas about human history were added
dubious ideas about human nature. In his *Treatise of Human
Nature* Hume argues with brilliance and at length that actions
cannot be either reasonable or unreasonable:

> Tis not contrary to reason to prefer the destruction of the whole
> world to the scratching of my little finger. Tis not contrary to
> reason for me to choose my total ruin, to prevent the least
> uneasiness of an *Indian* or person wholly unknown to me.[36]

If tendencies to benefit or harm can never provide reasons
for choosing one line of conduct rather than another, it seems
to follow that we can decide between them only by the
feelings the ideas of them excite in us. Hume underlines this
conclusion, and Adam Smith regards it as uncontroversial,
adding only that 'though of the greatest importance in
speculation, [it] is of none in practice', since it can have no
'influence on our notions of right and wrong in particular

cases'.[37] We may wonder if that is true in cases where we are judges in our own cause, as the upper class necessarily is on issues of social justice.

However that may be, there is a second consequence if human conduct cannot be reasonable or unreasonable. In Hume's own words, 'Reason is, and ought only to be, the slave of the passions.'[38] All our actions will be caused by feelings, emotions and desires.

> Tis universally acknowledged that the operations of external bodies are necessary, and that in the the communication of their motion, in their attraction, and mutual cohesion, there are not the least traces of indifference or liberty.

A major part of Hume's philosophical programme is to show that it is the same with the inner life of the mind: our choices and will are determined in a complex fashion by our feelings and desires. Gilbert Ryle has described well the attraction this programme has held for people like economists and social scientists:

> Thinking of their scientific mission as that of duplicating for the world of mind what physicists had done for the world of matter, they looked for mental counterparts to the forces in terms of which dynamic explanations were given of the movements of bodies. Which introspectible phenomena would do for purposive human conduct what pressure, impact, friction and attraction do for the accelerations and declarations of physical objects? Desire and pleasure, aversion and pain seemed admirably qualified to play the required parts.[39]

Like Hume's view on how we differentiate right and wrong, the opinion that human conduct can be explained in the same way as the phenomena of physics is a theoretical one; but it has practical consequences. An economic system will seem like a planetary system, something with its natural dynamism and balance, which we interfere with at our peril. And if the individual's choices are necessitated by his passions, it is an illusion to think we can interfere at all. Laissez-faire seems the only sane policy because anything else is either perilous or impossible. This sort of view issues in Malthus's defeatist verdict:

From the inevitable laws of human nature, some human beings will be exposed to want. These are the unhappy persons who, in the great lottery of life, have drawn a blank.[40]

Yet it would be a mistake to conclude this discussion on so defeatist a note. The extreme laissez-faire position was already being challenged, and being challenged by people who accepted the basic premiss of a competitive market system, before Malthus's famous essay was published. We referred earlier in this chapter to a category of social liberals. If only because of their growing importance throughout the last century, and now in this one, we cannot end this scene-setting chapter without saying a little more about them. For the reader needs to grasp at this early stage the existence and importance of a distinct tradition which has sought to combine the wealth-creating virtues of the competitive market system with traditional concerns for community solidarity and social welfare.

We may notice to begin with that for all his emphasis on the benefits of the invisible hand, Adam Smith grounds his *Theory of Moral Sentiments* unequivocally in the notion of our human sympathy for our fellows. Moreover both there and in *The Wealth of Nations* he makes it clear that the 'invisible hand' will only produce the desired results if people act with restraint in their business dealings. As Fred Hirsh reminded readers of *The Social Limits of Growth*[41] in the late 1970s, Adam Smith recognised, what some of his self-styled successors have missed, that a system of market capitalism will break down unless it is underpinned by traditional values of mutuality which both predate and are separate from it.

The step from this position to one which acknowledges the legitimacy of ameliorative interventions by government to modify the fiercer outcomes produced by market forces is not a large one. And it was taken quite publicly, well before the appearance of Malthus's essay, by the great democrat Tom Paine. We shall look at Paine's economic writings later in this book. Here it is enough to say that in the important (but frequently neglected) last chapter of the second part of *The Rights of Man*,[42] Paine puts forward a programme of social welfare, financed through public taxes, which has been called, without exaggeration, a 'Beveridge in embryo'.

Paine, in other words, should be seen not only as one of the first great genuine democrats but as one of the first great social liberals.

His most distinguished nineteenth-century English successor in this social liberal tradition is, of course, someone we have already introduced, John Stuart Mill. Once again we shall postpone a detailed discussion of his writing till later. Here it is enough to say that the popular picture of Mill as a great economist and, as the author of his famous essay *On Liberty*,[43] a great Liberal, is incomplete. It is incomplete because it leaves out Mill the self-styled socialist, Mill the champion of 'associations of labourers' (what we would today call workers' co-operatives) and Mill the pioneer propagandist for women's rights. It also leaves out Mill the, albeit qualified, democrat. Mill believed throughout his life in the necessity of a competitive market system, though he looked forward wistfully to the prospect of some reasonably tranquil steady state in the distant future. But he also came to believe that there was nothing sacrosanct about either the existing distribution of wealth or about the conventional capitalist structure of the firm. He is therefore, anyway towards the end of his life, an almost quintessential social liberal.

The next famous name in this tradition is Henry George, not an English but an American radical. George's commitment to democracy was less qualified than Mill's became in his later life. But what they both shared was their commitment to the benefits of a competitive market system on the one hand and a radical approach to other social and economic institutions on the other. Moreover the thinking of both, like that of Tom Paine, seems to have been impelled by a very real sympathy for the lot of poor working people. Today Henry George is largely remembered for his proposal to impose a 100 per cent tax on landlords' ground rents. But he deserves to be remembered for a wider contribution: as one of the founders of what later became the liberal wing in the American Democratic party; and as one of the most influential critics of the status quo over the two last decades of the nineteenth century, whose writings also played an important part in the sequence of events which led to the establishment of the Labour Party in Britain.

One of the now neglected figures who was much influenced by Henry George and in particular by his famous book *Progress and Poverty* was Philip Wicksteed (1844–1927). Wicksteed started his working life as a Unitarian minister. His interest in economic questions was awakened by reading *Progress and Poverty*, and he died with an international reputation as an economist. In between he played a notable part in the early years of the Fabian Society in the 1880s, and in the formation of the Labour Churches in the 1890s. He can be classified as a social liberal on precisely the same grounds as those which we have adduced in the case of Paine, Mill and George. For he recognised that it would be reckless folly to throw up the benefits of a competitive market system. But he also recognised that the outcomes of that system were likely to be unacceptably unfair unless remedial action was taken. And he too, as his work with the Labour Churches most obviously indicates, was impelled by a real sympathy with the poor.

At this stage we do no more than introduce the social liberals with a brief glance at these four key figures. But two points are worth emphasising in conclusion. The first is that the tradition did not end with Wicksteed. In our own century it embraces such great men of the first rank as Keynes and Beveridge in England and Roosevelt in the United States. It also includes Christians who have made notable contributions in the industrial relations field, whether as employers or trade union leaders. Seebohm Rowntree, the Quaker chocolate manufacturer, is a good example of the one. Joseph Arch, the Primitive Methodist and founder of the Agricultural Workers' Union in Britain, of the other.

The second and final point about social liberalism is a more general one. There are of course an array of commonsense and democratic arguments in favour of such a position. Indeed, it is doubtful whether a genuine democrat, one with a real feeling for the importance of the dignity of his fellows, can easily be comfortable in any other. But the key point is that it is obviously congruent with two paramount Christian values: the value of personal responsibility and the value of good neighbourly social concern – or of 'do to others as you would be done by' in an alternative formulation.

CHAPTER THREE

Britain Before 1855

What contribution, if any, did Britain's Protestant churches and individual Protestant Christians make to the progressive if painfully slow reforms which gradually softened the harshness of the country's industrial capitalism from about the second third of the nineteenth century, the period after the great 1832 Reform Bill, onwards? What contribution, again if any, did they make to the parallel processes of political and social reform as a result of which, by the middle of *this* century, a fully fledged political democracy was in place and was buttressed, more or less effectively in the economic and social spheres, by fairly comprehensive social welfare provisions on the one hand and by a fairly firm government commitment to policies of full employment on the other? What contribution, thirdly, have Britain's Protestant Christians made to the reform of industrial capitalism at the level of the individual enterprise? These are the questions on which the detailed discussion in this and the next chapter will chiefly focus.

But a number of introductory and anticipatory points are in order. First, what should occasion no surprise, there are diametrically conflicting views about the record of Britain's Protestant churches. According to the Marxist, and to some extent the popular working class tradition, the contribution of Britain's main Protestant churches has been either negligible, or negative, or, indeed for some, hypocritical as well as negative: while sometimes appearing to espouse the cause of working people, the Protestant churches, on this last view, have in fact intervened to protect privilege, and to sustain undemocratic inequalities. The Methodists and other non-conformist churches have perhaps been singled out for special attack in this respect. The chief intellectual protagonist of this position in today's world is, of course, E. P.

Thompson, and his attack is developed at considerable length in *The Making of the English Working Class*.[1] But there are passages in the novels of Dickens in which non-conformist business men are presented in a far from favourable light. It is worth remembering too Robert Tressell's grim portrait of the building foreman, Hunter, who was also a lay preacher at the 'Shining Light Chapel' in *The Ragged Trousered Philanthropist*. And it has also to be acknowledged that the otherwise progressive record of the high-minded English speaking Quakers is seriously flawed: as we shall see they were conspicuously unenthusiastic in their support for Lord Shaftesbury's Factory Act Reforms. John Fielden, Shaftesbury's chief confederate in those campaigns, actually renounced his Quaker upbringing, claiming that many members of the Society of Friends had relapsed into an 'inert conservatism'. It is true, no doubt, that the Quakers deserve great credit for their work in the progressive abolition of slavery. Yet it was as a result of an essentially Quaker decision that the institution of slavery was made legal in the state of Pennsylvania in the first place. Moreover it is salutary to recall Adam Smith's view about the subsequent Pennsylvanian decision to free its slaves:

> The late resolution of the Quakers in Pennsylvania to set at liberty all their slaves may satisfy us that their number cannot be very great. Had they made any considerable part of their property, such a resolution could never have been agreed to.[2]

But, of course, there are sympathetic as well as hostile interpreters of the record of Britain's (and other English speaking countries') Protestants over the period we are considering. Stafford Cripps was a committed non-sectarian Christian. He was also one of the leading members of Clement Attlee's reforming post-war Labour Government. Writing in 1945 and with the growth of government intervention in the economy over the previous century clearly in mind, he went so far as to claim:

> It was very largely the more active Christians in this country who insisted on the State introducing measures of control.[3]

In this and the following chapter we will not attempt any final judgement between the sympathetic and hostile interpretations of the record. Our aim is a more modest one: to supply at least an introduction to the evidence on which a fair-minded judgement must be based.

ANGLICANS

The period from the accession of George III to the Great Reform Bill was one of almost unqualified Erastian worldliness for the Church of England. It was the era of the landed clergy and the building of those fine Georgian rectories; a bishop at the top of the scale might receive £10,000 a year, equivalent to half a million tax free in our money. It was also the era of maximum clerical identification with the State and the social *status quo*. Whether as magistrates or as *de facto* poor law administrators the clergy in the countryside in large measure *were* the State.

In 1792, a year of social unrest on the far side of the Channel, a tract appeared entitled *Reasons for Contentment Addressed to the Labouring Poor of the British Public*. The author was William Paley, whose living at Monkwearmouth was worth £1,700 in money of the time, and who was also Archdeacon of Carlisle and a non-honorary Canon of Lincoln. But it would be unfair to judge Paley exclusively by a combination of his income and the title of his tract. Unlike some of his churchmen contemporaries he was an energetic campaigner for the abolition of the slave trade. Moreover there is a famous passage in his *Principles of Moral and Political Philosophy* which shows that he had a clear-sighted understanding of the workings of the economic system within which he lived:

> If you see a flock of pigeons in a field of corn; and instead of each picking where and what it liked (taking just as much as it would and no more) you should see ninety nine of them gathering all they got into a heap; reserving nothing for themselves but chaff and refuse; keeping this heap for one, and that the weakest, perhaps the worst pigeon in the flock; sitting round and looking on all winter, whilst this one was devouring, throwing about and wasting it; and if a pigeon more hardy and hungry than the rest touched a grain of the hoard, all the others instantly flying

upon it and tearing it to pieces; if you should see this you should see nothing more than what is practised and established among men.[4]

Paley's image has the merit of eschewing humbug. A friend advised him to excise it from the manuscript of his book before publication. 'That passage about the pigeons will not go down' John Law told him; 'it may prevent you becoming a bishop.'[5] To which Paley's rejoinder was unequivocal: 'Bishop or no bishop, it shall stand.' Nevertheless, in the end he accepted the conventional justification of the established practice:

Inequality of property in the degree in which it exists in most countries of Europe, abstractedly considered, is an evil: but it is an evil which flows from those rules concerning the acquisition and disposal of property, by which men are incited to industry, and by which the object of their industry is rendered secure and valuable.[6]

Although Bentham scoffed at Paley's qualifications to write on economics, he was not the first clergyman of the Established Church to venture into this field. As early as 1753, in *A Dissertation on the Numbers of Mankind,* Robert Wallace who was an Edinburgh Royal Chaplain, challenged Hume's optimistic view of progress, and remarked that the slaves of antiquity 'seem to have been more certain of subsistence, and to have had better food, not only than the beggars, but even many of the day-labourers and lower orders of the farmers and tradesmen of modern times'.[7]

In *Various Prospects of Mankind* (1761) he describes an ideal society in which land is not appropriated and government is minimal. He then argues, however, that the population would outstrip the food supply, and when that happened the chaos would be so frightful that it is lucky men's vices have hitherto prevented such a social order from emerging. To this reasoning, Malthus has nothing of substance to add.

Mention may be made too of William Ogilvie (1736-1813), Professor of Latin at Aberdeen, who in 1781 gave warning that the clergy' in almost every country of Europe' was at risk, and ought in its own interest to effect 'an alliance

between the church and the plough'. He lived many years
before his time. The Established Church was not wholly
indifferent to the mounting distress of the poor. The Relief
Committee to which Robert Owen submitted his first
proposals for industrial communes was chaired by a not
unfriendly Archbishop of Canterbury. But the attitudes
typified by Paley and Malthus himself were slow to change,
and the first Anglican clergymen, it could be said, to accept
the spirit of Ogilvie's advice were the Christian Socialists of
1848.

Though the Anglican evangelicals were no more inclined
than the clergy to challenge the foundations of the existing
order, they had a profound effect on the moral climate. This
was perhaps their greatest though their most intangible
achievment. Their direct contribution was very different.
Essentially it was to cleanse that order of its least defensible
and largely peripheral features. That is how Wilberforce's
anti-slavery campaign is probably best understood. The
work of Lord Ashley in his successive Factory Acts and other
measures of reform can also very largely be understood in the
same way.

William Wilberforce (1759-1833) was the only son of a
partner in a prosperous trading house in Hull, a town for
which he became Member of Parliament in 1780. His
evangelical enthusiasm was not confined to the single issue of
the anti-slavery campaign. He was closely involved in the
setting up of the Christian Missionary Society in 1798.
Moreover he showed some concern for the practical as well
as the spiritual needs of what today we would call the
underprivileged of the Third World. For example, he
corresponded with the Emperor Christophe of Haiti and
offered to procure a supply of 'professors, school masters and
governesses' for the island. The project appears not to have
come to much. But that is apparently explained not so much
by any dilatoriness on Wilberforce's part as by the sudden
overthrow of the Haitian emperor. At home his most
positive contribution as an evangelical seems to have been his
support for the Sunday school initiatives of Miss Hannah
More. It seems that he first met that remarkable woman in
1795. He was evidently impressed. For, three years later, he
decided to make available £400 annually to support her work.

Anthony Ashley Cooper was already 50 when he succeeded his father as seventh Earl of Shaftesbury in 1851. During the earlier part of his life he was known as Lord Ashley, and it was this name that was associated with work which his latest biographer, at the end of a not altogether uncritical study, sums up as follows:

> No man has in fact ever done more to lessen the extent of human misery or add to the sum total of human happiness.[8]

The justification for this encomium rests on an array of practical achievements, legislative and otherwise, covering an awesome range of different fields. Many of the great Victorian philanthropic reformers confined their attentions to one main area of social injustice: Elizabeth Fry to prisons, Chadwick to public health and sanitary matters, Octavia Hill to slum housing, and so on. The man who became the seventh Earl of Shaftesbury did not restrict the focus of either his concern or his action. No doubt he is most famous for the legislation which eventually limited the freedom of the factory and mine owners to employ labour, especially child and female labour, as they chose. But he was also the pioneer reformer of the country's lunatic asylums, as Florence Nightingale attests in a startling remark:

> Lord Shaftesbury would have been in a lunatic asylum if he had not devoted himself to reforming lunatic asylums.[9]

He made an outstanding contribution to sanitary reform. And as the promoter of the ragged schools movement he probably did as much for the education of poor children as any of his contemporaries before Foster's Education Act of 1870. And the list could be extended, almost indefinitely. But two other examples will have to suffice. He must share with his fellow evangelical Samuel Plimsoll much of the credit for the passage through Parliament of the Merchant Seamen Bill of 1876. He was also one of the earliest and most determined campaigners on behalf of child chimney sweeps.

Of the religious character of Ashley's motivation in all this, there can be no doubt:

He believed that factory children, chimney sweeps and lunatics all had souls to be saved and that very little time remained in which to save them. 'It is eternity work' said a Welsh Evangelical on his death-bed; men like Wilberforce and Ashley and indeed the Evangelicals as a whole, saw all social and charitable efforts as 'eternity work'.[10]

THE ANGLICAN CHRISTIAN SOCIALISTS

On the morning of 10 April 1848 the Rev Charles Kingsley, feeling cut off in his Hampshire parish of Eversley from the great unfolding of events in the capital, came up to London. The chief public event billed for the day was a gigantic mass meeting on Kennington Common. It had been arranged to supply a tumultuous send-off for the monster Chartist petition which was to be conveyed thence to Parliament. Both the authorities and the propertied classes were in a state of considerable alarm. Many of the latter had enrolled as special constables. Among them was Kingsley's older friend the Rev Frederick Denison Maurice.

But it was not with Maurice that Kingsley set out, later in the day, to see what was happening on Kennington Common. His special constable duties notwithstanding Maurice was discovered by Kingsley to be effectively confined to barracks in his home in Queen's Square with a cold. Maurice suggested that an appropriate and more contemporary alternative companion would be John Malcolm Ludlow. So, armed with a letter of introduction, Kingsley moved on from Queen's Square to Ludlow's chambers in Lincoln's Inn. Some time later, the two of them headed for Kennington Common. But they got no further than Waterloo. The great mass meeting had broken up: not through any intervention by the authorities but as a result of torrential rain. Later again, in the early evening, the two of them reported back to Maurice in Queen's Square. By that time, Canon Raven tells us, Kingsley and Ludlow were 'firm friends'.[11] More important, the events of the day had stirred all three to the point where they felt it was both necessary and desirable to act. Christian Socialism's beginning can be pinpointed in the meeting between the three of them at Maurice's house that night. The following day they posted up a placard which began: 'Workers of England, you have more friends than you think for', and which was signed 'A working parson'. Such a gesture of solidarity from the Established Church was unheard of, and astonishing to a degree hardly imaginable today. It may be claimed to mark the first radical Anglican response to industrial capitalism.

If we ask where the ideas of these Christian Socialists came from, it is clear that they found their intellectual inspiration in the writings not of the radicals but of such 'Tory' critics of the prevailing economic orthodoxy as Carlyle, Southey and Coleridge. In the heady days of their university youth Southey and Coleridge had planned to sail away from the Old World and to establish an experimental working community, a Pantisocracy, in the United States. The plans aborted for a number of reasons: one of them, it seems, was a conflict about whether domestic servants should be included on the ration strength of the proposed Pantisocracy and whether, if they were, they should eat in a separate mess. Yet Southey for one retained his special interest in possibilities of this kind. He met Robert Owen in 1816 and we are told by Canon Raven[12] that he recognised New Lanark as a genuine Pantisocracy in action. But what Kingsley and Maurice chiefly took from Coleridge and Southey was not their youthful blueprints of ideal working communities; it was the essentially *social* character of their conservatism. Southey and Coleridge were among the earliest and most outspoken critics of the political economy of laissez-faire individualism.

> As for the Political Economists, no words can express the thorough contempt which I feel for them. They discard all moral considerations from their philosophy, and in their practice they have no compassion for flesh and blood.[13]

Similarly Carlyle:

> Laissez-faire, Supply-and-Demand – one begins to be weary of all that. Leave it to egoism, to ravenous greed of money, of pleasure of applause: – it is the Gospel of Despair.[14]

In their influence on Kingsley and Maurice it is probably Carlyle's *Signs of the Times* (1829) and above all his essay 'Chartism' which appeared in book form ten years later,[15] which are most important. The latter is especially notable for its fierce hostility to the reformed Poor Law of 1834, and to the Poor Law's assumption that working people who really want jobs will find them.

Of the five key figures in the Christian Socialist movement, Maurice, Ludlow, Neale, Kingsley and Hughes, three have already been mentioned. Maurice's father was a minister of the Unitarian persuasion. During his adolescence both his mother and his sister underwent conversions and transferred their allegiance from the Unitarians to the Evangelicals. After taking a degree at Cambridge, Maurice himself entered the Church of England, but without aligning himself with its Evangelical wing. He was much attracted by Coleridge's idea of a national 'clerisy', a divinely ordained priesthood of a divinely constituted State. We shall see that a similar idea attracted Christians in Germany who shared Maurice's mistrust of parliamentary democracy of the orthodox liberal type.

Ludlow was born in India and brought up and educated in France. He had contacts with French liberal Catholics as well as with French Protestants. His interest in the possibility of co-operative workshops was first kindled by Fourier. Later in England he came to know about Robert Owen. When, however, he persuaded Maurice to endorse his co-operative promoting initiative, neither Owen's 'home colonies' nor Fourier's 'phalansteries' provided the model. His co-operative workshops were modelled on the attempts to realise the plans of Buchez and Louis Blanc in Paris in 1848.

The main contribution of Edward Vansittart Neale was perhaps to supply capital from his considerable fortune to help get the co-operatives off the ground. There is some doubt about just how much of his patrimony Neale devoted to co-operative promotion and never recovered. A figure of £60,000 was apparently published in the 1860s, but Neale himself said, 'I do not estimate it at more than £40,000' (more than £1m in money of the 1980s). In any case, his evangelical background was every whit as important a precondition for the character of his life and work as his wealth was. That came mainly from his father. But it was reinforced from his mother's side by no less a person than William Wilberforce, her brother. Later in life Neale left behind him the more

specifically religious elements of this evangelical background. But in doing so he transferred to the co-operative
movement something close to a religious commitment.
Philip N. Backstrom neatly contrasts Neale's subsequent
attitudes with those of Maurice and the other Christian
Socialists:

> Neale, unlike Maurice and his disciples, was not trying to
> Christianise Socialism, for to him Socialism *was* the fulfilment of
> Christianity.[16]

Kingsley had a real and rare capacity of becoming
passionately involved in the issues which he took up. His
great talent was literary. Had either his passion or his pen
been missing, it must be doubtful whether that placard
would ever have been hoisted on 11 April 1848. Though his
contribution to Christian Socialism was less sustained than
Neale's, it was both dazzling and decisive in its initial impact.
As Parson Lot he wrote extensively for the periodicals which
followed the placard: *Politics for the People* (1848) and the
Christian Socialist (1850–1). His fairly early withdrawal from
the active team of Christian Socialists is persuasively explained by Canon Raven: as a conscientious parish priest and
aspiring writer, there were other compelling claims on his
time.

The last of the five white knights of Christian Socialism
was Thomas Hughes, author of *Tom Brown's School Days* and
star pupil of Thomas Arnold of Rugby. The character of his
particular brand of Anglican Christianity is indicated by the
title of a series of lectures which he delivered on the New
Testament. The title was 'The Manliness of Christ'. Canon
Raven's account of his recruitment is worth quoting:

> He was an asset of incalculable value in his effect both upon his
> fellow members and the public. A movement for reform
> invariably attracts to it all the available freaks in the community
> . . . And to them had come Tom Hughes, the 'blue' with the
> healthy mind and healthy body . . . the ideal hero of the British
> public and the sporting press . . .; they could not be so bad after
> all if a man like that was among them.[17]

In June 1850, following the launch in January of a Working
Tailors' Association, the Christian Socialists set up the
Society for Promoting Working Men's Associations with
Maurice as President. Early in 1853, after the passing of the
Industrial and Provident Societies Act in the previous year,
the promotional body changed its name and became the
Association for Promoting Industrial and Provident
Societies. That in turn held its final meeting on 25 November
1855 when it handed over its functions to the Executive
Committee of the national Co-operative Conference. Thus
the Christian Socialist initiatives for the promotion of actual
productive enterprises fall between early 1850 and 1855. In
fact well over half of the dozen or so enterprises with which
they were directly involved started life within the first 18
months of that period. They were mostly artisanal ventures,
tailors, bootmakers and the like, though Neale and his cousin
A. A. Vansittart were also active in promoting the Atlas
Ironworks in Manchester and the East London Ironworks in
Mile End.

Only in one case, The Manchester Hatters, was a
reasonably long business life – some 20 years – achieved. A
passage from what amounts to the first annual report of the
promoting body has been widely quoted as evidence of the
promotors' candour as well as failure:

> In the first nine months of our life as a society we set up three
> sets of shoemakers in association, supplying in two instances the
> whole of the funds, in the other all but £5. None of the men
> were picked; we accepted them just as they came to us. We gave
> them absolute self-government, merely reserving to ourselves
> certain rights of interference in any cases of dispute or
> mismanagement while any capital remained to us. Each of these
> associations quarrelled with and turned out its original manager
> within six months; one, the West End Bootmakers, went to
> pieces altogether before nine months had gone. The other two
> struggled on until the beginning of the next year, never paying
> their way and continually quarrelling.[18]

Perhaps the kindest judgement is the one assigned by Canon
Raven to the promotors themselves:

The promotors were forced to confess that their enterprise had been premature and that though the ideal was, as they still unanimously maintained, right and worthy, it was not yet capable of being put into practice, and that education must be extended and developed before a successful result could be obtained.[19]

Kingsley's verdict, written in 1856, was more succinct. It also reflects the distinctive values of his social Toryism: 'It will require two generations of training both in morality and drill.'[20]

By 1855 the key promotors had had enough of the direct sponsorship of productive ventures. Even if Neale's money had not by then more or less run out (which it had) it must be doubtful whether they would have chosen to go on trying to achieve their ends by those direct methods. As it was, in the immediate subsequent period, Ludlow threw his main energies behind helping Maurice to launch his major educational experiment, the Working Men's College in Red Lion Square. Neale for his part turned his main energies into helping the largely consumer co-operative movement to come together and build its own central institutions. From 1873 to 1891 he was General Secretary of the Co-operative Union. Especially toward the end of their lives both were to reappear on the public stage as veteran champions of co-operative *production*. And Thomas Hughes both in and out of Parliament demonstrated a similarly abiding commitment to the ideals of the Society of Promoters. He was even to be associated in the 1890s with a semi-utopian, semi-Owenite venture in the United States, and supported a scheme for settling Tom Browns in a pioneering colony of yeomen co-operators carved out of the Appalachian uplands in Rugby, Tennessee.

If Neale, Ludlow and Hughes had been asked, after 1855, to define their specific goals, the same two main answers would almost certainly have been given by all three of them: to persuade the new trade unions to swing their support behind initiatives for co-operative production; and to persuade the new co-operative movement to give priority to self-governing co-operative productive enterprise rather than to consumer stores and wholesale distribution. In both of these endeavours their efforts were at least 95 per cent unsuccessful. A largely token commitment to co-operative production can still be found in the now venerable rule-books of some of the earlier trade unions. And perhaps a dozen artisan production co-ops have survived into today's world from the last decades of the last century.

The success of the Christian Socialists lies in the challenge which they mounted and sustained to the prevailing attitudes of the Church of England in particular and of their middle and upper class contemporaries in general. It was not so easy to preach resignation to the poor after Kingsley had written:

> We have used the Bible as if it were a mere special constable's handbook – an opium dose for keeping beasts of burden patient while they were being overloaded – a mere book to keep the poor in order . . . We have told you that the Bible preached the rights of property and the duties of labour, when (God knows!) for once that it does that, it preaches ten times over the *duties of property* and the *rights of labour.*[21]

More positively the Christian Socialists must take the credit for being the first to put the social and economic questions posed by industrial capitalism firmly on the Church of England's agenda. No doubt the tradition they began has never been more than a minority one within the Church of England. But whether we look at working class education, or at the growth of the great working class institutions – the trade unions and the co-operatives – or at the origins of the Welfare State itself, we see its influence. Jo Grimond once had the job of examining the speeches from the bench of bishops in the House of Lords in the second half of the last century. His recollection of the central finding is very clear. The bishops were never 'ahead of progress' during this time; but nor were they very frequently all that far behind it. Without the influence of Maurice and his friends the bishops might well have fallen 'behind progress' more frequently.

OLD DISSENT

Before they were overtaken by the rise of Methodism, the Baptists and the Congregationalists (originally known as the Independents) were the most numerous sects of Britain's

'Old Dissent', and probably the most accessible to ordinary folk. Though both are the offspring of the Reformation and of seventeenth-century Puritans, they have rather different origins. Most of the later Baptist congregations can link their origins with the sect's pioneering chapel set up in Spitalfields by Thomas Helwys in 1612. By contrast the Congregationalists are the outcome not of the initiative of a single individual but of an Act of Parliament. They came into existence following the Act of Conformity 1662. As many as 1,900 of the Church of England's then population of clergymen found themselves unable to accept this measure of Charles II and broke away accordingly. The justification for considering them and the Baptists together is that at crucial periods their response to events in the outside world has been remarkably similar, and they share a common, more or less democratic form of chapel government. By contrast it would be odd if the main issue which has divided them, infant baptism, had affected their respective responses to industrial capitalism.

Both the Baptists and the Congregationalists suffered severe persecution between 1662 and the Act of Toleration in 1689. John Bunyan, who is claimed by both denominations, was himself in prison on more than one occasion and for a number of years. In this respect their early history closely resembles that of the Quakers. But they were less interested in social and economic questions than the followers of George Fox. Efforts have been made by Christopher Hill and E. P. Thompson to present a social side to Bunyan's writing. It is no doubt true, as Hill writes, that 'In *The Life and Death of Mr Badman* Bunyan tried to keep small men in the paths of commercial morality'.[22] But the Bedford tinker seems to have been a good deal less interested in such matters than George Fox was. His main concern was with his own titanic struggle for religious peace of mind. For the period from the Act of Toleration to the beginnings of the impact upon them of Wesley's evangelical revival, a recent Baptist historian, A. C. Underwood, in *A History of the English Baptists*, gives his chapter an unusually candid heading – 'Toleration and Decline'.[23] 'Little did they dream' he says of the General and Particular Baptists[24] 'that the granting (of toleration) would be followed by a leanness in their souls'. Moreover he makes it clear that the decline covers not only the Baptists but also the other principal denominations of 'Old Dissent': 'lethargy had come over them'.[25]

No doubt they still exhibited both democratic and intellectual virtues. The famous Dissenting Academies remind us of the second. Evidence of their commitment to democracy is supplied by the attitudes of Baptist Ministers to the American War of Independence. Apparently only three cases are known where they 'did not stand for freedom'.[26] But when it mattered, in the aftermath of the French Revolution, the vast majority of dissenting ministers rallied to the support of the *status quo*. The only notable exception was the Rev Joseph Priestly, F.R.S. (1736–1803). Priestly was originally a Baptist minister, but switched to the Unitarians later in life. Such was the unpopularity of his republican views that in the face of the Birmingham mob he prudently decided to leave the country. He was apparently helped with his packing by the Rev Michael Maurice, a fellow Unitarian minister, and the father of the leader of the Anglican Christian Socialists.

If this analysis is correct, it seems far fetched, to suggest, as E. P. Thompson does, that the eighteenth century religious revival could have emerged out of 'Old Dissent'. It seems altogether more plausible to follow the contrary view: that without Wesley's revival the old dissenting chapels would have simply petered out, anyway as forces to be reckoned with in a national context. In its article in the 1962 edition, the *Encyclopaedia Britannica* asserts flatly that the Congregationalists were 'rescued' by the evangelical revival. Underwood says the same at greater length about the Baptists.[27]

The changes which took place in 'Old Dissent' as a result of exposure to Wesley's evangelical revival included an awakening of interest in those social and moral issues which could be tackled without posing a serious threat to the *status quo*. From towards the end of the eighteenth century onwards Baptists and Congregationalists start playing their part in national anti-slavery and temperance campaigns. In the case of the Congregationalists their 'scorecard' in this respect goes further, and includes one notable 'first'. John Howard (1726–90) was a member of their Bedford chapel. His initiatives in relation to prison reform substantially predate those of Lord Shaftesbury and Elizabeth Fry. His name is justly commemorated by the Howard League for

Penal Reform. His family lives on in Bedford. But it is not until the second half of the nineteenth century that a real interest in social problems by Baptists and Congregationalists gathers momentum. For the most part before then the influence of both denominations was scarcely felt outside their own chapel congregations though the Baptists can claim that a tiny minority of ministers spoke up for the short lived Chartist Churches in the 1840s.

METHODISTS

Any account of the Methodist response to industrial capitalism must take in its important contribution as a school for trade union leaders, particularly in the last century, but even to some extent today. It must examine the hypothesis, first advanced in 1912 by Eli Halevy,[28] that it was the Methodists who in some sense saved Britain from a violent political revolution during those turbulent years between the fall of the Bastille and the Reform Bill of 1832. More generally it must consider the charge, argued most forcefully and with passion and eloquence by E. P. Thompson in *The Making of the English Working Class*, that anyway over its first 100 years to 1839, Methodism is best understood as an agency by which working people were more or less duped.

Wesley's followers are widely and correctly seen as being closer to the Church of England than are the other nonconformists. For one thing John Wesley himself (1703–91) was an ordained Anglican clergyman and remained one throughout his long life. The break with the Established Church came only after his death. Equally important, he took from the Church of England its unequivocally hierarchical set-up. At the apex of the organisation he created there was, during his own lifetime, himself, and subsequently the 'conference', a plenipotentiary and self-perpetuating body of Methodist ministers, of whom the original 100 members were all his personal appointees. It was precisely over the issue of democratic accountability to the membership that splits away from the 'Wesleyan Connexion' took place from the last years of the eighteenth century onwards: most importantly, the New Connexion and then, from 1812 onwards, the Primitive Connexion.

Wesley did not enshrine the democratic virtues in his

movement, and Thompson is surely more right than wrong when he suggests that Wesley set it off in a non- (if not an anti-) intellectual direction. Its defining characteristic is the total priority which it assigned to the struggle against personal sin. Wesley, like Ashley, believed that his was 'eternity work' and that he was in the business of saving souls. It is easy to see how people who thought in these ways could be disinclined to allocate resources, financial or intellectual, to ameliorative social programmes. At the same time to argue that his converts were largely duped by Wesley, the salesman of tickets of escape from hell fire, is to ignore the 'witness' of people like George Eliot's Dinah in *Adam Bede* and a multitude of real Methodist activists to whom we are introduced by Robert Wearmouth. No one can read his *Methodism and the Common People of the Eighteenth Century* without being struck by its examples of a genuinely luminous Christian kindness extended especially, though not exclusively, to prisoners in the condemned cells of the country's jails.

Wesley's 'genius for organisation' was at least the equal, in Halevy's view, of his 'genius for preaching'.[29] The movement or 'connexion' as a whole was divided into a country-wide population of 'circuits'. The constituent bodies of the circuits were the individual and local Wesleyan societies or chapels.

> At the head of the circuit were placed under the authority of a superintendent two or three travelling or itinerant preachers who . . . journeyed from one society to another, . . . supervising all and preaching as the representatives of a higher authority.[30]

To this extent the system reflected what Thompson calls a 'sacerdotal approach'. But more distinctive and important is the use it made of the services of the laity below the level of the individual chapel. The ratio between the number of chapels and chapel services (three a Sunday) on the one hand and the number of full-time itinerant ministers on the other was such that the great bulk of religious work had to be delegated to lay preachers. For example in 1851 we can see from the Census of Religious Worship that not much more

than one service out of twenty was taken or preached at by
full-time ministers. The amount of religious work which had
to be undertaken by lay preachers was correspondingly
enormous. Moreover the involvement of the laity extended
to the whole membership and not just to the lay preachers.
The membership of each chapel was subdivided into little
groups called 'classes', each with its class leader, and each
required to hold a weekly meeting for instruction, bible
reading, prayers and debate.

Halevy says this lay contribution reflected Wesley's inten-
tion to institute 'a species of lay third order' to complete the
evangelising work of the clergy. Obvious to us now is its
potential as a training for work in other spheres. As training
grounds these Methodist classes had an unforeseen, but
crucially important, result in providing leaders for the
growing trade union movement in the second half of the last
century.

Between Wesley's launching of the movement in 1739 and
the 1851 Census of Religious Worship, the Methodists grew
in numbers to become a body a third of the size of the
Church of England, and larger than all the other Protestant
groups put together. As Halevy emphasises, there was
nothing on the Continent which remotely corresponded to
this religious phenomenon. To explain it, says Thompson, at
least in the crucial years 1790–1830:

> Three reasons may be adduced: direct indoctrination, the
> Methodist community-sense, and the psychic consequences of
> the counter-revolution.[31]

The second of these can unquestionably be accepted. With
their lay preachers, their class leaders and their Sunday school
teachers the local Methodist chapels constituted highly
organised little communities. We can also be confident that
for the most part they were communities in which at least the
more prosperous and the more skilled of the manual
workforce – as well as businessmen and other middle class
people – could feel at home. But what of the first and third?

As the main agent of indoctrination, Thompson gives
Sunday Schools. It is true that in 1851 the Wesleyan

Methodists had 644,000 Sunday School scholars, with a pupil-teacher ratio of 5:1, while the Church of England, though thrice the size, had only 936,00 pupils and a ratio of 12:1. But this is evidence only for effort, and there are grounds for scepticism about indoctrination. Almost half of the Sunday Schools used in 1851 had been established only in the last 20 years. Whereas the Connexion membership increased by roughly 50 per cent between 1830 and 1850, the number of schools increased by nearly 100 per cent. If those schools were really engaged in direct indoctrination, then there was much more of that going on after the Reform Bill than before it. To look at it the other way round, can Thompson seriously invite us to believe that a whole generation of working class children were duped and 'directly indoctrinated by the Wesleyan Methodist Sunday Schools from the 1790s onwards'? There were less than 200 of these schools covering the whole country in 1801. To impute more than marginal influence to the group of dedicated, but totally untrained teachers and to see them as skilled in 'direct indoctrination' seems simply absurd.

Thompson's third component 'the psychic consequences of the counter-revolution', seems unhelpfully elusive, but perhaps Thompson means merely that Methodism offered pie in the sky to those who despaired of getting any here? He says, at least: 'There is a sense in which any religion which places great emphasis on the after life is the chiliasm of the defeated and hopeless.'[32] This analysis, however, does not fit the actual composition of the Methodist Connexions. Even their working class members, who were never a majority, came less from the big industrial towns where conditions were most desperate, than from small towns and villages where employers and employees lived fairly close to each other. Evidence for this can be found in Wearmouth,[33] K. S. Inglis[34] and W. Jessop.[35]

More plausible is Halevy's contention about Methodism's role in containing pressures which might otherwise have spilled over into revolution.[36] To begin with, the political conservatism of the Wesleyan Methodist leadership is well documented. Wesley himself at least twice offered to raise 'volunteers' to assist the armed forces, and it was not for nothing that, during the War of American Independence, he wrote a 'Calm address to our American Colonies'. At the Annual Conference of 1792 it was resolved that:

1. None of us shall, either in writing or conversation, speak lightly or irreverently of the Government under which he lives.
2 We are to observe that the Oracles of God command to be faithful to the higher powers, and that honour to the King is there connected with the fear of God.[37]

Jabez Bunting, when he said: 'Methodism is as much opposed to democracy as to sin'[38] was doing no more than maintain the already established tradition.

But aside from their endorsement of the political *status quo*, what precisely was the nature of the influence which the evangelical Methodists exerted on their own chapel congregations in the first place, and by their example, Halevy argues, on the Church of England and on the sects of Old Dissent as well? An appealing aspect of their message is its implicit emphasis on the values of personal responsibility and personal restraint. Halevy finds in these essentially moral notions the source of British social and political stability. It was their influence that . . .

. . . invested the English Aristocracy with an almost Stoic dignity, restrained the plutocrats who had newly risen from the masses from vulgar ostentation and debauchery, and placed over the proletariat a select body of workmen enamoured of virtue and capable of self restraint.[39]

At the heart of Halevy's analysis are the linked ideas of freedom and restraint. They were, in his view, ultimately a legacy inherited from the Puritan sects. But between the eighteenth and the nineteenth centuries, there was a subtle change in the meaning of the words 'freedom' and 'liberty'. For most of the eighteenth century those words had meant freedom from a tyrannical monarchy, the freedom of a free press, the freedoms demanded by John Wilkes. During the first fifteen years of the nineteenth century people came to understand by them:

Restraint self imposed and freely accepted as opposed to restraint forcibly imposed by the Government. England was contrasted

with Napoleonic France, as being at once the home of liberty
and virtue . . . And this change in the opinion entertained of
themselves by the English was undoubtedly the result of the
Methodist propaganda continued by the Evangelicals.[40]

The political message of the Wesleyan Methodists on the side
of the *status quo* was complemented and underpinned by a
workaday message which legitimised the bourgeois values of
hard work, personal responsibility and a self restraint
bordering on the ascetic. The Wesley brothers rejected
Calvin's doctrine of Predestination and followed the Dutch
Protestant Arminius in allowing that individuals could, with
the help of God's grace, escape eternal punishment and save
their souls. But a *Methodist Pocket Book* for 1813 exactly
illustrates what Weber meant by 'the spirit of capitalism'. G.
E. Milburn describes it in a recent paper as follows:

> Each week of the year . . . is allotted a double-page spread – on
> the left a diary page, headed by a biblical text and a verse of a
> hymn, and opposite a page ruled in columns for weekly cash
> accounting. Piety on the left, profit on the right.[41]

Milburn's paper includes ample evidence, if evidence is
needed, that the numbers of Methodist businessmen far
exceeded the number of their trade unionists.

The economic, no less than the political message of
Methodism is inimical to revolution. Whether the success of
that message between 1789 and 1832 prevented a revolution
in England, whether the maintenance of civil peace in this
period really needs any explaining, are further questions
which the present study cannot aspire to settle.

QUAKERS

The Quakers provide us with a tradition which has now
lasted for well over 300 years and which has combined hard
work in the real world with progressive social reform. With
only one main exception, Lord Shaftesbury's campaigns for
his Factory Acts, they have been ahead of their time. On
today's salient issue of Women's Liberation they may claim
to have been ahead by 300 years. As anti-slavery campaigners
they anticipated Wilberforce by two generations. As employers concerned about the housing and other welfare needs

of their employees they anticipated Robert Owen by at least 40 years. Of their more theoretical contributions to the study and analysis of social and economic arrangements those of John Bellers and Seebohm Rowntree in particular have been outstandingly influential.

Standard denominational histories usually include a kind of score card of the great and famous whom they can claim as being 'theirs'. How far is this legitimate and worthwhile? So far, clearly, as the actions writings or utterances of the persons concerned reflect their Christian or denominational position. The Quakers meet this requirement well. In the writings of their founder, George Fox, himself, we frequently find a definite movement (even if not a definitely argued one) from a religious premiss to a conclusion in the field of social action:

> How are you in pure religion . . . when both blind and sick and halt and lame lie up and down, cry up and down, in every corner of the city? . . . You know that you are one mould and blood that dwell on the face of the earth. Would not a little out of your abundance maintain these poor children, halt lame and blind, and set them at work that can work, and they that cannot, find a place of relief for them?[42]

'Set them at work that can work': this attention to practical and detailed specifics is one of the strongest and most admirable features of the Quaker tradition. Braithwaite supplies[43] a wide range of examples. In 1678 in Cork 'Friends of the clothing and spinning trade' are warned against paying wages in kind. In 1695 there are injunctions against letting lands at rack rents. And often a precept is reinforced by a reference to 'precious truth':

> In the time of harvest . . . remember that the portion of the poor be not gathered: Leviticus XIX.9
> Lay no more upon your servants than you would be willing to be laid upon you.

Arrangements for providing work date back at least to 1677. In that year under the influence of John Taylor of York, Friends agreed to raise a stock for the occupation and maintenance of prisoners. In London £100 was allocated to

buying flax for Friends to spin at home. Between 1679 and
1684 when the experiment came to an end, it was administered by John Bellers (1655–1725), a man who was described by
no less a personage than Karl Marx as 'a veritable phenomenon in the history of political economy'.

Bellers was the son of a London grocer of good standing,
and was himself apprenticed to a cloth-merchant. The
religious motivation of his many and varied reforming
proposals is always plain. In attacking, for instance, the laws
which prescribed the death penalty for theft he says (1699)
that the life of a man is of greater value to God than many
pounds.[44] In 1695 he published his celebrated pamphlet
entitled:

> Proposals for Raising a College of Industry of All Useful Trades
> and Husbandry with Profit for the Rich and Plentiful Living for
> the Poor and a Good Education for the Youth.

The 'College' which Bellers proposed was essentially a
working settlement. It would have a total population of 300,
including men, women and boys. Bellers argued that the
work of no more than 200 would provide:

a) his 'plentiful living' for all;
b) the necessary house rents; and
c) the rent on farm land.

The work of the remaining 100 would provide a profit,
according to Bellers's calculations, of between 5.5 per cent
and 8 per cent for those who financed the enterprise.
However he covers himself against contingencies:

> But if it should require 220 people to provide Necessaries for
> 300, it will pay the Undertakers well enough.

(Note the substitution of 'necessaries' for the 'plentiful living'
of his title page.) He goes on to suggest that:

> Colleges could at once be established at Colchester where they
> make Bayes [sc. baize] and Perpetuanoes, Taunton, for Serges,
> Stroud for Cloth and Devonshire for Kersies.

It is easy to see the hand of Bellers the ex-cloth merchant's apprentice as well as Bellers the social reformer in the proposals.

A critic might raise the question whether the proposed colleges were substantially different from the nineteenth century workhouses of grim repute. No college of the Bellers type was actually set up, but experiments like the flax-spinning one which Bellers superintended are sometimes known as 'Work House' schemes. Arthur Raistrick uses this heading to introduce the topic in *Quakers in Science and Industry*.[45] In the absence of much evidence it can only be said that the Quaker schemes, however paternalistic, were essentially voluntary, and that Bellers's own character seems to have been more genial than the reverse. In his last letter to Friends before his death he urges the Yearly Meeting to treat the poor prisoners of London each year to a 'dinner of baked legs and shins of beef and ox-cheeks'.[46]

Besides introducing the idea of productive communities, Bellers seems to have been the first to propose a kind of labour currency or labour system of value:

> This college-fellowship will make labour and not money the standard to value all necessaries by.[47]

It is notable also that his eagerness to create employment did not make him a Luddite. In 1723 he deplores 'the suppressing of saw-mills' and laws against labour-saving machinery generally; on the contrary, encouragement should be 'given by the legislature for any new discovery in mechanics and husbandry'.[48]

A further field in which he was a pioneer was public health. In 1714 he called for a far-reaching, State-supported national health system, including hospitals at the universities, a Royal Society for the promotion of medicine, and 'hospitals in London for the poor, preferably for each class of disease, with registration of each patient and a record of the case.'[49] To justify State intervention of this kind he says:

> The sending of ambassadors abroad in time of peace, or spies in time of war, or the supporting of any foreign trade, are not more necesary, nor of greater advantage to a prince or State, than it is

for them to procure all knowledge of the art of healing that the universe can possibly supply.[50]

Although it was centuries before Bellers's programme was carried out, the Quakers repeatedly offered practical leads. It was they, in the person of Henry Tuke, who established the first modern lunatic asylum, the Retreat in York, in 1796. They also initiated social welfare provision in industry.

An example of this is provided by Raistrick[51] in his account of the ironworks of the Darby dynasty at Coalbrookdale in the eighteenth century. From the beginning the Darbys 'were concerned that their work people should be adequately housed, and the works estate included workmen's cottages as well as a house for the Darbys'. Richard Reynolds, who directed the ironworks from 1756 to 1768, bought a neighbouring property and laid out parks for the work people. Schools were provided, and also houses for the old and distressed. In addition, the Darbys dispensed with work on Sundays, despite the costs and deleterious effects of letting out the furnaces. It is clear that when industrialisation was carried out under the influence of Christian moral principles in this way – as it was at other Quaker ironworks too – the problems of transition were very much reduced.

Quaker industry was distinguished not only by solicitude for the work force, but also by a high standard of business ethics. The same high standard marks and partly explains the success of the Quaker banks. Some of these, such as Barclay, Freame, Gould and Hoare, descended from earlier goldsmith firms; others like Lloyds and Gurney, arose during the eighteenth century in conjunction with Quaker industries and providing services to them.[52]

Quaker banking may be said to have been one of the factors which facilitated the development of industrial capitalism, and the Quakers of the eighteenth and nineteenth centuries may be presented as capitalists *par excellence*. At the same time it must be recognised that capitalism is a better system for those who live under it when high standards of business ethics prevail than when they are sacrificed to unlimited acquisitiveness.

By the late eighteenth century, the British Quaker community had established sucessful undertakings across the whole spectrum of business activity. The family business, normally structured as a partnership, was almost always the chosen vehicle. Among others they included, besides the banks already referred to, Allbright and Wilson, Reckitt and Coleman, Wedgewoods the pottery manufacturers, and Allen and Hanbury in pharmaceuticals. The founder of this last firm deserves further mention.

William Allen (1770-1843) was a younger contemporary of Henry Tuke. He was an early enthusiast for public initiatives in the field of education. Robert Owen sought and received his help to buy out his partners and establish a progressive educational system at New Lanark. There was an 'institution for the formation of character' which took children from the age of two or even younger, and a school for older children. Unfortunately Allen and other Quaker supporters later fell out with Owen over his introduction of dancing and the wearing of light, comfortable clothes. Allen also launched and endowed his own scheme for training and education in agriculture at Lingfield in Surrey. It is a measure of the social acceptance which Quaker business had achieved by the 1820s that Allen had close links with the Royal family and, as a Trustee of the Duke of Kent, had responsibilities, after the Duke's death, for his infant daughter Victoria.

More germane for our purposes here was his largely unsuccessful attempt in the early 1830s to swing Quaker business opinion behind the campaign to limit child labour. He was one of the most important members of the shortlived Quaker society for the 'Improvement of Conditions of Factory Children' which was founded in 1833.

How far does this failure require us to revise our basically favourable assessment of Quaker business practice?

The short answer is that the failure of the Quakers to rally behind Lord Shaftesbury should make us wary of an over-naive interpretation of the motives behind their general commitment to progressive and enlightened business practices. For whether that commitment came mainly from their hearts or their heads, there seems little doubt that the actions which resulted from it were for the most part, in the present jargon, cost effective. It is tempting to deduce from their notable failure to side with progressive forces in this case that Quaker businessmen calculated that to do so would adversely effect their financial results and impair their competitive position. They may also have felt politically inhibited about breaking ranks with the great majority of their fellow businessmen on this issue. And some may also have themselves experienced (as we shall see John Fielden did) factory work from a young age and have believed that since they had survived it so could others. But that is unlikely to be the main explanation. Adam Smith was presumably right in his notably unstarry-eyed comment, which we quoted earlier, about the decision of the Pennsylvanian Quakers to free their own slaves. A similar approach, to what might otherwise be something of a puzzle, seems appropriate here.

UNITARIANS

Thomas Firmin (1632-97) was an elder contemporary of John Bellers. By his mid-forties he had accumulated a small fortune as a successful merchant in the City of London. But he is chiefly notable for the money and effort which he devoted to charitable schemes that provided productive work for the unemployed poor. He had been alerted to the need for such schemes by no less a figure than John Biddle (or Bidle), by tradition the first of England's Unitarians. For from Biddle he learnt 'to distrust mere alms giving but rather to further the condition of the poor by personal investigation and *to reduce the causes of social distress by economic effort*'.[53] During the year of the Great Plague (1665) he provided work, making up clothing, for those thrown out of their jobs by its ravages. Later, on a more permanent basis, he set up a similar project in which the work was linen manufacture. At its zenith it is said to have provided employment for the phenomenal number of 1,700 spinners, to say nothing of flax dressers and weavers. Remuneration was on a piece-work basis and the going market rates were paid. But Firmin soon discovered that these were so low that 15 hours were normally needed to earn 6d. He then supplemented the going market rate with bonus payments.

For that and other reasons the scheme lost money and was eventually discontinued. But Firmin resembles Bellers in the subject matter of his only known published work as well as in his projects and values. Written in the form of a sequence of letters it was entitled:

Some proposals for employing the poor, especially in and about
London, and for the prevention of begging.

Like Bellers, in other words, Firmin was both intellectually
and practically interested in the problem of the unemployed
poor. Moreover there is almost a ring of the 1980s about his
discovery that if people 'price themselves into jobs' by
accepting going rates set by a fully competitive labour
market, they may find themselves unable to earn enough
even for customary subsistence.

The parallel between Firmin and Bellers is a striking
individual one. But there are more general Unitarian/Quaker
parallels. Both were religious groupings which appealed only
to a small minority. In each case their approach was neither
enthusiastic nor evangeligal but a combination of cerebral
and practical. At the same time there are differences. One is
that the Unitarians seem to have been much more politically
active, especially in their support for the long agitation which
eventually produced the Great Reform Bill, but also subsequently. If we are talking about the antecedents of the 1832
Reform Bill, the famous Unitarian names are those of Joseph
Priestly (1739–1804) and Major John Cartwright. A second
difference is that while the Quakers have been more
prominent in business, the Unitarians have been more
prominent in professional and intellectual fields. One name
must suffice: Dr Thomas Southwood Smith. He made a
mark in public health which is probably second only to that
of Edwin Chadwick, and can reasonably claim to have been
one of the founding fathers of the great mid-Victorian
movement for sanitary reform. He was also in advance of his
time in recognising the importance of publicity. He not only
dissected Jeremy Bentham's corpse but did so in public
before a gathering which included the banker and historian
George Grote and the young John Stuart Mill.

But in the reform of industrial capitalism it is probably the
name of John Fielden (1798?–1848), the successful cotton
manufacturer and radical Member of Parliament which
stands highest in the Unitarian record. For the enactment of
controls on the use of child labour in factories, and for the
eventual regulation by the State of maximum working
hours, Fielden's efforts and contributions were probably

second only to Shaftesbury's. Moreover they were efforts by which he personally, as a cotton manufacturer, could have been expected to lose.

Fielden came from a Quaker family which combined yeoman farming with manufacture, first of woollen goods and then of cotton cloth, in the neighbourhood of Todmorden in the Pennine Hills. We do not know by what arguments Richard Wright converted him to Unitarianism in 1818. But we know that he was dissatisfied with what he saw as a conservative inertia exhibited by many of his Quaker contemporaries. And we have his own account of why he entered political life:

> When I consented to become a member of Parliament it was not with a view to joining party men or aiding in party movements, but in order to assist by my vote in doing such things as I thought would benefit the labouring people . . . I have all my years of manhood been a Radical reformer because I thought that reform would give the people power in the House of Commons that would secure to them that better condition of which they are worthy.[54]

What convinced him of the need to control the employment of child labour was his own experience in being sent, like other Quaker children, to work in his father's mill at 'little more than ten years old'.[55] In his *The Curse of the Factory System* he says:

> The object of the following pages is to show that the work people have been and are cruelly treated, that they have not idly asked for protection, but that humanity and justice require it; that we shall do ourselves no harm by granting it to them; but always avowing that I would cast manufacturers to the winds rather than see the work people enslaved, maimed, vilified and broken in constitution and heart.[56]

APPENDIX: AMERICAN PROTESTANT COMMUNITIES.
In the eighteenth and nineteenth centuries a number of communities were set up in the United States under religious inspiration which were genuinely communistic. They were not intended as alternatives to capitalism. Their purpose was entirely religious, their members simply wishing to lead the

kind of life they believed Christianity demanded of them, and most of them were established under the pressure of persecution. Nevertheless we cannot ignore them because their example was extremely influential in the nineteenth century. Engels, for example, appealed to them to prove that Communism really works. We consider them at this juncture because the earliest were founded before the Declaration of Independence, and the most important, the Shaker Communities, were founded by English immigrants.

The Shakers originated in England as a sect of Quakers. In 1774 the prophetess Ann Lee with eight companions moved to America, and in 1787, three years after her death, the first Shaker Society was set up at Mount Lebanon, New York. A good number of further Societies were founded in the next 50 years, and at one time America had 5,000 Shakers. In 1907 there were still 15 Societies comprising 700 persons, and although at one time the sect was reduced to a few old ladies, younger men have been joining it in recent years. A major reason for the decline was that although their Societies contained both men and women – enjoying, moreover, complete equality of status – they were celibate: their children were brought in by new members or adopted. They had all their goods in common, and their Societies were economically successful. They seem also to have been well disciplined and contented, in spite of the fact that Shakerism lends itself to extravagant manifestations of religious enthusiasm: not merely dancing and shaking, but whirling like a top with the eyes shut, mass possession by the spirits of long dead Indians and so forth.

It is clear that the Shakers should be regarded as a Protestant religious order, and their success compared with that of those religious foundations of the Dark Middle Ages, like Whitby, which contained both monks and nuns. Much the same can be said of the other successful American religious communities.

A tradition of such communities goes back to the seventeenth century. The earliest establishment to have a long duration was Ephrata, Pennsylvania. It was founded by Conrad Beissel, who came from Germany and joined the Dunkers (so called from their method of baptism) in 1724. In 1732 he led away a splinter group to found his community. It was celibate for a time, but later permitted marriage, and still existed, though with only 17 members, in 1900. Less ancient but also long-lived and important was the community of George Rapp (1759–1847). Rapp was a German religious leader who brought his followers to the United States in 1804 to escape harassment from the Lutherans at home. His foundation remained solidly German, 300 families having emigrated with him. At one time it had 1,800 members. They settled first in Pennsylvania, then moved to Indiana, and then returned to Pennsylvania selling Harmony, their Indiana settlement, to Robert Owen. Community of goods was adopted on their arrival in America, and celibacy in 1807. Persons joining signed a covenant by which they resigned any claim to wages and, after 1836, to the capital they had brought in; in return they were guaranteed 'the necessities of life' not only 'in their days of health and strength' but 'when any of them shall become sick, infirm or otherwise unfit for labour'. They prospered economically, but membership fell off, and in 1907 there were only four or five left, all far advanced in age.

In the nineteenth century the open spaces of the United States attracted a variety of immigrant religious communities. Besides Rapp's Harmonists there were Hutterite Mennonites from Russia, the Zoar Separatists and Amana Inspirationists from Germany and Holland, the Devotionalists of Bishop's Hill from Sweden (whose colony was disorganised by the murder of their leader in open court by a violent litigant), and the German Catholics of St Nazianz, Wisconsin. But more closely in touch with secular thinking were some native products.

In 1841 the Universalist minister Adin Ballou set up the Hopedale community in Massachusetts. It lasted until 1856 and at one time had 235 members. It described itself as 'actualising as well as promulgating practical Christian socialism', and aspired to being 'a miniature Christian republic' (Ballou, 1851). Also in 1841, Brook Farm was founded by the Unitarian minister George Ripley. Its original aim, in the words of a sympathetic observer (*The Dial*, October 1841) was to establish 'the Kingdom of Heaven, as it lay in the clear spirit of Jesus of Nazareth'; it soon, however, lowered its sights to the phalanx as described in the works of Fourier, and we shall return to it in connection with that. Among later religious communities may be mentioned Martha McWhirter's Women's Commonwealth, celibate and fairly successful though small, and the Perfectionist communities of Oneida, New York, and Wallingford, Connecticut, founded by John Humphrey Noyes (1811–86).

Oneida and Wallingford are well documented since Noyes and his follower W. A. Hinds wrote the fullest accounts we have of the American communities. Their books show them to have been reasonable men, and in addition Noyes appears as a gifted writer. According to his own account, he was influenced both by the Revivalism and by the Fourierism of Brook Farm. Oneida was set up in 1848 and Wallingford, an offshoot with which it was closely united, in 1851. They were financially successful, and membership rose to over 300. Two things distinguished them from other communities. First, although they had 600 acres of land they were not primarily agricultural. Oneida, says Noyes,[57] 'made its fortune by first sinking forty thousand dollars in training a set of young men as machinists'. Its principal product was steel traps, but 'we can make tools for all other businesses, and the whole range of modern enterprise is open to us'. Secondly, they extended communism from goods to their own bodies and had what they called 'complex marriage'. Besides holding that this is in accordance with Christianity, Noyes considered that conventional monogamy is disruptive of communal life, and his system, which was carefully supervised and seems to have involved no forcing of people against their inclinations, may well have had the same practical effect as celibacy. Nevertheless it continued to scandalise more orthodox Protestants, and after holding out against formidable pressure for many years, the Perfectionists abandoned it in 1879. The communal way of life immediately began to break up. In 1881 they turned themselves into a joint stock company. They adopted a constitution, however, which made it rather a common ownership venture than a conventional capitalist firm, and according to Hinds, who by then had himself become president of the company, in 1907 it was thriving.

The success achieved by these communities, unsupported

as they were by the population around them, and encumber-
ed, in the case of the Perfectionists, by a hitherto untried
system of sexual relations, is impressive. Two things,
however, limit their value as models. First, hardly less than
Catholic monasteries and convents, they were religious
communities: they were motivated by a degree of religious
fervour which has always been exceptional in Christian
societies at large, and their internal harmony seems to have
been proportional to their exclusion of ordinary marriage.
Secondly, their communism was for internal use only. In
relation to the outside world they were enlightend employers, but still employers of the conventional type. The
Rappists, for example, owned a cutlery business which
employed 200 Chinese; the Perfectionists, even before they
became a joint stock company, had a workforce roughly
equal in numbers to themselves to do the less interesting
work in their factories and on their land.

CHAPTER FOUR

Britain After 1855

1855–1918

Metaphorically, though not in any formal sense, the period from 1855 to 1918 witnessed what G. Kitson Clark has called 'the progressive disestablishment of the Church of England'.[1] In practice and in popular estimation the Anglican church began to lose its august status as a pillar of the realm. Thoughts about its clergy becoming a genuine 'national clerisy' may perhaps still have seemed realistic in the 1830s. They could hardly have seemed other than ridiculous in the 1860s. In parallel, anyway from the late 1850s onwards, there was a shift to the left among the country's intellectual leaders. In its early stages there was no real question that this second process should extend to the point where it reached full blooded socialism in the sense of the State ownership of the means of production. Rather it was a move from the laissez-faire to social liberalism. Even the commitment of the Trades Union Congress (TUC) to public ownership, which has never been other than ambiguous, was surprisingly late (1893) rather than otherwise. The man with the best claim to have initiated the intellectual movement to the left is, of course, John Stuart Mill. We describe elsewhere the evolution of his position, and the controversy which still surrounds it. There is no need to repeat that here. But the point to stress is a simple one. Particularly in the early stages of the leftward movement of intellectual opinion the boundary line between social liberalism and full blooded socialism was fluid and in some sense ill-defined. Moreover even when, with the spread of Marx's ideas in the 1880s, a clear theoretical definition became available only a minority of serious political figures chose to emphasise or take their stand upon it. Within that minority the most famous name is William Morris.

The second key figure in promoting the leftward shift of

opinion in the final quarter of the last century was not so much Marx as the American Henry George. Here again, since we have already outlined both his general pro-market position and his most eye catching proposal – for a 100 per cent tax on landlords' ground rents – there is no need to repeat that discussion. For our purposes at this point it is the impact rather than the content of his views and those of the later Mill which is important.

That impact was probably most consequential in its effect on two bodies of opinion: the TUC and the newly formed Fabian society. In 1888 the TUC passed a 'Georgite' resolution, committing itself to the nationalisation of land. As we have just noticed it was another five years before Congress took the full blooded step of committing itself to public ownership across the board. It did so by approving a resolution which permitted it to support at General Elections only those parliamentary candidates who were themselves pledged to wholesale public ownership.

The impact on the Fabian society merits rather more extended treatment. The society itself came into existence early in 1884 following a split in its antecedent organisation, the Fellowship of the New Life. The latter has been described by Henry Pelling, the historian of the Labour Party, as having been 'vaguely Ruskinian' in outlook. Those who split away were evidently inspired by less romantic and more politically realisable social concerns. They were joined shortly afterwards by two most notable new recruits. One, George Bernard Shaw, was later to become internationally famous as a playwright. The second was Sidney Webb. Webb saw himself explicitly as a disciple of the later Mill.

It was Sidney Webb who a generation later drafted the new constitution of the Labour Party, at the request of its then general secretary, Arthur Henderson. Because that constitution formally committed the party to wholesale public ownership and because of Webb's later reputation as the embodiment of bureaucratic socialism, it is sometimes assumed that the Fabian society was committed to a more or less Marxist, though non-revolutionary, ideological position from the start. But a reading of its early history does not support this view. The society in its early days encompassed a wide range of tendencies. If anything it was almost certainly more Georgite than Marxist (or bureaucratic socialist) over the first ten years. In a famous published exchange Shaw, for example, conceded that his earlier acceptance of Marx's labour theory of value had just been plain wrong. The man who convinced Shaw of this error has already been mentioned: the economist and former Unitarian minister, Philip Wicksteed. We shall return to him later in this chapter. But the point to recall here is that Wicksteed, like George and Mill, has to be classified as a social liberal rather than a full blooded socialist.

The early Fabian Society, in short, is best seen as evidence not of a mass conversion of British intellectuals to full blooded socialism in the 1880s and 1890s but as evidence of a more diffuse leftward shift of opinion. Moreover this interpretation is confirmed by its early political stance. It was a relatively late convert to the case for a fully independent Labour Party. In its early days it aimed to influence and permeate the existing parties rather than join in forming a new one.

It would be outside the scope of this book to attempt to trace in any detail either the gradual evolution of Fabian Society policies or the sequence of steps which resulted in the eventual establishment of what became in 1906 the country's Labour Party. But it would be wrong to leave the impression that the impact of the 'new thinking', which we have mainly associated with George and Mill, was confined to the TUC and the Fabians. It was much more diffused. As we shall see in a moment it had a widespread impact across the spectrum of the country's Protestant churches. And it was a key influence on the early thinking of the Lanarkshire miner James Keir Hardie (1856–1915), the man who, more than any other, was the architect of the Labour Party.

Keir Hardie's childhood must have been unusually tough. An illegitimate child, he went out to work at the age of eight. He obtained a job as a trapper in a coal mine and learnt to read and write at night school. Though hostile throughout his life to the Established Church, the young Keir Hardie became an active member of local chapel and temperance groups before throwing himself into the work of the local miners' union branch. Henry Pelling makes a point of telling us that George's writing was an important early influence upon him. The chapel and the miners' union would have predisposed him in favour of the Liberal Party. It is thus entirely plausible to accept Pelling's contention that the future founder of the Labour Party was only deflected from standing as a Liberal candidate by the party's refusal to offer him a nomination. As it was he formed the Independent Labour Party and entered Parliament as its only member in 1893.

It will be important to remember how nearly Hardie came to the point of aligning himself with the Liberals when we consider a remarkable bunch of 'Lib-Lab' trade union leaders later in this chapter. But here what needs to be emphasised is a parallel ideological point. All the evidence is that it was the social liberal Henry George, and not Karl Marx, who mainly influenced the Labour Party's founder in his formative years. Henry Pelling reports Hardie's brief contact with the Marxist Social Democratic Federation (SDF) in London in the 1880s. Evidently the former Lanarkshire miner felt uncomfortable in that company.

Of course this is not to claim that Marx's thought was without influence on British opinion in the 1880s and 1890s. The TUC's 1893 resolution, which has already been mentioned, is sufficient warning against making that mistake. It is to claim no more than that other influences, and notably the social liberal ones which we have identified, were more important. For what it's worth the semi-romantic influence of Ruskin was probably also more influential at this time than anything which came directly or indirectly (via William Morris) from Marx.

The trade unions' decision to name their own educational establishment in Oxford after that singular, romantic moralist and sage was almost certainly no accident. But it has attracted less attention than it deserves.

However from the viewpoint of the country's Protestant Christians what was important was simply an undifferentiated leftward shift in the climate of opinion. In the political world it is best typified by the famous pronouncement of the Liberal Minister Sir William Harcourt, in 1889: 'We are all socialists now.' Similar noises were starting to come from churchmen as well.

ANGLICANS

We saw that after the failure of the Christian Socialist workshops Maurice devoted his energies to the Working Men's College. John Ruskin taught there, and although he was not an orthodox Anglican, Maurice and Ludlow almost certainly influenced his economic writings in the 1860s and 1870s and confirmed his support for what has since been called 'organic socialism'. In *Unto This Last* (1870)[2] Ruskin attacks Mill's laissez-faire economic theories, advocates the establishment of government workshops, and calls for State education. The same call was coming from such prominent Anglicans as Archdeacon Sandford of Coventry and Parliament took the decisive step with the Forster Act of 1870.

The tradition which runs from the Christian Socialists through Ruskin was first revived within the Church of England itself by the Rev Stuart Headlam. In 1877, when curate of St Matthew's, Bethnal Green, he founded the Guild of St Matthew to propagate a message of Christian Socialism both within the Church and outside it.

Headlam is an unusual figure even after one has made full allowance for the rich diversity of characters in the Church of England. He combined a radically High Church position with a political approach which was much in advance of his age. Henry Pelling quotes a remarkably radical resolution which was approved by the Guild in 1884:

> That whereas the present contrast between the condition of the great body of workers who produce much and consume little and of those classes who produce little and consume much is contrary to the Christian doctrines of Brotherhood and Justice, this meeting urges on all Churchmen the duty of supporting such measures as will tend:
> a) to restore to the people the value which they give to the land [the influence of George is obvious here];
> b) to bring about a better distribution of the wealth created by labour;
> c) to give the whole body of the people a voice in their own government; and
> d) to abolish false standards of worth and dignity.[3]

Pelling observes that as well as contributing a tract to the Fabian Society, Headlam remained Georgite all his life. It is

safe to assume that *Progress and Poverty*[4] was also a factor
behind the setting up, in 1889, of a second body to promote
Christian Socialism within the Anglican church. This was the
Christian Social Union (CSU) and its founder was Canon
Henry Scott Holland. It was from the first distinctly less
radical than the Guild of St Matthew. But its members rapidly
overtook those of the Guild, and at its peak probably reached
well over 2,000, or roughly five times the maximum figure
achieved by Headlam. Moreover within the Church it was
the more influential, probably because it was the less radical
of the two bodies. Both Charles Gore, later Bishop of
Oxford, and William Temple were members.

But whatever the effectiveness of the CSU as a body there
can be no doubt about the subsequent influence, within the
Church of England and outside it, of its leading members,
and notably of Charles Gore and William Temple. The latter
will be discussed later in this chapter. But a word needs to be
said about Gore and particularly about an important collection of essays which he sponsored and for which, when it
was first published in 1913, he contributed an introduction.
The collection is entitled: *Property, its Duties and Rights*.[5]

Some contributors adopt an historical approach to the
subject, others start from a philosophical or religious
standpoint. In his introduction Gore attempts to draw out
what he sees as the most important conclusions. He begins
by commending a key distinction between 'property for use'
and 'property for power'. And he goes on to a crucial passage
which deserves to be quoted at length:

> The conviction rises in our minds as we contemplate the facts
> that something has gone wrong with our tenure of property:
> that we need by peaceful means, and, it may be, by general
> consent, to accomplish such a redistribution of property as shall
> reduce the inordinate amount of 'property for power' in the
> hands of the few and to give all men, as far as may be, in
> reasonable measure 'property for use'. Then we ask ourselves,
> are we in entertaining such an ambition violating any sacred
> rights of property. We interrogate . . . the philosophers and we
> find . . . that we can discern no absolute right of property. *Its
> justification must depend upon no a priori principle but upon its social
> effects.*[6]

There is nothing mealy-mouthed about this introduction of Gore's. For example he asserts without qualification: 'The modern church has generally been on the wrong side.' But what gives it almost a contemporary ring in the 1980s is Gore's insistence that it is just as important to spread 'property for use' among the many as to curtail the 'property for power' of the few. He considers the counter argument that the unrestricted right to accumulate property is a necessary condition for the prosperity of industry; and he neatly turns the argument on its head:

> But what about the energy of the masses of men who can acquire no property or no sufficient property to give them secure status and hope. If you go some way to equalising opportunity . . . will you not stimulate a thousand energies and interests to one you may check.

Gore's introduction to *Property, its Duties and Rights* is reticent in only one respect. He leaves his readers in some doubt about whether the proposed redistribution of 'property for use' can be reconciled with the public or State ownership of the means of production. On the other hand he is clearly alive to the dangers of State tyranny:

> No doubt . . . it is a difficult process to guard against State tyranny on the one hand, and on the other to prevent the excess of individualism which means in practice the enslavement of the many to the few.

If only because of the circumstances of his times Gore was more conscious of the second set of dangers than the first. Moreover, as we shall see, that was if anything even more true of those, like his friends Temple and Tawney, who carried on the CSU tradition in the Church of England between the two world wars. With important qualifications both men were in principle prepared to accept public ownership. Quite possibly, and if only on a provisional basis, Gore would have accepted it as well. Plausible evidence for this view is supplied by his particularly close relationship with Tawney. He was responsible for persuading Tawney to join an important committee on 'Christianity and Industrial Problems', established by the then Archbishop of Canterbury, Randall Davidson, in 1916; a committee the report of which paved the way for two important conferences on much the same subject between the wars. They will be considered later on in this chapter. Here it is necessary to add one last word about the links between Gore and Tawney. It is not as widely known as it should be that the latter's famous *Religion and the Rise of Capitalism* was originally presented in the form of the Scott-Holland lectures in 1922 and that Charles Gore contributed a prefatory note to its first published edition.[7]

Nevertheless Gore's position is probably best seen as representing a kind of half-way house between Sir William Harcourt's 'socialism' and the qualified acceptance of public ownership by progressive Anglicans like Tawney and Temple between the wars. It was in that direction, in the period up to 1918, that the majority of progressive Anglicans were clearly moving. Yet there were Anglican voices, and not only reactionary ones, which spoke out against this trend of progressive opinion. One was that of Archdeacon Cunningham. His chief objection to State socialism was the belief that it was incompatible with Christian voluntaryism. He could well have accepted voluntary socialism or 'socialism without the State'. John Neville Figgis the philosopher, who was also first an Anglican priest and then an Anglican monk, spoke up against State socialism on much the same grounds. Yet he was one of the fiercest and most eloquent of his generation's critics of industrial capitalism. Nevertheless he objected to State socialism, on the grounds of its excessive centralisation as well as because of its non-voluntary character. Space, alas, does not permit us to do justice to either of these far-sighted Christians.

THE METHODISTS AND OTHER NON-CONFORMISTS

Both in popular recollection and according to professional historians the 'non-conformist vote' was one of the decisive factors in the Liberals' landslide electoral victory in 1906. According to a recent study more than half the Members of Parliament elected either as Liberals or with the backing of the Labour Representation Committee (LRC) – with which the Liberals had reached an informal pre-election pact – had non-conformist connections of one kind and another. It is true that this arithmetic includes, for example, both Asquith and Lloyd George. And there may have been others whose chapel affiliation was overshadowed by their political ambition and zeal. It is also true that non-conformist support for Liberal and LRC candidates was in part attributable to specialist free church concerns, to temperance legislation, for example, and to education. All the same it is reasonable to see the results of the 1906 election as evidence for the spread among the electorate in general, and among chapel congregations in particular, of a growing acceptance of Sir William Harcourt's brand of 'socialism'. No doubt the achievements in this direction of the succession of Liberal governments which followed the 1906 landslide were modest enough. The pension and national insurance schemes introduced by Lloyd George as chancellor are the only substantial examples. Nevertheless they can reasonably be seen as measures of 'social liberalism' in support of which both Liberal and Labour members could, at least at this stage of the latter's evolution, be expected to combine. For even though the LRC Members of Parliament formally reconstituted themselves as the Labour Party on the morrow of the election, the party's Clause IV constitution was still a dozen years and a world war away in the future.

However it is not this groundswell movement of non-conformist and other opinion which is chiefly interesting, for our purposes, important though it clearly is. Two rather more specific phenomena are what will mainly concern us.

The first is a movement of non-conformist clerical opinion parallel to that represented among Anglicans by the Guild of St Matthew and the CSU. Secondly we shall focus on an important group of non-conformist and mainly Primitive Methodist trade union leaders who emerged over this period. As we would expect some of these men eventually joined the Labour Party. Others remained unshakably Liberal throughout their lives.

Hugh Price Hughes (1847–1902) was the prime mover behind a loose grouping of younger Methodist ministers in the 1880s who called themselves the 'Forward Movement' and whose views found their main expression in a new weekly, the *Methodist Times*, of which, in 1885, Hughes became the first editor. His concern to be identified with the

leftward shift of opinion is indicated clearly enough by the
title of a collection of sermons which he published in 1889.
He called it *Social Christianity* and what he meant by that is
neatly summed up in a sentence quoted by Inglis:

> Jesus Christ came into this world to save human society as well
> as to save individuals, indeed you cannot effectually save the one
> without saving the other.[8]

In Hughes's own case the extent of his commitment to 'social
Christianity' seems, in fact, to have been severely restricted.
Inglis remarks that he 'put more trust in personal compassion
than in communal interference as a solution for social
distress'.[9] But his younger contemporary John Scott Lidgett
took a more radical view. He was the founder of the
Methodist settlement in Bermondsey and he remained its
warden for more than half a century (1891–1949). He was for
some years, after 1918, leader of the progressives in what was
then the London County Council. A warm admirer of
Maurice, he delivered the Maurice lectures in 1935. Finally
his book *The Fatherhood of God*, published in 1902, made him
the first Wesleyan 'whose social theory can be judged fully
collectivist'.[10]

Further to the left again was Samuel Keeble (1853–1946).
He is likely to have been one of a very small minority of
Methodist ministers who had read Marx's *Das Capital* before
the end of the last century. With the possible exception of
Lord Soper in our own day, Keeble probably went as far as any
ordained Methodist minister, at any time, in his endorsement
of a non-Marxist collectivist position.

The immediate influence of the Forward Movement, and
of Keeble in particular, was limited. Keeble's most important
book *Industrial Day Dreams* (1896) sold only 208 copies, and
he had to close down the *Methodist Weekly* in 1903 for lack of
readers. He is said, however, to have greatly influenced
Philip Snowden, and he and the Forward Movement
generally are important for initiating a new social conscious-
ness in the Methodist community. They enabled members of
that community, both clerical and lay, to come to terms with
the evolving views of the Fabians and eventually to accept –
and in the case of important individuals actively to work for –
the post-war reforms of the Attlee government.

This having been said, a caution should be reiterated. The general character of Methodism was much more capitalist, or at least 'shopocratic', than socialist or even working class. Working class leaders formed only a tiny minority of the Methodist leadership. At least until 1945 the graduates of Methodist Sunday Schools are typified not by intellectual social reformers but by that formidable master grocer and Mayor of Grantham Alfred Roberts, father of Margaret Thatcher.

Parallels to the Methodist Forward Movement can be found in Old Dissent. The views of the Congregationalist minister Dr R. F. Horton were very similar to those of John Scott Lidgett. We find him forming a 'Social Reform League' which campaigned for sanitary improvements in the neighbourhood and which was responsible for introducing the Adult School Movement into Hampstead and Kentish Town.[11] He lectured on subjects like 'the unemployed, the eight hour day and the housing question'. More unusually:

> During one of his lectures Horton spoke of Jesus as the leader of the labour party [or Labour Party – reports differed].[12]

These moves, of course, did not endear Horton to Protestants of more conservative views in politics and theology. Courage was needed to take up these positions. It was not a quality lacking in the make up of the Baptist minister Dr John Clifford. Clifford had a forceful personality and from working class beginnings came to be a Companion of Honour. In the middle of this career he joined the Fabian Society and contributed to one of its pamphlets a piece entitled 'Socialism and the Teaching of Christ'. He here expresses the hope that:

> The era of Individualism . . . may give place to one in which State-industrialism . . . will issue in a completely equipped co-operative scenario . . . Human nature is very intractable. But British Society may pass by certain stages from the limited collectivism which now exists to one which covers the whole machinery of the lower part of life and provides that physical basis of human existence on which the spiritual structure is slowly reared.[13]

This apparently bleak collectivism, he claims, has four merits:

1. It destroys the occasions of many of the evils of modern society.
2. It advances, elevates and ennobles the struggle for life.
3. It offers a better environment for the development of Christ's teaching concerning wealth and brotherhood.
4. It fosters a higher ideal of human and social wealth and well being.

The experience of the twentieth century, it may be thought, has failed to provide a notable confirmation of these judgements. But it would be wrong to leave the impression that Clifford's bleak collectivism is typical even of 'progressive' non-conformist opinion at this time. It has much more in common with the values of bureaucratic socialism which were later to become associated with the Webbs. The bulk of progressive non-conformist opinion, in this period and subsequently, endorsed a position not of State socialism but of what we have called social liberalism, or alternatively, of welfare capitalism.

And that is true as much of the Unitarians as it is of the other non-conformist denominations. Joseph Chamberlain (1836–1914) is now mainly remembered as the man who split the Liberal Party over Irish Home Rule and then became the champion of the Empire and the advocate of tariff reforms to introduce Imperial preference. His earlier political career in Birmingham and the policies of 'social managerialism' implemented there under his leadership are largely forgotten. So is his strong commitment, at least in his younger days, to the Unitarianism in which he was brought up. Yet we are assured by Holt[14] that he taught in the Sunday School of Birmingham's Unitarian Church of the Messiah for many years. His work there has two parts. First, he was instrumental in introducing into the city what later became known sometimes as 'gas and water' and sometimes as 'municipal' socialism. This involved the takeover by the local authority, from more or less short sighted local private monopolies, of the assets and operations of gas and water undertakings. If this seems an odd policy for a man who spent the later part of his political career in alliance with the Conservatives, we may recall that he proposed marriage to Beatrice Potter some

years before she met her eventual husband Sidney Webb. His
Birmingham policies reflect a genuine social concern as well
as a commitment to efficient methods of management.
Secondly, he was the first civic leader in one of the country's
major industrial cities to inaugurate a major programme of
slum clearance and rebuilding.

In addition to these local activities, Chamberlain became a
chief figure in the National Educational League in 1869. Its
main purposes were first to make propaganda for the basic
principles of State financed, universal and compulsory
education which were enshrined in the Forster Education Act
of the following year. Secondly it campaigned for a new
system of religious education: State schools should themselves be non-sectarian, but each and every religious sect
should be free to provide religious education on State school
premises, to children whose parents chose that they should
receive it.

The reforming efforts of another distinguished Unitarian,
Sir James Stansfield, were concentrated in a narrower area. J.
L. and B. Hammond, who wrote a biography of him, gave it
the sub-title 'A Victorian Champion of Sex Equality'. He
made his name through championing the repeal, accom-
plished in 1886, of the Contagious Diseases Act of 1864. This
had empowered police and magistrates to arrest and detail for
examination and treatment any woman suspected of promiscuity.

But the most remarkable Unitarian figure of the period
1855–1918 is Philip Wicksteed. Besides being one of the
leading Unitarian ministers in London, he was a distinguished classical and medieval scholar, an outstanding economist, and one of the founders of the Labour Church
movement of the 1890s. It is only the last two facets of his
career which concern us here.

Wicksteed's interest in economics, like that of the Fabians,
was kindled by Henry George. His principal work, *The
Common Sense of Political Economy*, was published in 1910[15]
well after his resignation from the ministry, but does not
reflect any movement away from Christian ethical ideas. He
is a defender, and a compelling one, of the market system.
For he believes that when a system of competitive markets is
functioning properly it will produce an optimum output of

goods and services. In this respect he stands in the classic tradition of liberal economists, and his position is mainly distinctive only because of his elegant and exhaustive elucidation (in opposition to Marx's labour-theory of value) of the theory of marginal utility. On the other hand he sees nothing sacrosanct in those features of the *status quo* which have nothing to do with the proper functioning of a market system. He sees neither theoretical nor moral objections to the redistribution of *unearned* income; and none to the progressive taxation of those incomes which are actually earned. He seems to favour the eventual acquisition by the community of the ownership of land, and he is not altogether opposed to further extensions of public ownership so far as these can be made compatible with the proper functioning of markets. But reformers should arrange things in such a way that market forces are working for them and not against them.

Wicksteed recognises that market forces may depress wages below the level even of subsistence for unskilled workers. But he rejects any suggestion that a correct solution lies in the imposition by the State of a minimum wage. He also, unlike Ruskin and William Morris, believes in unlimited division of labour. 'Society', he says, 'is enriched by it.' We must keep it. But there is a crucial proviso which Wicksteed insists is necessary if we are to 'accept without either terror or reproach a competitive system'.[16] The proviso has two parts. First, such a competitive system is morally acceptable only if privilege is eliminated and a democratic equality of opportunity prevails. Secondly, it must be possible for positions at the bottom to be filled 'with dignity and satisfaction'.

Wicksteed is exceptional if not unique among the reformers we have considered in that he had the energy and capacity to study the inner workings of the competitive system, and having done so concluded that the system should stand. His is the most distinguished intellectual contribution of Unitarianism to the issues raised in this book.

On the practical side Wicksteed's contribution was to join John Trevor (1855–1929) in starting the Labour Churches movement. Trevor was of English birth, but studied for the Unitarian ministry in America (where he visited, but was apparently unimpressed by, Oneida). Returning to England he lived for a while as an agnostic, but resumed his ministry to work first with Wicksteed in London and then on his own in Manchester. In Manchester he launched the first Labour church with Wicksteed's help and probably under his inspiration. In *What do the Labour Churches Stand For?* (1892) Wicksteed writes:

> What workman can walk into a middle class congregation with the consciousness that the underlying assumptions, both in the pew and in the pulpit, as to the proper organisation of active industrial life and the justification of social and industrial institutions, are in a militant sense his own? And if he cannot do that, then in asking him to join in the worship you are not asking him to express and nourish the religious aspects of his own higher life but to suppress or suspend that life in order that he may share in the devotions of others, who cheerfully accept, and in many cases would stubbornly defend, the things against which it is his mission to fight.[17]

The Labour churches were founded to meet this need of working men for a church in which they could feel at home. That such a need existed is proved by the fact that 22 were opened in the next four years. Some 50 years earlier the so-called Chartist churches had sprung up for the same reason, and there are close parallels between the two movements. Unitarian ministers were active in the Chartist churches too. In Chartist churches it was usual to pick a text from the Bible which had some relevance to political or social problems, and using it as a starting point try to find a solution along Christian lines.[18]

Services in the Labour churches seem to have been similar: there were addresses on politico-religious subjects, and readings from the Bible and from works by progressive writers. Keir Hardie, who was, as we have seen, hostile to the Established Church and to Methodism, strongly supported Trevor. So did Ben Tillett and other activist union leaders. This is the basis for Pelling's claim[19] that the Labour churches were mainly a protest against the Methodist alliance with the Liberal Party. It is arguable, however, that Pelling confuses a consequence with a cause. The Labour churches may have helped to detach non-conformists from Liberalism and win them to the idea of a Labour party; but they arose to satisfy a desire and a need on the part of working people in the last century to have their own religious institutions, instead of attending as second rank citizens in churches organised by other classes. Horace Mann, in his famous commentary on the Census of Religious Worship in 1851, provides a striking official acknowledgement of this need. It has its parallel in our own day in the establishment of their own churches by Christians among the country's ethnic minorities.

In this respect the Labour churches contrast with other unorthodox religious ventures started by social reformers in the 1890s. An example is the Brotherhood Church founded in 1892 by J. Bruce Wallace. Branches were later opened in Croydon and elsewhere for the purpose of replacing exhortation by thought and sacraments by five o'clock tea. But at the original building in Southgate Road, North London events were less anaemic. It was there that Bertrand Russell, the radical philosopher and godson of John Stuart Mill, was besieged by women with nail-studded boards, and there that not only Lenin but also Stalin took part in the Fifth Congress of the Russian Social Democratic Party.[20]

Of Christians outside the Unitarian fold Trevor seems to have had most admiration for William Booth (1829–1912). Insofar as the Salvation Army was designed rather to relieve effects of social problems than to remove their causes, though it is an important Christian response to those problems, it falls outside our scope; but Booth's activity was not in fact limited to works of charity.

Booth was partly of Jewish descent and started life as a pawnbroker. He was converted to Methodism and in the 1850s he and Catherine, his equally dynamic wife, were itinerant preachers in the New Connexion. Feeling, however, that they were not reaching the masses, they became evangelical freelances, and in 1865 inaugurated their Christian Mission in Whitechapel. Their methods of attracting attention by bands, hymns and advertising literature were novel and not unsuccessful. The weekly paper *War Cry* reached a circulation of 350,000 copies in 1883. At this time their activity was purely religious; it was only in the later

1880s that they started to set up 'slum posts' and 'night shelters' for the down and out.

By 1890, however, when he published *In Darkest England and the Way Out*, Booth had come to see that it was useless to provide . . .

> . . . temples and meeting houses to save men from perdition in a world which is to come, while never a helping hand is stretched out to save them from the inferno of their present life . . . [It was necessary to] change the circumstances of the individual when they are the cause of his wretched condition and lie beyond his control.[21]

For this he proposed 'self helping and self sustaining communities' in cities, in the country and overseas. Booth estimated the number of chronically unemployed at 3,000,000, and hoped in the long run to provide a livelihood for all.

This hope, of course, was not fulfilled. Nevertheless with the help of another Unitarian minister, Herbert Mills, a pilot agricultural project was tried at Hadleigh, Essex, which had 325 colonists in 1892. The Salvation Army also started some industrial workshops which they optimistically called 'elevators'. Some of them lasted at least until 1914, and Frederick Coutts, a recently retired General, is probably justified in claiming them as pioneering experiments in the provision of 'sheltered employment'.

INFLUENCE IN THE TRADES UNIONS AND LABOUR MOVEMENTS

Trevor's Labour churches tell us that the distinctions of social class are not miraculously transcended when people cross the threshold of church or chapel. The work of the Salvation Army in the period before the First World War reminds us how far the industrial capitalism of those days was from the welfare capitalism of today. The Forward Movement among the Methodists, and the CSU and the Guild of St Matthew among the Anglicans, tell us, at the very least, that something like a social conscience was starting to develop among progressive Christians towards the end of the nineteenth century. The proliferation during this period of

Christian (usually denominational) settlements in what we would today call 'deprived inner city areas' is further evidence of the same thing. John Scott Lidgett's Methodist settlement in Bermondsey was only one. Toynbee Hall, founded seven years earlier (1884) in Whitechapel as a result of Anglican Christian socialist initiatives (and with help from Balliol College) is probably more famous. There was even a Unitarian settlement, with which Mrs Humphrey Ward, as well as Philip Wicksteed, were associated. Their impact, even in their immediate vicinities, was probably never more than quite modest. Their importance was rather that they offered 'exposure' to working class conditions of life to young middle class Christians with a social conscience. (In this sense they can be compared with the Industrial Mission of the British churches of the last 30 years. For, as we shall see, this is mainly important in that it provides clergymen with some exposure to industrial life.)

Yet it is arguable that from the standpoint of Britain's subsequent economic and social development none of these was really important. Of much greater consequence, or so it has been argued, was Christian and Methodist influence on the trade unions and the Labour movement. Indeed in his *Social and Political Influence of Methodism in the Twentieth Century* Robert Wearmouth comes close to presenting Methodism in general, and the Primitive Methodists in particular, as the chief parent of Britain's labour movement from the 1850s onwards.[22] Wearmouth's interpretation can perhaps be partly discounted. He was essentially the 'official' historian of Methodism in his day and he perhaps fails to put adequate emphasis on the distinction between social liberalism on the one hand and Clause IV socialism on the other. But in their writings on trade union history the Webbs lay great stress on the importance of the Methodist contribution. Moreover towards the end of his long life Arthur Henderson chose to highlight the non-conformist influence on his generation of Labour leaders in no uncertain terms.

> When I first became a member of the Trade Union Movement, close on 50 years ago, the majority of the leaders locally and nationally were actively engaged in religious work as lay preachers, church deacons etc. . . . The political Labour

Movement, which developed out of the Trade Union Movement, and drew the majority of its early Parliamentary leaders
from it, received much of its driving force and inspiration from
radical non-conformists.[23]

At least at the statistical level there is good evidence about the
size of the Methodist and other non-conformist contribution
to the development of the trade unions after 1850. According
to Wearmouth[24] 'recent investigation has produced a list of
eighty Trade Union leaders who owed their career, position
and influence to their religious experience'. Their allegiances
were:

Primitive Methodists: 46
United Methodists: 14
Wesleyan Methodists: 9
Independent Methodists: 1
Other Denominations: 10

Methodists were especially numerous and influential in the
various miners' organisations in the north-east of England.
Thomas Burt (1837–1922) and William Straker (1855–1941)
are probably the most famous. Both grew up in the
Northumberland coalfields where Burt became the general
secretary of what was then the Northumbrian Miners'
Mutual Confidence Association and Straker succeeded him as
general secretary in the early years of this century.

Both their record and their own testimony are such as to
leave us in no doubt about the importance to them of their
Primitive Methodism. Straker became a local preacher and
though Burt appears not to have done so – indeed he has been
claimed by the Unitarians – he attended Methodist chapel
twice on Sundays and was a total abstainer. Further evidence
of his commitment to Methodist goals is provided by the
inclusion of two more or less standard non-conformist
demands in his first address to the voters of Morpeth in 1874:

– The disestablishment and disendowment of the Church of
  England
– Free and non sectarian religious education.

Burt and another miner, Alexander Macdonald, were the
first two working men to be elected to Parliament. Burt held

Morpeth from 1874 to 1918 and Wearmouth concedes that he was 'a staunch Liberal all his days'.[25] Of course he was not a laissez-faire Liberal who believed in the unfettered free play of market forces. Rather he was a social liberal and believed that market forces should be tempered by the ameliorative action of the State and in other ways. Though he was one of the most outspoken opponents of the bill to introduce a statutory eight hour day into the mining industry, he was closely associated with the Employers' Liability Act in 1880 and active in his support for an array of new measures dealing with safety in the mines. It goes without saying that he refused to join the Labour Party; and though, against his opposition, the Northumberland Miners eventually joined the Miners' Federation of Great Britain, he declined to do so himself. Of his career as a union leader Straker wrote:

> Burt never shirked a fight, but would never advise one until every other means of reaching a reasonable settlement had been tried in vain . . . Throughout his whole career he was noted for his conciliatory methods in all trade disputes.[26]

Unlike Burt, Straker like all or almost all of the union leaders of his own generation, joined the Labour Party. But the Liberal – even Libertarian – principles of his youth shine through his evidence to the 1919 Hankey Commission on the future of coalmining:

> Wages and conditions have improved but the discontent and unrest have not disappeared. The unrest is deeper than the pounds shillings and pence, necessary as they are. The root of the matter is the straining of the spirit of man to be free.

The difference between Burt and Straker can be explained, at least in part, by differences of generation. The younger man's views, and his decision to join the Labour Party, reflect the progressive leftward movement of intellectual and trade union opinion over the period up to 1914 which we have already outlined. Closer in both age and outlook to Thomas Burt were two other prominent trade union leaders and Liberal Members of Parliament: John Wilson (1837–1915) and Joseph Arch (1826–1919). Wilson (who was converted to Primitive Methodism after an intemperate youth and became a local preacher in 1870) was first elected a Liberal Member of Parliament in 1885. He became Secretary of the Durham Miners in 1896. Joseph Arch, who came from the family of a farm labourer and whose father was exceptional in that he regularly attended the Church of England, was also converted to Primitive Methodism and became a local preacher in 1847. He is chiefly famous for having founded first the Warwickshire Agricultural Labourers' Union and then the National Union, in 1872. He was twice elected Liberal Member of Parliament for North West Norfolk.

It was to men of the stamp and outlook of Joseph Arch and John Wilson that Arthur Henderson referred when he wrote, as we quoted earlier, that in his youth the 'majority of [trade union] leaders locally and nationally were actively engaged in religious work'. It seems perverse not to accept that their policies and values were coloured by their religious beliefs. Putting the same point in a different way it seems certain that their policies and values would have been quite other than they actually were if their chapel membership had been non-existent or unimportant. For one thing it is easy to believe that, like Keir Hardie, they were not men who felt any instinctive sympathy for the Marxist SDF. But had their chapel commitment been weak or absent their antipathy for the SDF would also, most probably, have been less pronounced.

But we still have to ask what did their chapel membership mean to them? One plausible answer is that it gave them a combination of both self respect and social respect. Others, starting from the Webbs and continuing down to our own day, have stressed the importance of Methodist (and particularly Primitive Methodist) membership, with its class meetings and public speaking, as a school for political and trade union organisation. That was, of course, immensely important. But it fails to capture the specific impact of their Methodism upon them. Local Chartist societies could supply training in organisational and political skills. But they could not supply a specifically Methodist ingredient.

There is evidence that both John Wilson and Joseph Arch spoke or preached on Robert Burns's famous text: 'a man's a man for a' that'. The text, it need hardly be said, is an affirmation of mens' rights to the respect of both themselves and their fellows and to an acknowledgement of their intrinsic worth and status as human beings. It is easy to see how directly Burns's text must have 'spoken to the condition' of working people in the period we are talking about. And it is not difficult to imagine its impact.

But, of course, if the message is 'a man's a man for a' that' it may carry with it an important corollary. As Durham miners' leader, John Wilson came to enjoy the respect not only of his fellow citizens in general but of the majority of the Durham coal owners in particular. Those who identify themselves with Robert Burns's text may well be that much more able to be reconciled to a world in which some are capitalists and some are trade union leaders, some are more and some are much less economically privileged. They may well be the more ready, in short, to reconcile themselves with outcomes which, even assuming moderate government intervention, are mainly the result of a market system.

That, at any rate, seems to have been more or less the position of Thomas Burt and John Wilson. Moreover as Robert Moore[27] has shown in his excellent study of three Durham mining villages which were dominated by the Primitive Methodists from about 1870 to 1926, the views of these two men were not untypical. There was at least a limited acceptance of a market system. In the miners' lodges and the Primitive Methodist chapels there was also the feeling that within a mainly market system it was still possible for a working man to follow an honourable calling, whether as a miner or as a union leader.

This was then perhaps the classic working class Liberal (or Lib-Lab) position down to 1918 or, in the case of the Durham pit villages studied by Robert Moore, down to the final collapse of the great miners' strike in 1926. It recalls Philip Wicksteed's objective: a system in which market forces continue to operate but in which there is also real dignity for all callings, including those which might otherwise be dismissed as lowly.

But it would be quite wrong to leave the impression that all Primitive Methodists (let alone all non-conformists) shared the views of men like Thomas Burt and John Wilson during this period. For one thing, not even all Primitive Methodists, let alone all Methodists, were working people and members of trade unions. As a recent study has shown there were immeasurably more successful Methodist businessmen than Methodist trade union leaders during this period. There was at least one Primitive Methodist who, if he didn't quite become a millionaire, was close to doing so. Moreover there is no evidence that the Primitive Methodist membership looked askance at business success and profit making: very much the reverse. As early as the middle of the nineteenth century the Methodists are said, by a historian of the generation before Robert Wearmouth's to have embarked on their 'mahogany age'. William Booth and his wife regularly complained that Methodism in their day had become a 'shopocracy'. We should remember too that it was his pre-1914 Methodist upbringing which exerted a profound influence on the future Mayor of Grantham, the formidable Alfred Roberts.

Nor, switching to the opposite end of the political spectrum, would it be correct to leave the impression that the views of men like Burt and Wilson represent the farthest point on the left to which Primitive Methodists (or other non-conformists) were prepared to venture. We have already noticed that Straker were significantly more radical than Burt. So was Joseph Arch who, though he fundamentally accepted the system, campaigned with his union and in Parliament to improve it, by strengthening the organisations of working people and by government intervention. And there were Methodist trade union leaders during this period, even if perhaps only a minority, who like Samuel Keeble were committed to a fully fledged socialist position. In short, then as now, you could find Methodists and other non-conformists, you could find free churchmen at all points of the political spectrum. Mr Tony Benn, and Dr Rhodes Boyson, are good examples of the same phenomenon today.

Nevertheless, for our purposes in this book, it is legitimate to highlight the lives and views of those working class Liberals in the period before 1914 who were also committed Christians and mainly, though not invariably, Primitive Methodists. It is legitimate to do so because they seem to have made a real effort to reconcile their Christian principles with at least a modified version of a market system. They did so, essentially, by stressing the equal worth – in a human and democratic sense of equal – of all who contributed within such a system. It may be no accident that Philip Baxendale, in our own day, has indicated that similar considerations were among those in his mind when he converted his highly successful family business, Richard Baxendale and Sons, into the Baxi Partnership in 1982. Mr Baxendale would not claim that he was a regularly practising Methodist. But he acknowledges the important influence of his Methodist upbringing and schooldays. Finally it is worth noting that a similar combination of values is reflected in the work of those two great Quaker industrialists, Joseph Rowntree and his son Seebohm. However for various reasons we shall consider their contributions elsewhere.

1918–1951: TEMPLE AND TAWNEY

Progressive Anglican thought in the period after 1918 was dominated by two men whose names have already been mentioned: William Temple and R. H. Tawney. Both became paid up members of the Labour Party at the moment when, in 1918 as we have already seen, it became formally committed by its new constitution to the public ownership of the means of production. When under Clement Attlee the party came to power in 1945 and proceeded to carry out a reorganisation of society, the reorganisation, of course, very much reflected that commitment. From 1918 onwards Tawney and Temple made important contributions to shaping the features of the society which the Labour Party was trying to bring to birth. At the same time they did much to prepare the Church of England to accept and even support the Attlee reforms.

Temple and Tawney were more or less exact contemporaries. Born in the early 1880s they went to the same school, Rugby and the same Oxford College, Balliol, and early became great friends. Temple followed his father into the church. Tawney's career was essentially an academic one, but it was unusual for someone of his background in that it included a long early spell in the Workers' Educational Association and two years serving in the ranks, rather than as an officer, in the First World War. Temple became Bishop of Manchester in 1921, Archbishop of York in 1929, and finally, like his father before him, Archbishop of Canterbury in 1942. Tawney had immense personal influence on the leaders of the Attlee administration. Moreover he was married to the sister of William (eventually Lord) Beveridge, the chief architect of the Welfare State.

Within the Church of England, Tawney and Temple exercised their main influence partly with their writings and partly through two important conferences, the first early and the second late in the inter-war period. Despite their different titles both conferences were chiefly concerned with the subject matter of this book: the Christian response to industrial capitalism. Both can be seen as having developed out of Randall Davidson's committee on Christianity and Industry, the work of which we noticed early on in this chapter. As well as Tawney, the future Labour Party leader, George Lansbury, had been a member of that committee.

There is something of a 1980s ring about the second of two specific initiatives which, Temple tells us, followed the 'Conference on Christian Politics, Economics and Citizenship' (COPEC) held in Birmingham in 1924:

> . . . the Christian ratepayers of a London Borough approached their Borough Council with a demand that their rates be *increased* in order that some very bad housing in the Borough might be improved. When it became apparent . . . that the Chancellor of the Exchequer would, for the first time in several years, have a surplus to dispose of, a great number of Christian income tax-payers wrote to their Members of Parliament to urge that restoration of the 'cuts' in unemployment relief should take precedence of any reduction in the rate of income tax.[28]

However it was the second conference, an international one held in Oxford in 1937, which came closest to defining Christian policies on 'the social question' which were in line with those of the then Labour Party. Tawney and Temple were perhaps the two key figures at this Oxford gathering. According to Ronald Preston[29] the former expressed some dissatisfaction that the conference did not formally commit the churches even to selective nationalisation. On the other hand its final documents include a list of 'points in the economic sphere at which the purpose of God is challenged'.

And they show considerable overlap with the official thinking of the Labour Party at the time:

1. The ordering of economic life has tended to enhance acquisitiveness and to set up a false standard of economic and social success.
2. Indefensible inequalities of opportunity in regard to education, leisure and health continue to prevail; and the existence of economic classes presents an obstacle to human fellowship which cannot be tolerated by the Christian conscience.
3. Centres of economic power have been formed which are not responsible to any organ of the community and which cannot be tolerated by the Christian conscience.
4. The only form of employment open to many men and women, or the fact that none is open at all, prevent them finding a sense of Christian vocation in their daily lives. [30]

The fact that the conference committed itself to this list of critical points, which Tawney almost certainly helped to draft, is the best evidence for his own and Temple's impact on fellow Christians of their generation. But, of course, they were also influential because of their writings and other actions.

Temple was among the group of Church leaders who attempted to bring the coal miners' union and the coal owners together in 1926 to find a solution to the coal strike, one as bitter even if not as protracted, as its successor in 1984–5. And though he conceded, in a letter to Seebohm Rowntree many years later, that the intervention had perhaps been ill advised, he always asserted the Church's right to speak out on social political and economic issues. He does so most forcefully in the opening chapter of his *Christianity and Social Order*, first published in 1942.

Temple is careful to distinguish between the main body of the text, the 'substance' of which, he asserts, 'every Christian might endorse' and a set of detailed personal proposals which are added as an appendix and which Christians are free to accept or reject. Even the latter, however, are marked by a most notable balance:

The question now is not – shall we be socialists or shall we be individualists. But – how socialist and how individualist shall we be. [31]

And again a page later:

> Our need is to find channels for right self interest which does not
> encourage exaggeration of it as our present order does.
> Communal ownership would entirely close one channel to it and
> open others – especially the road to the bureaucratic aristocracy
> which is an evident feature of the Russian system. [32]

The two quotations suggest the values of social liberalism.
But, unlike Philip Wicksteed, Temple was not a convinced
believer in the virtues of the competitive market system.
Moreover he makes no secret of his belief in government
intervention and planning:

> No one doubts that in the post-war world our economic life
> must be 'planned' in a way and to an extent that Mr Gladstone
> (for example) would have regarded and condemned as
> socialistic. [33]

Temple in fact desires enough 'planning' to provide social
security and full employment, and will countenance a
measure of nationalisation. Among his most specific proposals, two are particularly noteworthy. As regards investment
capital, he recommends a fixed maximum rate of dividends,
and a principle of amortisation according to which:

> As soon as the interest paid on any investment is equal to the
> sum invested, the principal should be reduced by a specified
> amount each year until the claim of the investor to interest or
> dividends was extinguished. [34]

Secondly, in anticipation of the industrial democracy proposals put forward by Lord Bullock in the 1970s he suggests a
'specially created Planning Authority' which should . . .

> . . . regulate the Articles of Association of limited liability
> companies and should be instructed to ensure that labour is
> effectively represented on their directorates. Thus the wage
> earners in any given concern would be represented, if not
> directly, then through the great labour organisations. [35]

The reader of the 1980s will be struck by the originality of
these proposals, but also by what Temple leaves out. His

book contains no adequate acknowledgement of the evils of monopoly, private or public. Neither does he consider the possibility that 'small' might be 'beautiful'. On the contrary:

> There is a sentimental value in these little firms. But they are a hindrance to progress in the science and art of management. Under our proposals men will be less likely to 'start a little business' because it is more respectable; so much the better.[36]

At the same time there is an important and frequently neglected passage in the body of the book in which Temple directs attention to the value of groups intermediate between the individual and the State as a whole. Modern democracy, he says . . .

> . . . has been impatient of those intermediate groupings and has moved towards 'individualism' or 'collectivism' *as if there were no third alternative*. But it seems scarcely too much to say that neither individualism nor collectivism is compatible with a truly Christian understanding of man or life.[37]

In fact Temple seems to be running two quite separate points into one. The first is the need for a third *system*, a system which is neither laissez-faire capitalism nor State socialism. The second is the need to foster institutions (of whatever kind) intermediate between the individual and the State. But he offers his readers no very clear guidance about how these needs are to be met. On the other hand there are hints about his thinking when he discusses the 'participation by labour in the conduct of the actual work of production':

> The ideal arrangement would be a revival of something like the mediaeval guilds on the basis of national charters.[38]

But if this suggests a sympathy for syndicalism or guild socialism the following sentence points to a rather different solution:

> An alluring illustration of this was afforded by the Zeiss glassworks at Jena before 1914; I do not know what happened to this admirable scheme and I hope it still flourishes.[39]

That particular scheme was in operation at the level of an individual works or enterprise. It had nothing to do with a national charter or national guilds. However it evidently incorporated a high degree of worker participation in both ownership and control.

Given our own pre-occupation with schemes like that at the Jena glassworks, Temple's reference to it is a valuable pointer. But it would be a mistake to assign it more than a rather peripheral position in his thinking. Moreover, though, as we have seen, he addressed himself at some length to questions about the ownership and control of industrial establishments these were probably never his main preoccupations at least between the wars. For he was clearly more concerned to correct manifest evils than with more fair weather initiatives of social engineering:

> Unemployment is the most hideous of our social evils and has lately seemed to have become established in a peculiarly vicious form. We have long been acquainted with transitional, seasonal and cyclical unemployment – in which catalogue the adjectives represent a *crescendo* of evil; but now we have also to face long term unemployment.[40]

Moreover Temple backed up his denunciation of the evils of unemployment with action. When Archbishop of York he was instrumental in persuading the Pilgrim Trust to finance an important study. Its main object was to collect information about the effects of unemployment on men and women who had lost their jobs and on their families and communities. Of course there have been many similar enquiries and research projects since then, and especially over the last 15 years. But when it was published, in 1938, as *Men Without Work*[41] the study had all the impact of a pioneering piece of social research. By the time of its publication the unemployed totals had fallen quite sharply; in part because of a slow rearmament build-up; in part for other reasons. Nevertheless the study attracted considerable attention when it first appeared. Nor is it surprising that there has been a marked renewal of interest in it in recent years: so much so that a new edition of *Men Without Work* is due to be published shortly in the United States.

Like his friends the Webbs, to whom he dedicated his book *Equality* (1931), Tawney was and remained to the end of his life in large measure a Clause IV socialist. But, as we shall see, his position in this respect rested more on technical than ideological grounds. Moreover, in sharp contrast to the Webbs, he was a critic rather than an admirer of the Soviet system. And it would be quite wrong to conclude, from his devotion to the Labour Party, that his political philosophy can be summarised in the two propositions: 'the unions right or wrong' and 'public ownership right or wrong'. That would be at the very least a gross oversimplification. As regards the first, in *The Attack* one of the very few of his post-war publications which deals with contemporary issues he writes:

> If the condition of something approaching full employment were established, both the power and responsibility of organised labour would be greatly increased. It might abuse the former and ignore the latter.[42]

Tawney's starting point about ownership, if we consider not merely *Equality* but his earlier work *The Acquisitive Society* (1921) recalls the views of Bishop Gore quoted earlier in this chapter. It is that we need to distinguish between its 'active' and 'passive' varieties. Ownership is of the first kind, for our purposes, when it enables someone to perform a socially useful function. It is of the second kind when it carries with it no productive or other socially useful obligations at all. Only then is it 'corrupting to the principle of industry'.[43] But:

> The characteristic fact, which differentiates most modern property from that of the pre-industrial age, and which turns against it the very reasoning by which formerly it was supported is that in modern economic conditions ownership is not active but passive, that to most of those who own property today it is not a means of work but an instrument for the acquisition of gain or the exercise of power.[44]

This distinction is central both to Tawney's analysis in *The Acquisitive Society* and to his policy proposals:

> As far as property is concerned, such a policy would possess two edges. On the one hand it would aim at abolishing those forms of property in which ownership is divorced from obligations.

On the other it would seek to encourage those forms of economic organisation under which the worker, whether owner or not, is free to carry on his work without sharing its control or its profits with the mere rentier . . . Insofar as it abolishes those kinds of property which are merely parasitic, it facilitates the restoration of the small property owners in those kinds of industry for which small ownership is adapted. A socialistic policy to the former is not antagonistic to the 'distributist state' but, in modern economic conditions, a necessary preliminary to it.[45]

But how can we reconcile these views with Tawney's undoubted commitment to the public ownership and nationalisation measures of the Attlee government? The answer is clear enough. He happened to believe that worker ownership arrangements were applicable only to small or very small undertakings. He could not imagine a set of structures which would make them applicable to medium-sized, let alone to really large organisations. For the latter he believed that some form of public ownership was the only practicable solution. Since he rejected conventional private capitalist ownership of medium and large scale undertakings – on the double grounds that it was inescapably tyrannical and bound to involve parasitic wealth – he had no alternative position to adopt. Thus he was a public ownership man for essentially technical rather than ideological or fundamentalist reasons.

It may be added that even in *Equality* Tawney is quite clear that democracy comes before socialism:

If these laudable improvements [sc. nationalisation of banks and key industries] leave the British public cold, an enlightened minority has neither the right nor the power to force them down reluctant throats.[46]

Tawney then is a democratic socialist. Doubtless it is this that both explains and justifies the choice of him by the Social Democratic Party (SDP) as their Patron Sage and the naming of their counterpart to the Fabian Society after him. His placing of his commitment to democracy before that of his commitment to socialism must reflect, among other things, the fundamental Christian values which he shared with his friend Temple and to which the latter gives due emphasis in *Christianity and Social Order*:

> . . . it is worthwhile to notice how absolute was Christ's respect for the freedom of personal choice. He would neither bribe nor coerce men to become his followers. Judas was allowed to betray him if he so determined. Not even to save a man from that will the Lord over-ride his freedom. For in freedom all spiritual life utterly depends.[47]

THE POST-ATTLEE WORLD

Almost certainly since the early 1950s as well as before, a majority of practising Anglicans, both lay and clerical, have voted Conservative at elections. To that extent Disraeli's happy description of the Church of England as the Tory party at prayer has still some aptitude. But equally, over the last 30 years as well as earlier, an articulate minority of Anglican clergymen has spoken up in favour of the current programmes of the Labour Party and its allies. Bishop Stockwood and the late Canon Collins are two of the most well known names in recent times. Moreover the party's ranks in Parliament have continued to include a number of committed Anglicans in the tradition of George Lansbury. Mary Hamilton says of Lansbury in the *Dictionary of National Biography*:

> In his own person and in the wide devotion which he inspired within the Labour movement and beyond it, he represented the truth that the inspiration of British Socialism is derived rather from the Bible than from Karl Marx.

But the attention of socially concerned Anglicans has shifted substantially in the post-Attlee world: away from domestic issues and in the direction of Third World ones in general and of those associated with the racial tyranny in South Africa in particular. Bishop Huddleston is the classic representative figure of this change of preoccupations and priorities. The impact of his work and writing about South Africa, Tanzania and Mauritius has been incomparably greater than anything which occurred during his spell as Bishop of Stepney in London's East End.

There have also been distinguished contributions by

Anglican laymen in the same direction, awakening the Church's conscience to the poverty of the Third World and to the iniquity of racial tyranny. Among the most notable of these lay Anglicans are the married team of Guy Clutton-Brock and his wife Molly. It may not be an accident that they spent the early years of their married life between the wars in London where Guy was employed in social and youth work. But from the middle 1950s till the early 1970s they worked in Southern Africa, in what are now Botswana, Malawi and Zimbabwe. Their work embraced both rural development and political opposition to the white settler regime in what was then Southern Rhodesia. It came to an end only when Guy was physically deported from Southern Rhodesia by Mr Ian Smith in 1971 and had to give up his agricultural development work at Cold Comfort Farm.

Guy and Molly Clutton-Brock's move from Bethnal Green to the banks of the Limpopo can be taken as a symbol of the changing priorities of those socially committed Anglicans which we are talking about. The change has not been confined to the Church of England. Among Methodists, perhaps the leading example is the Rev Colin Morris, sometime adviser to President Kaunda of Zambia and co-author of the latter's book *Zambian Humanism*.

In Chapter VI of our book we shall record a parallel shift of direction in the social teaching of the Catholic Church. It is outside our scope to describe the work of Christians in the Third World in any detail, but two quite short observations are in order.

First, there is some evidence that Christians working in the Third World are coming increasingly to favour co-operative organisations as the best mechanisms for both agricultural and non-agricultural development. The Clutton-Brocks's Cold Comfort Farm was structured as a co-operative. Indication of a more general as well as a Roman Catholic predisposition in favour of co-ops in the Third World was an international conference devoted to Workers' Co-ops and held at the Coady International Institute at the University of Antigonish in Nova Scotia during the late summer of 1982. The Institute was founded in the 1950s in memory of Moses Coady whose work in promoting co-operative initiatives in Canada's isolated maritime provinces is described later.

Those who attended the 1982 conference could hardly fail to have been struck by the commitment to the promotion of co-operatives expressed by a wide diversity of people, ranging from Indian Jesuits working in rural Kerala to leaders of active women's groups in Zimbabwe.

The second point is a more negative one. Christian and Anglican commitment to Third World causes, both those which have to do with poverty and those connected with racial tyranny, was the subject of a powerful and widely publicised challenge at the end of the 1970s. The author of the challenge was the Rev Edward Norman, Dean of Peterhouse, Cambridge. Dr Norman presented the BBC's Reith Lectures in 1979 under the title 'Christianity and the World Order'. Both here and in his earlier (1976) *Church and Society in England, 1770–1970* he makes clear his loyalty to the political and economic tradition of laissez-faire.[48]

Dr Norman apart, Bishop David Sheppard was the only senior Anglican to publish a full account of his views on the social and economic issues faced by Britain at present, until the broadcast and publication of the 1985 Hibbert lecture by the recently appointed Bishop of Durham, the Rt Rev David Jenkins.

Sheppard has spent most of his ordained life in Britain's older inner cities; in London and, since his appointment as its bishop in 1975, in Liverpool. His *Bias to the Poor* (1983) strongly reflects that experience.[49] Its social values are clearly on the well left-of-centre tradition of Temple and Tawney. Its most frequently reiterated message is:

> We must listen to the poor, exist with them, try to stand in their shoes; and then be willing for them to take a full share in leadership and decision making.[50]

Not that the Church should allow itself to become the representative of a special interest group. The Bishop of Liverpool remains committed to the age old catholicity of his Church's position. Though, in the name of 'affirmative action' he accepts the idea that the churches of Christian immigrant communities should be permitted a phase of something like 'separate development', he would want them in the long run to be fully part of a universal Church community. But for our purposes here the chief interest of *Bias to the Poor* is rather different. It lies in what he has to say about contemporary capitalism and contemporary Marxism.

He emphasises that 'Christians have important common ground with Marxists'. This includes, among other things, the belief that man is a social being, a recognition of the influence on minds and destinies of economic and social structures, an indignation at 'unequal distribution of wealth and opportunity'.[51] But he also indicates several fundamental points of difference. Of these one of the most interesting concerns the concept and reality of class, and Marxists' 'often dogmatic views about the proletariat'. He continues:

> Marx saw the proletariat as an economic concept, defined by the workers' relationship to the means of production. The reality of inner city life in Britain today does not reveal one main stream of working class life. Different groups who would claim to be working class have different attitudes which are greatly influenced by their particular local situation. In particular, minority groups frequently do not respond to those who speak of them as being involved in a class struggle.[52]

Roughly halfway through *Bias to the Poor* the bishop has a chapter headed 'A Crisis for Capitalism'. Its main thrust is to challenge the fashionable contemporary revival of the doctrine that the 'market' will provide the optimum solution for all or almost all our own and other people's economic problems. Far from that:

> At present the market does not need the labour of 30 per cent of the labour force in many areas of Merseyside and many other cities in developed countries. It does not need the labour of possibly 30 per cent of the whole labour force of Third World Countries.[53]

Public ownership is not mentioned as a remedy. But government intervention of a Keynesian and New Deal variety are put forward as the best way of making good where market forces have failed. Bishop Sheppard favours substantial public investments directed as a priority to areas of high unemployment. Apart from that, 'fairer distribution' should be attempted 'more by an open prices and incomes policy which took in everyone than by indirect and hidden intervention'.

These policy suggestions seem to place the bishop firmly with the Labour party moderates or even with the SDP in the current political line-up. Certainly there is no hint of fellow feeling for the views of Mr Arthur Scargill or Mr Tony Benn.

In view of his dissatisfaction with both Marxism and capitalism, it is surprising that he does not explore the possibility of any third way. It is true that evidence of some revival in the setting up of small new businesses, on Merseyside and elsewhere, is noticed and commended. So is the St Helen's Trust which works to help midwife these new small firms. But the bishop shows no real knowledge of or interest in the growth of co-operative ventures over the last few years. The strengths of his treatment of contemporary capitalism do not lie in his policy proposals. They come rather from his reassertion of moral values and his theology: from his refurbishment of the old Lutheran concept of a 'calling', and his insistence that:

> If we are to find our way through this sensitive time of widespread change in employment patterns, individualistic incentives must give way to much stronger concern for the community as a whole. [54]

The writings of Bishop Sheppard constitute one exception to our generalisation that Christian social concern in England has been transferred to the Third World. A second, the report of the Archbishop of Canterbury's commission on the country's inner cities, *Faith in the City*, was published too late for more than a passing reference here. It will have to suffice to say that in its analysis, its values and its recommendations, it is very much in line with *Bias to the Poor*. Bishop Sheppard was, in fact, the commission's vice-chairman.

A third exception is what the Churches themselves call their 'industrial mission'. The clergy involved whether full-time or part-time, are known as industrial chaplains. In 1981 they evidently totalled 324, a figure which breaks down [55] as follows:

Full time: 129
Half time: 26
Part time: 169

The first impetus which resulted in the development of this new Church activity was Anglican. But from quite early on other churches became involved so that there are now chaplains who are Roman Catholics, Baptists, Methodists and ministers of the United Reformed Churches. The claim that this is a genuinely ecumenical undertaking seems fair enough.

We should not think of an industrial chaplain as having the same kind of functions in relation to the firms or other undertakings to which he or she is informally accredited as those performed by a prison or hospital chaplain or one in the armed services. It is apparently the case that at least up to the outbreak of the Second World War some of the Royal Ordnance Factories included a chaplain on their payroll. And it is a curious fact that the pioneer industrial chaplain or industrial missioner, the Rev E. R. Wickham (later Bishop of Middleton) was himself briefly employed as a chaplain to one of those factories.

But the work of industrial chaplains is not the provision of church services within the factory gates. The Scott Bader Commonwealth once briefly experimented with industrial 'church parades'. It was evidently unpopular. Chaplains are warned against seeing themselves in these terms. It was with the aim simply of establishing some kind of Church presence in industry, and thus of bringing some Church influence to bear on the shopfloor and in the boardroom that Bishop Hunter of Sheffield, in 1944, invited Wickham to launch a pilot industrial mission in Sheffield. This was close to the aim of the French hierarchy in starting the worker-priest missions in Paris and in other industrial centres at the same time. Wickham in fact later visited the Paris Mission and reported on his experience.[56]

Although, however, a few Anglican clergymen did, like the French priests, become genuine full-time industrial workers, this was not quite Wickham's aim. He had two objectives. First, contacts and relationships were to be built up with the decision makers on both sides of industry: with directors and senior executives on the one side and with full time trade union officials, convenors and shop stewards on the other. We may note in parenthesis that this approach was evolved in Sheffield in the 1940s and 1950s when unions would have figured prominently in all industrial establishments of any size. Today's high technology, large scale and non-unionised companies, like Hewlett Packard for example or IBM, were not a feature of the Sheffield industrial landscape which Hunter and Wickham surveyed. Neither are they mentioned in the 1982 guidelines for industrial chaplains. Secondly, in the last section of his famous *Church and People in an Industrial City*[57] Wickham makes it clear that the industrial mission cannot be limited to the 'principalities and powers' at the top of the twin union and management hierarchies: it must include within its scope the 'centurions' (middle management) and 'other ranks' of the industrial army. He suggests, with appropriate qualifications, that the missioner should seek to build up, on the model of Wesley's organisation, small groups of Christians in factories and offices who will meet quite frequently, or at least regularly, and will attempt at those meetings to bring their Christian beliefs and values to bear on the issues of industrial life, both day to day and long term. And this also seems to have been the broad aim of individual mission activities even in those parts of the country, South London for example, where both the methods used and the individual environment have been rather different from those in Wickham's Sheffield.

What has been the impact of this initiative and of all the work which has gone into it? In the absence of any objective data there is no alternative but to fall back on information made available *ad hoc* by individuals. This suggests that there may have been a significant number of *local* successes. For example the greatly respected Frank Scuffham has clearly been doing most valuable work in Corby over a number of years and played an important part in containing the demoralisation of the town at the time of the great steel closure in 1981. Scuffham has also been closely involved in a number of initiatives aimed at revitalising the town's economy. And, as an outside director of the common ownership company Scott Bader, he has played, and continues to play, an important part in its evolution.

Other chaplains have made names for themselves particularly perhaps in relation to industrial training and retraining. By contrast they seem to have been less closely involved with recent 'progressive' developments in established and relatively flourishing businesses. For example we know of no evidence that industrial chaplains have played any part in helping businesses to move to single status employment and away from the differential treatment of white collar and blue collar workers.

But it is perhaps too early to reach a trustworthy opinion. Wickham himself said that ten years would be needed in any particular locality to bring forth worthwhile results. In fact, it may be the end of the century before we can really judge what the Churches' industrial mission has achieved.

On the other hand given the resources available to it, realism suggests that we should not expect too much from the Churches' industrial mission. In particular it seems unrealistic to suppose that industry will be much changed, for better or worse, by the work of industrial chaplains.

Does any other realistic source of possible change present itself in the Britain of the 1980s? Judged both by his writings and his actions Mr Tony Benn clearly believes that the answer is 'yes'. Put crudely, he believes that a Labour government committed to 'socialism' could transform British society in such a way that we would wake up to find ourselves living in a world which embodied both socialist and Christian values. In his *Arguments for Socialism* he makes an eloquent case for the view that for practical purposes (ignoring theology) Christian and socialist values are identical. In any case:

> Christian, humanist and socialist moralities have in fact co-existed and co-operated throughout history and they co-exist and co-operate today most fruitfully and not only within the Christian Socialist movement itself. The British trade union and Labour movement, like Anglicans, Presbyterians, Catholics, Methodists, Congregationalists, Baptists, Jews and campaigners for civil rights have all gained inspiration from these twin traditions of Christianity and humanistic socialism.[58]

Mr Benn is, of course, entitled to remind his readers of the historical links between and the overlapping values of Christianity and non-coercive socialism. He is also entitled, as he does in *Arguments for Socialism*, to emphasise the ferment of moral and altruistic enthusiasm associated with the Levellers and others in the 1640s – which fall outside the scope of this book. Maybe Mr Benn and those who think as he does will succeed in the triple task which his whole project seems to require. Maybe they will succeed in taking over the Labour Party, in winning a general election and thirdly in transforming society along the lines of his humanist-Christian-socialist blueprint. It seems improbable in the same way that a victory for the Greens in a West German election, followed by the introduction of new arrangements based on Ms Petra Kelly's principles of 'eco-feminism' seems improbable.

The parallel is in some ways instructive. But at least at the theoretical level it seems to us to work to Mr Benn's disadvantage. It does so because, as we understand it, the State apparatus would play a much larger part in Mr Benn's transformed society than in Ms Petra Kelly's. Moreover, whatever else is true, it seems to us that there is no warrant in the Christian tradition for State socialism. There is, as we have seen, a cautious warrant for voluntary socialism or for 'socialism without the State'. However that is clearly something else.

There is too a second charge against Mr Benn's blueprint. It can be expressed in the view that his ideas take insufficient account of the *necessity* for incorporating at least a measure of self-interest in any set of arrangements for organising the economy. Mao failed to grasp this point. So, perhaps with even more cynicism did Stalin and the majority of his successors in the leadership of the Soviet Union. William Temple, on the other hand, was in no doubt about this necessity:

> . . . a statesman who supposes that a mass of citizens can be governed without appeal to their self-interest is living in a dreamland and is a public menace. The art of government is the art of so ordering life that self-interest prompts what justice demands . . . [59]

Temple brings us back to Philip Wicksteed and the latter's objective of making the economic system work on the side of social reform. No easy task to be sure. But it is an endeavour, from what we have seen about the evolution of progressive Christian thought in Britain over the last two centuries, which is more likely to produce change for the better than Mr Benn's blueprint.

Grigor McClelland is not a Labour Party politician and socialist but a Quaker businessman and academic. But his cautious little book *And a New Earth*[60] with its subtitle, 'Making tomorrow's society better than today's' seems to us to offer guidance which is more realistic and more congruent with the Christian tradition than Tony Benn's *Arguments for Socialism*.

We simply haven't got the space even to summarise McClelland's excellent discussion of, in effect, what should be the responsible Churchman's response to contemporary industrial capitalism. A brief extract from his treatment of the related questions of income and wealth distribution must suffice. He begins with a scarcely controversial summary of the background:

> The radical egalitarian view does not favour equality regardless of needs: it could be summed up in the phrase 'to each according to his needs . . .' Such 'Christian communism' was practised among groups of early Christians and more recently has been practiced in Kibbutzim and certain other relatively small scale communities. It has not, so far, been attempted on a national scale, though any Welfare State is a move in that direction and it is the declared intention in the long term of modern communists. It goes beyond what George Fox or any other Quaker leaders advocated for their country or even any community within the country, nor has it so far been advocated or practiced by the Society of Friends or any of its constituent bodies.[61]

Then comes the realistic objection:

> There certainly seem to be massive practical obstacles – on all the evidence we have at present about human behaviour – to the adoption in the foreseeable future of such a principle for a community on any substantial scale.[62]

And then he goes on:

> Our present society may fall short not only of radical egalitarianism, the distribution to each according to his needs; *but also of equity, the distribution to each according to his deserts, the requirement*

of justice. For the two are not necessarily the same. What is justice?[63]

McClelland is clearly attempting to arrive at a distinction between just and unjust (or fair and unfair) inequalities. We should not be surprised by his implicit acknowledgment that if we are looking for a distribution which can be expressed in terms of a mathematical formula we will fail to find a persuasive solution. On the other hand McClelland is in no doubt that Britain's income and wealth inequalities in the middle 1970s were still unacceptably great. He is clear that the right direction is the one which leads to narrower differentials. And he warns eloquently against the dangers of 'gross disparity'.

> Gross disparity in material circumstances constitutes a barrier to mutual understanding no less difficult to surmount than those of distance, language and culture. This applies not only between individuals but between whole strata (defined by material circumstances) of the population. Such divisions must lead to conflict. Is it really any better to be part of a society marked by economic apartheid than of one marked by racial apartheid?[64]

Towards the end of his discussion of income and wealth distribution McClelland introduces his readers to the famous proposals put forward by the American philosopher John Rawls and argues that Rawls's test question – reduced to its most basic formulation 'Would you swap?' – is a fair one. But McClelland's chief point is the one which we have already emphasised: that in his view the differentials of wealth and income prevailing in the middle 1970s were still too large. It should go without saying that following a combination of Mrs Thatcher's tax changes and the huge increases in unemployment over the last ten years those disparities are larger now than they were when Grigor McClelland was writing.

However for our purposes here the relevant message of McClelland's book is the simple one that differentials of wealth and income need to be narrowed. At least in respect of the former it is hard to see how this could be achieved except through some redistribution of the ownership of productive assets.

In a speech in the House of Commons early in 1985 the former Conservative Prime Minister, Mr Edward Heath, criticised Mrs Thatcher's government for ignoring the lesson of two hundred years of industrial capitalism: the lesson that if capitalism is left to itself the disparities of income and wealth become inexorably larger and the divisions in society become inexorably sharper. In words reminiscent of William Temple, Mr Heath also attacked the government for what he saw as its failure to introduce policies to reverse the upward trend of unemployment. Mr Heath and fellow Tories who think like him serve to remind us that there is an honourable British tradition of social Conservatism which goes back at least to Shaftesbury and Coleridge.

CHAPTER FIVE

Catholic Thinking Before 1891

THE PAPACY

The first formal teaching by the Catholic Church on the social problems which followed the Industrial Revolution was in 1891. Since the effects of industrialisation had been visible even in Catholic countries since the 1820s, this response may seem tardy. Why did the Church not speak out before?

One reason is that the countries first affected were north-eastern France and Belgium. Even in northern Italy there was little industry before railways arrived in the 1850s. The real transformation of life in central Italy hardly began before 1870 and was at its height in the last 20 years of the nineteenth century. Before then the Bishop of Rome could hardly have had the urgency of social problems borne in on him. Another reason is probably the rapid multiplication, in Italy, France, Ireland and elsewhere, of religious orders devoted to teaching, nursing and social work. Saints Vincent de Paul and Louise de Marillac had founded the first order of nuns for full-time service among the poor in 1633, but after 1800 there was an explosion of new foundations of teaching Brothers, Sisters of Charity, Sisters of Mercy and so forth. In France the number of nuns rose from 12,400 to 25,000 between 1815 and 1830. Those who were concerned at social conditions applied themselves to works of relief before thinking of trying to change the system. But a third factor was that at the beginning of the nineteenth century the Papacy had placed itself in a position in which it was almost impossible for it to support any kind of reform.

In the second half of the eighteenth century, though critical eyes were turned on ecclesiastical wealth and privilege in all Catholic countries, and although Church property had been confiscated and monasteries suppressed in Austria and

Tuscany, the Church was not in general committed to a defensive conservatism. It contained both conservatives and progressives within it. The Abbé Gabriel Bonnot de Mably (1709–85), for example, besides advocating political freedom and religious toleration, attacked the laissez-faire economics of Quesnay and his disciple Mercier de la Rivière. Private property, Mably held, was an evil; the earliest human societies had probably been communistic; and although it was impossible to revert to Communism, it was urgent to reduce inequalities in wealth, for instance by splitting up estates on the death of their proprietors.

In 1789 the majority of the French clergy supported the Revolution. Support came not only from middle class curés but from aristocratic abbés and bishops, men like the radical Sieyès, Fauchet who advocated redistribution of land in 1790, and Talleyrand, then Bishop of Autun; indeed, if the clergy had not ranged themselves with the Third Estate, the Revolution could hardly have taken place, at least in the orderly way in which it did. It was Talleyrand who proposed the confiscation of Church property, and the clergy accepted this on the understanding that the State would pay them salaries in return. Many were even prepared to accept the Civil Constitution of the Clergy in 1790, ill-judged as the proposal to make bishops and parish priests into civil servants may have been.

But then in the spring of 1791 Pope Pius VI issued the briefs *Quod Aliquantulum* and *Caritas*. In these he not only forbade the French clergy to accept the Civil Constitution, thereby placing them in an impossible position; *Quod Aliquantulum* also condemned the Assembly's cherished Declaration of the Rights of Man. The condemnation seems to have been based partly on a misunderstanding. The Declaration is now recognised to be rather liberal than radical in character. Property, according to Article 17, is an 'inviolable and sacred right'.[1]

Pius took particular exception to the claim that 'men have a right to think, say, write and print what they like about religion'. But as the Abbé Bouvet pointed out in his aggressive reply, *Le Pape Hérétique* (1791), the Pope overlooks the vital qualification 'provided that this does not disturb the public order'. On the other hand when Bouvet maintains that 'Christ had no other view in the preaching of his gospel than to make men masters of their thoughts', he is wrong to represent Pius as denying this. What Pius says on the positive side is that men have to live in society and use their reason. He is not opposing authority to being master of one's thoughts, but rationalism tinged with socialism to a kind of random, irresponsible individualism.

In the heat of the debate, these fine shades were lost. All that was seen was that the Pope had condemned the Rights of Man, and in the eyes of loyalists and rebels alike this cut the Church off from the whole current of social reform. When the first lay Catholic response to the Revolution came in 1796 from Joseph de Maistre and Louis de Bonald, it was an uncompromising attack on republicanism. 'What distinguishes the French Revolution and makes it an event unique in history' says Maistre[2] 'is that it is radically *bad*. No element of good disturbs the eye of the observer; it is the highest degree of corruption ever known; it is pure impurity'. It was to be a hundred years almost to the day before the harm done by Pius VI was repaired.

The quarrel between the Papacy and liberal politics was kept alive and exacerbated by a series of events it will suffice to recall briefly. Pius VI was active in stimulating Austria and Prussia to invade France and put down the Revolution, action for which France has never entirely forgiven the Church. In due course the French invaded Italy. Pius was taken prisoner and died in captivity. His successor Pius VII (1800–23) was more accommodating to new ideas, and by conceding the right of appointing all bishops to the State, he negotiated a concordat with France. He failed, however, to prevent large-scale expropriation of Church property in Germany in 1803 and in Spain in 1812, and was himself a captive of the French from 1809 until the restoration of the Bourbons in 1814.

Of the popes who came after him, Leo XII (1823–29) and Gregory XVI (1831–46) were conservatives, the latter effectively killing the liberal Catholic movement in France and Belgium. Pius IX (1846–78) gave the Papal States a constitution, but within a few months the prime minister had been assassinated and Pius himself had fled from mounting civil disorder. A combination of Catholic states restored him, but he lost the Papal States in 1860 and Rome in 1870. In 1867 he issued an Instruction, known as the *non expedit*, in which Catholics were told not to take any part in public life in the new Italy. This remained a serious obstacle to any Catholic social policy in Italy until the ban was lifted in 1918. Still more regrettable, because its effects were world-wide, in 1864 he published the famous *Syllabus Errorum*, a wholly negative document which ends by condemning as erroneous the proposition that: 'The Roman Pontiff can and should come to terms with progress, liberalism and modern civilisation.'[3]

Catholics in Italy divided into so-called Intransigents, who accepted the *Syllabus* and the *non expedit*, and Transigents who worked with the liberals that formed the Italian government. The former showed more social concern than the latter. In 1874, largely through the initiative of G. B. Paganuzzi (1841–1923) and G. Acquaderni (1838–1922) they started a series of congresses, the purpose of which was not only to unite Italian Catholics in defence of the Pope, but also to consider the plight of the working classes. A. Gambasin has called attention to the accuracy with which, at these congresses, the Marchese Sassoli Tomba traced social problems to defects in the system of industrial capitalism. The congresses developed a permanent organisation with a section for the systematic study of social questions. In this, however, Italy was far behind, and profiting from the experience of, Catholics elsewhere.

FRANCE BEFORE 1870

Disturbing effects of industrialisation began to appear in France, particularly in and around Paris, Lille and Lyon, in the 1820s. The first specifically Catholic response discernible was small and down to earth: the establishment of the Society of St Joseph by the Abbé Lowenbruck in 1822. This was for the benefit of working men, particularly for those coming to Paris from the country; it aimed at preventing them from losing touch with religion and being debauched by the lax morals of the capital. The Abbé de Bervanger became director in 1825. With the aid of Count Victor de Noailles he set up a school for apprentices which was still flourishing, teaching 15 trades to 800 boarders, in 1890. This 'oeuvre', moral and educational rather than political, and proceeding from private benevolence, was typical of by far the greatest part of Catholic social action in the nineteenth century. (As an English example one might give the 'industrial schools' for destitute or delinquent children run by priests or nuns after 1860.)

The French clergy in the 1820s tended to be devout rather than intellectual, and intensely royalist and conservative. The same, indeed, could be said of the Catholic clergy throughout Europe except in Ireland, where for centuries the monarchy and the established order of things had been the Catholic Church's declared enemy. But liberal Irish bishops like James Doyle of Kildare and Leighlin (1786–1834) and John MacHale of Tuam (1791–1881) had other things to occupy them besides the Industrial Revolution, and Irish influence on Catholic social thinking outside Ireland was slight and indirect.

In July 1830 the backward-looking Charles X was replaced by the more progressive Louis Philippe. In October Paris was greeted by a new daily paper, entitled *L'Avenir*. Its message was simple and challenging. The concordat of 1801 must be broken off, and the clergy must repudiate the salaries they were receiving from the government: only so could the twin objectives be achieved of liberal political reform and genuine religious renewal. The editors signed themselves, not without a flourish: F. de La Mennais, priest; Ph. Gerbet, priest; H. Lacordaire, priest; C. de Coux; Comte Ch. de Montalembert; Daguerre; E. d'Ault-Dumesnil; Waille.

It was these men who gave Catholic thinking in the nineteenth century its first impulse. The most famous are Montalembert (1810–70), a distinguished historian, Lacordaire (1802–61), who later refounded the Dominican order in France, and La Mennais (1782–1854) (or Lamennais in the less aristocratic style he later adopted), the initiator of *L'Avenir* and a writer who combined a passionate love of liberty with outstanding force and lucidity of style. They had contacts with liberal Catholics in other countries. Montalembert visited Daniel O'Connell (1774–1847) in Ireland in September 1830, and later married Elizabeth de Merode, a member of one of the Belgian Catholic families which in

1828 formed an alliance with the anti-clerical liberals to cast off Dutch rule.

The proposal to separate Church and State caused turmoil among the French clergy. The hierarchy took fright, and a series of unfavourable statements was obtained from Rome. In November 1831 Lamennais was obliged to suspend publication, and he, Lacordaire and Montalembert went to Rome to plead their paper's case in person. They were unsuccessful. In August 1832 the Encyclical *Mirari Vos* condemned not only the paper's theological but its political views. The editors all accepted the Vatican ruling, but the French hierarchy humiliated Lamennais by requiring him to repeat his submission no less than four times. He became embittered, left the Church in 1834, and remained unreconciled until his death in 1854.

L'Avenir more than once promised to offer a full scale alternative to laissez-faire economics, but was always distracted by more straightforwardly political issues. In his editorial of 30 June 1831, however, Lamennais brilliantly outlines ideas which were to be central in Catholic thinking in France and Germany:

> Whether one develops the system of agricultural colonies, already tried with success, or applies in industry, for the benefit of the poor, the principle of association, or, as is probable, by a happy combination reunites agriculture and industry: the intervention of the priest will always be necessary, not only to give these associations the moral character on which their political utility and material prosperity depend, but also in order that a disinterested third party should serve as a bond between the two contracting parties, the rich who provide the land and the money, and the poor who contribute to the common fund only their labour.

It was only after he left the Church that Lamennais applied himself to social problems directly, and even then his approach is more political than economic. In his short essay *De l'esclavage moderne* (1839), having compared the condition of French workers unfavourably with that of slaves in antiquity, he argues that the remedy lies in electoral reform. The immediate cause of the distress of the poor is that they cannot combine for collective bargaining. They cannot

combine because it is illegal, and the law cannot be changed
until they are enfranchised. Lamennais points out that out of
a population of 33 million persons, only 200,000 have the
vote. *Du passé et de l'avenir du peuple* (1841) contains his fullest
examination of the problem. He criticises the socialist
proposal to abolish private property in acutely prophetic
words:

> Since liberty is individual . . . it follows that property, in its
> essence, must be individual too.

Where all property belongs nominally to the State:

> There will be those who have in fact the disposal not only of the
> common property but of persons, in order that the production
> which is necessary may be assured;

and these will not be willing to surrender their powers. The
task, then, is to bring it about that everyone owns property.
Lamennais proposes a three-point plan: legalisation of workers' association, better education, and the raising of capital on
security of future labour – though on the important question
whether it is the State that is to supply this capital he is not
explicit.

Although Lamennais himself did not go deeper into social
problems than this, friends and people influenced by him did.
The writer for *L'Avenir* on economic matters was Charles de
Coux (1787–1864). He held that the measure of a nation's
wealth was 'the notion of what is necessary', something
corresponding to what we call 'the standard of living'; and
identified industrial capitalism as the main cause of the
present misery of the poor and the 'silent war' between them
and the rich. Like Lamennais after him, he urged the repeal of
the laws against trade unions. When *L'Avenir* was suspended,
he and Gerbet organised a course of lectures on political
economy. Some things they said foreshadow the *Communist
Manifesto*. Gerbet held that the classes which had destroyed
feudalism had replaced it by a 'feudalism of wealth'. De
Coux predicted a proletarian revolution – until universal
suffrage was finally achieved, the growth of the franchise
looked like a mechanism which would produce such a
revolution. But there were the differences we should

anticipate. The class war, though an actuality, was not something inevitable, and universal suffrage would have a stable and happy issue only if all parts of society accepted a Christian view of life.

After *Mirari Vos* and Lamennais's withdrawal from the Church, de Coux seems to have given priority to remaining a Catholic, and although he took the chair of economics at the new University of Louvain, little more of value survives from his pen. His and Gerbet's course, however, had one practical result. It was attended by, and certainly influenced, Frederick Ozanam. Besides providing inspiration to the Catholic republican parties which began to form in the second half of the nineteenth century, Ozanam in 1833 founded the Society of St Vincent de Paul. This provided, and still does throughout the world, an irreplaceable service for casualties of industrial capitalism.

In 1834 Vicomte Alban de Villeneuve-Bargemont (1784–1850) published his three-volume *Traité d'économie politique chrétienne*. He was influenced by Gerbet and still more[4] by de Coux, with whom he later collaborated on the review *L'Université catholique*. In 1828–30 he had been prefect of the industrialised Department du Nord, and the sufferings there of the poor had convinced him of the evil of industrialisation on the English model. In opposition to laissez-faire theory he maintained that the State has a duty to protect the working classes.[5] His chapter 'Laws to prevent indigence'[6] contains a legislative programme which looks forward, however distantly, to the modern Welfare State. There should be compulsory education free of charge. Firms employing more than 50 employees should be required to keep their factories healthy and submit to regular inspection. They should also be required to provide adult education, to admit no worker under the age of 14 without a doctor's certificate, to employ no one illiterate, to separate the sexes, and to set up savings banks to which employees would be obliged to contribute. Workers' associations should be legalised, but for purposes of welfare, not[7] for collective bargaining.

Villeneuve-Bargemont had a high opinion of agriculture as a vocation. He had visited the model agricultural colonies established near Steewyck in Holland in 1818 and in 1822 he set up a model farm. He devotes the last book of his *Traité* to advocating agricultural co-operatives in France. There was, he argues, more than ten times as much land lying idle as would be needed to settle all the available industrial poor. Although nothing came of this scheme he was able to have some influence on events. In 1840 he was elected Deputy for Hazebrouck, and in 1841 he was a leading sponsor of a law to limit child labour. (Catholics, it should be said, were not the only French Christians concerned about child labour at this time; Protestant industrialists in Alsace, such as Daniel Legrand, also pressed energetically for reform.)

L'Avenir ceased publication on 15 November 1831. On 3 December the torch was taken up by a new weekly, first called the *Journal des sciences morales et politiques*, and later *L'Européen*. Its first edition announced the project of 'realising on earth the principles of Christian equality'. The editor, B. J. B. Buchez, was a very different man from the aristocratic editors of *L'Avenir*. Born in Corsica, an ardent revolutionary in his twenties, Buchez was the person chiefly responsible for importing Italian secret societies into France. He had narrowly escaped execution in 1822 for his part in an unsuccessful insurrection. Qualifying then as a doctor, in 1825 he turned from conspiracy to the socialism of Saint-Simon, and during the next few years contributed saint-simonist articles to *Le Producteur* and his own *Journal des progrès des sciences et institutions médicales*. In 1829, however, he broke with the saint-simonists on religious grounds and although, it appears, he never became a churchgoer, his subsequent thinking was based on the unreserved acceptance of Catholic theological doctrines. Protestantism, he thought, encouraged individualism and egotism, whereas Catholicism recognised and made sense of the essentially social nature of man.

A prolific writer, Buchez campaigned for his ideas partly in his journals *L'Européen* (1831–2, 1835–7) and *La revue nationale* (1847–8), and partly in prefaces to his mammoth *Histoire parlementaire de la revolution française*, published in 40 volumes. He gained a considerable following among the skilled workers of Paris. From 1840 to 1850 (when the government made it impossible for them to continue) these workers ran a monthly called *L'Atelier*, the main aim of which was to encourage producers' co-operatives. As we shall see, its influence extended beyond France to England and America. Corbon, the chief editor, was a close friend of Buchez, and in 1848 *L'Atelier* was proud to say that 'it should be regarded as the expression of the thought of Buchez' (12 May). After the fall of Louis Philippe in February 1848 Buchez was elected to the National Assembly. The time called more for a man of action than for one of ideas, and he failed to make his mark on public life. An opponent of Louis Napoleon, after Napoleon's coup d'état in 1851 he was arrested, and though soon released he took no further part in public life.

In the first month of *L'Européen* Buchez put forward proposals for 'improving the condition of wage-earners in towns' which he later elaborated but never substantially changed. He divides workers into two categories. First, there are skilled men who need little plant, such as carpenters. To these, the capitalist is a sheer parasite. They should form associations which enable one or two men to sign for the rest, but continue to receive pay as before. At the end of the year the profits are to be divided into two parts. One fifth is added to the capital of the enterprise, which must be indivisible and inalienable. (After February 1848 Buchez tried to introduce a law to permit the creation of such inalienable funds, something impossible under French law as it then stood.) The remaining profit is apportioned between an insurance fund and bonuses. No one may be employed for more than a year without being admitted to membership. By these means Buchez hoped to establish what his follower Henri Feugueray called, 'la republique dans l'atelier'. On the matter of credit, he was prepared to have co-operatives borrow at interest provided that the lenders (unless they became working members) had no share in the profits. But he preferred a State bank, financed by having the taxes paid into it.

In 1825 Robert Owen tried to start a self-sufficient community in America, and William Thompson, partly under his influence, urged workers to form co-operatives in England. It is not clear whether Buchez knew of these initiatives. His co-operatives are different from Thompson's, which were to depend on trade unions, and Owen's, which were to be created by philanthropists from on high. Perhaps

Buchez' ideas arose from discussions with French working men. They were carefully worked out and practicable. Feugueray says some ten Buchezian co-operatives were attempted. Only one, the Ouvriers Bijoutiers en Doré, did reasonably well, lasting from 1834 to 1873. One was suppressed by the local magistrates, apparently by mistake; the rest seem to have failed less through lack of capital than because the members had insufficient preparation. It is an indication of the good sense of Buchez' system that some of its key features are followed by the most successful co-operatives today, those at Mondragon in Spain.

Buchez' second category was of workers who depended on substantially heavier capital investment. Most of these, he thought, would need private capitalists for the foreseeable future (300 years, according to a reminiscence of his disciple Auguste Ott), and he therefore proposed other arrangements. The State should set up unions with compulsory membership which would organise savings schemes. It would also establish councils of delegates from capital and labour. These councils should be presided over by government officials, and should regulate rates of pay and arrange for movements of labour.

The Revolution of February 1848 summoned social reformers to Paris from all over Europe; it also brought Lamennais out of retirement. On 27 February he started a daily, Le peuple constituant, which ran until it was suppressed on 11 July. In five articles on 'Work' (26–30 April) Lamennais says that the aim should be not to abolish property but to distribute it, and calls for education financed by the State, and co-operatives financed by local authorities. Auguste Barbet, Le peuple's chief writer on economics, claimed to have advocated this scheme as far back as in 1826, and to have tried it successfully in 1830.

The Second Empire was the product of a general reaction against revolutionary ideas, and French Catholics mostly turned from seeking changes in social and economic structures to private charity and paternalistic good works. The fact that the Archbishop of Paris had been killed trying to mediate between the workers and the government troops in 1848 doubtless helped to damp their revolutionary fire. However that may be, by 1870 when it began to be realised that good works were not enough, a generation of workers had grown up to which the Church was quite alien.

One figure who straddles the gap from 1848 to 1870 deserves mention. Frederick Le Play (1806–82) qualified as a mining engineer, and travelling in that capacity acquired first-hand knowledge of Britain, Scandinavia, Russia, Spain, Austria, Hungary and northern Italy. In 1855, under the title *Les ouvriers européens* he published some 40 full scale case studies of workers' families in different countries. By this work, and by starting the Society for Studies in Social Economy in the same year, he helped to found the modern discipline of sociology.

Le Play was both a convinced Catholic and a sincere social reformer, though contrary to what that may suggest, for the central part of his life he was not a churchgoer, and his proposals for reform were dominated by the belief that parental authority within families is the crucial factor for a society's morale. He was an early warner against bureaucracy, not only in Russia where he found a sympathetic listener in Nicholas I, but also in France where he seems to have introduced the word.[8] His chief importance, however, lay in his vast personal experience, which drew to him social reformers of all kinds. Before 1848 he had among his associates Montalembert and Louis Blanc; in the 1850s he collaborated with Ducpétiaux; after 1870 Leon Harmel, La Tour du Pin and Lemire were his pupils.

GERMANY AND AUSTRIA

In Germany in 1850 manufacturing industry still accounted for only 5 per cent of the work force, and workers' associations of a medieval kind lingered on until 1869. The social problem, therefore, was less urgent in the first half of the nineteenth century than in France, and Catholic thinking about it developed more slowly.

The first important figure is Adam Müller (1779–1829). A Protestant by birth, Müller was initially enthusiastic about the ideas of Adam Smith and Rousseau. By 1800, however, he was disenchanted and in 1805 he became a Catholic. This change of religion was attended by an espousal of the idea of a corporative State, and Müller was the first Catholic to propose this as a solution to social problems.

A number of rather different systems are reckoned as corporativist, but three features may be singled out as typical. First, there is an attempt to substitute vertical divisions of society between different vocations or economic sectors, for horizontal divisions like that between proprietors and property-less workers. Secondly, whereas liberals like to have nothing between the individual and the State, corporativists favour a graduated structure of intermediate or 'partial' associations. Thirdly, they wish parliamentary representation of constituencies defined by geographical location to be supplemented or replaced by representation of economic groups.

In Germany the development of the idea of a corporative state was probably due more to Protestants than to Catholics. In the 1860s Otto von Gierke argued in an influential historical work[9] that the germ of it goes back to the Calvinist Johannes Althusius (or Althaus) of Wittgenstein (1557–1638). In 1603 Althusius envisages[10] a socialist, not to say totalitarian, State, and Gierke may be right to read him as desiring that governing bodies should be elected not directly by the people but by intermediate bodies. Corporativism is, strictly speaking, the viewing of the State as an organic body, and Althusius does speak[11] of the mercantile class as 'the feet of the body politic'.

Müller's corporativism probably derives not from Althusius but from the Protestant philosopher Fichte. In 1800 Fichte published *Der geschlossene Handelstaat* (*The Closed Commercial State*).[12] In this he maintained that the State was, or should be, constituted by a contract not between individuals but between organised estates ('stände'), the agriculturalists, the manufacturers and the merchants, these in turn being sub-divided by trades. In a State so formed, the government would not laissez-faire but control the economy, and distribute the wealth created in proportion to functions.

Fichte's proposals were authoritarian and open to a suspicion of being imperfectly disinterested.

> The man who concerns himself with deep reflection [we are told] would not even have the necessities of life if he were to maintain himself like the tiller of the soil . . . He requires food which satisfies when taken in smaller quantities . . . more varied and stimulating food, and surroundings which continually

present to his outer eye the purity and nobility that are to reign within him.[13]

Müller does not demand caviare for philosophers. Instead he gives a special role to the Church. But otherwise his system, unfolded in *Die Elemente der Staatskunst* is similar. There are to be four 'stände': clergy, landed aristocracy, manufacturers and merchants.[14] These are to play roles in the State analogous to roles played by individuals in families. The clergy are like the senior members of the family, and do the thinking; the nobles stand to the productive commons as a wife to her husband. The system is explicitly totalitarian: 'The State is the totality of human affairs'.[15]

Müller's ideas are usually called Romantic, and had no chance of practical realisation. He was followed, however, by a number of German Catholics in the nineteenth century. Of these some were not merely unrealistic but outrageous, for instance Karl Ludwig von Haller (1768–1854) who held it to be a natural law that states should be ruled by those with inherited wealth. Nevertheless Müller's basic claim that, 'it is not possible to conceive man outside the State'[16] is in line with modern thinking.

One of the most sympathetic of the early Catholic corporativists is Franz von Baader (1765–1841). In 1828 he and others in Munich started a journal *Eos* to advocate Christian and corporative measures. In 1834 he submitted a memorandum to the Bavarian government on the state of the proletariat, and in 1835 he published his short but arresting essay *Concerning the Present Disproportion between the Proletariat and the Propertied Classes*. He had worked in England and Scotland as a mining engineer in 1794–6, and this enabled him to give his compatriots some first-hand information about 'our allegedly most educated and cultivated countries'.[17]

How often have I, for instance, assisted at 'meetings' and 'associations' of factory owners in England which regularly ended by establishing maximum wages and minimum sales prices and therefore were no better than conspiracies against the proletarians . . . The worst way to try to remedy this manifest iniquity is through the chambers and parliaments, for here more than anywhere else the factory owners are at the same time

contending parties and judges, while they exclude the representation of the interests of the poor wage-earning masses.[18]

The Munich group included the historian Joseph Goerres
(1776–1848) and had contacts with the French liberals.
Baader corresponded with Lacordaire. Lamennais was in
Munich on his way home from Italy when *Mirari Vos* was
issued, and it was from an article by him in the local
Kirchenzeitung in 1831 that Baader derived his view that the
Church should undertake the function of representing the
interests of the working classes, and for this purpose should
restore the diaconate.

The next generation of Catholic corporativists included
Franz Joseph Ritter von Buss (1803–78). He had contacts not
only with the Munich Catholics but with Buchez. His ideal
of restoring guilds in which 'the journeymen would again sit
down at table with the masters' (speech to the German
Catholic Convention at Mainz in 1848) was not to be
realised, but he may be claimed as the first German to
propose a piece of social legislation: in 1837 he moved a
limitation of working hours in factories in the Diet of Baden.
He was also active in organising church-funded social work,
and translated Baron de Gerando's three volume *System of
Comprehensive Services for the Poor.*

In 1848, the year when Marx and Engels issued the
Communist Manifesto, a series of sermons on social questions
was delivered at the cathedral of Mainz by Baron Wilhelm
Emmanuel von Ketteler, priest of the rural parish of
Hopsten. It could be argued that Ketteler had a greater
influence on Catholic social thinking than any other individual since the Renaissance. That was not only because he
had a powerful, flexible and practical mind, but also because
from 1850 onwards he was bishop of the important diocese
of Mainz. Before the encyclical *Rerum Novarum* he was the
only Catholic reformer who spoke with an official voice. As
the Ordinary of a diocese he possessed what is called
'magisterium', teaching authority, something for which
there is no substitute in the Roman Catholic Church.

Ketteler was born in 1811, studied law, and entered the
Prussian civil service. He resigned when the government
imprisoned the Archbishop of Cologne in 1837. He then

turned to the priesthood and was ordained in 1844. Six years later he became Bishop of Mainz and held the see until his death in 1878. Besides these careers in the civil service and the Church, he had a career in politics. In 1848 he was elected to the National Assembly at Frankfurt. During the 1860s he was trying to set up a Catholic political party, and in 1870 there came into being the Centre Party which, though non-confessional, represented German Catholics in the so called Kulturkampf with Bismarck over the next decade. Ketteler drew up the official programme for this party in 1871 and was himself elected to the first Reichstag, but retired because of the difficulty of combining the rough and tumble of political life with his episcopal duties.

From the beginning, in his 1848 sermons, Ketteler declares that men never have unrestricted ownership rights but only usufruct. He adds:

> The ill-fated dictum that 'property is theft' is not just a lie. Alongside of a great lie it contains a terrible truth.[19]

His most influential work was his short book on 'the labour question', *Die Arbeiterfrage und das Christenthum* (1864), in which he establishes the Catholic position as one opposed both to laissez-faire liberalism and to State socialism.

Starting with the question whether as a bishop he has any business to pronounce on such matters, his reply is simple: he is obliged to do so by the oath he took at his consecration 'to be *affabilis* and *misericors*, accessible and helpful, to the poor'. He proceeds to give as his diagnosis of the present malaise of society precisely the system of industrial capitalism: there exists a free labour-market in which labour is treated as a commodity and its price is fixed by competition.[20] He then considers the liberal and socialist solutions advocated respectively by Schulze-Delitzsch and Ferdinand Lassalle. He agrees with Lassalle that the liberal strategy, with its highbrow educational programme and its unctuous emphasis on 'self-help', is wholly inadequate: he notes that at a recent conference for the benefit of working men there had been present 25 civil servants, 11 professors, 16 lawyers, 8 bankers, 14 journalists, 30 doctors of various sciences, 16 businessmen and 2 workers. He is more sympathetic to Lassalle's proposal to use tax-payers' money to set up producers' co-operatives, but decides that it would be unethical.[21] It would be better to look for funds from the Church. Anyhow, he proposes[22] the following programme. There should be establishments for the old and sick. Steps should be taken to restore respect for marriage and to improve moral and religious education. There should be a range of workers' 'associations', including consumers' co-operatives, banks and societies for buying raw materials. In this connection Ketteler speaks favourably both of Schulze-Delitzsch's loan-associations and of the societies for journeymen which had been set up from 1847 onwards by his old fellow-student Adolph Kolping (1813–65). Finally, he recommends producers' co-operatives, of which there were already examples, he says, in England and France.

In his programme for the Centre Party Ketteler seems to have taken a step in the direction of State intervention in that the State is given[23] the task of 'corporate reorganisation of the working classes'. In a pamphlet on which he was working at the end of his life he lists five conditions for an organisation of the kind he favours: it must grow naturally out of the character and circumstances of the people; it must have purely economic ends; there must be a sense of collective honour and responsibility; all members of the same vocation must belong; and the State, having once set up an association, should refrain from interfering.[24]

After Ketteler, Catholic social thought in Germany was mainly channelled into the Centre Party. At first, two streams can be distinguished. Some people advocated a corporative State: so the Jesuit Heinrich Pesch (1854–1926), one of the chief theorists in the Party, and Franz Hitze (1851–1921) in his *Kapital und Arbeit und der Reorganisation der Gesellschaft* (1880). Hitze was perhaps Ketteler's chief successor. Of peasant background he was ordained in 1878 and well fulfilled Baader's idea of a social diaconate by being a member of the Reichstag for 40 years. The other stream of thought, represented by Baron Georg von Hertling (1843–1919) favoured what is called 'meliorism', the English strategy of working for gradual, piecemeal reform within the existing constitution. The issue between the corporativists and the meliorists was effectively decided in the early 1880s, when Hitze came over to Hertling's view.

Besides working through social legislation, Hitze, Windthorst, the official leader of the Centre Party, and others set up in 1890 the Volksverein for German Catholics. This was a sophisticated successor to Kolping's associations: a well equipped and highly efficient institution for adult education in social and economic matters. By 1914 it had 800,000 members. It made possible the powerful Catholic trade unions which were suppressed along with it by the National Socialists in 1933.

While corporative ideas lost ground in Germany after 1880, they exercised a persisting influence on Austrian Catholic thought. This was largely thanks to Count Karl von Vogelsang (1818–90). Vogelsang came from a Protestant family in Mechlenburg, and was in the Prussian civil service until 1848. He was on friendly terms, however, with Ketteler and the Munich Catholic intellectuals, and became a Catholic in 1850. In 1864 he settled in Austria and ran journals devoted to attacking all forms of liberalism and advocating a corporative State. In 1877 he was joined by Rudolph Meyer, a Prussian who had left Germany in consequence of antagonising Bismarck, and who though a Protestant worked with the Catholic politicians. In due course he had to leave Austria too for attacking Count Taafe, and went to Paris where he probably reinforced the corporativist thinking of La Tour du Pin. During the 1880s the Catholic politicians of Austria obtained legislation for the re-establishing of corporations and for limiting hours of work.

Both industrialisation and a Catholic response to it came later in Austria than in Germany, but 1888 saw the genesis of the Christian Social Party.

BELGIUM

The Industrial Revolution in Belgium broke earlier in a country already partly industrialised. In the Walloon area the seventeenth-century mining industry, with its worker-only associations, had been transformed by steam machines introduced in the 1780s, and by the early-nineteenth century was taking the lead in Europe. By 1820 the Cockerill complex was manufacturing all types of industrial machinery and in the 1830s railway construction was expanding two or three times faster than anywhere else in Europe. The state to which the population of Flanders was progressively reduced from 1820 was primarily due to the importation of English machinery and goods, which undermined both the home textile industry and the supplementary rural employment. Bad harvests and the potato famine completed a process which reached its horrific apogee in the 1840s and came to be known as the 'maladie de Flandres'.

In the thirteenth and fourteenth centuries industrialisation had established Belgian towns as economic entities and episodic democratic revolutions had secured the importance of democratically organised corporations within them. The notions of privilege and of freedom had become, and remained, inextricably confused ranged as they were against exploitation by local rulers and the central power alike. A system of rural 'communes' developed, linked to the towns and likewise administered locally. Through local customs and institutions, of which the Church was one, the country as a whole clung to a sense of identity through successive occupations. The communes still retain their administrative importance and in some Brabantine towns a few corporations survived to the 1870s when corporativism became central to Catholic thought.

This past goes some way to explaining the depth of traditionalism in the Belgian Church throughout the nineteenth century. It was rooted in custom, defensive and voiceless, until given intellectual expression by the Jesuit Abbé Francois-Xavier Feller (1735–1802), who emerged as a leading light of the Patriot Party in the Brabantine Revolution of 1789 when the 'United States of Belgium' declared their independence from Austria. His influences were Bellarmin, Suarez and, above all, Burke. His ideas incorporated a version of the Volkgeist view of history but drew their energy from the real world. In his hatred of Gallicanism and in his Ultramontanism he voiced the bias of the Belgian Church. In 1774 he founded the first organ of Catholic thought, the *Journal Historique et Litteraire* which was succeeded by the *Spectateur Belge* of his disciple the Abbé Foere (1787–1851).

Apart from Foere there emerged a group of writers, predominantly aristocratic, led by Henri Count de Merode-Westerloo (1787–1851). Bonald and de Maestre cast a brief spell over them, but their traditionalism was rather that of Feller and Foere, and eventually gave way to the liberalism of Lammenais and the *L'Avenir* group, with whom they were in close contact. They formed the nucleus of Catholic Liberalism, which flourished despite *Mirari Vos* until the 1880s. The Merode group still supported Lammenais, and the Belgian Church as a whole regarded itself as exempt from the strictures of the encyclical. It did however signal a split in the ranks of the Catholics, already roughly divided between the progressive, liberal faction and those who were nostalgic for the institutions of the Ancien Regime.[25]

In 1830 a popular rising which coincided with an alliance of leading Catholics and Liberals had secured independence of Belgium from Dutch rule, and the new constitution drew the admiration of liberals and democrats alike for its justice and clarity. Known as 'Unionism' the Liberal/Catholic alliance was extolled by Lammenais and the advanced Catholic thinkers but was largely misunderstood. As a working alliance it was a barter of concessions rather than a genuine compromise, and neither side properly appreciated the gravity of the 'social problem'. Moreover, although liberty of association was guaranteed for all, the clause was effectively negated by articles in the civil and penal codes where they applied to labour.

Against this background of bourgeois complacency the figure of Edouard Ducpétiaux (1804–68) stands out. His father owned a lace factory and the family were reasonably well off. At 23 Ducpétiaux took his doctorate in law and became the editor of the liberal *Courrier des Pays-Bas*. He was imprisoned shortly afterwards with Louis de Potter for his anti-absolutionist anti-Dutch sympathies. For a while he left the Church until re-converted by his second wife, but always remained Christian and was never anti-clerical. Released by the revolution he took part in the drawing up of the constitution, as did Adolph Bartels, and was appointed Inspector of Prisons and Charities by the provisional government, a post which he held until 1861. Initially concerned with prison reform, he eventually turned the force of his

attention on the problems of the industrial working population.

The reforms he urged the government to implement
covered all aspects of work from child labour to supervision
of contracts, and included compulsory education to the age
of 15 for boys and girls. In his early writing Ducpétiaux
proposed a 'Homocentric economy'. At the beginning of his
*De la condition physique et morale des jeunes ouvriers et des moyens
de l'améliorer* (published in 1843, the year before Marx wrote
his Paris Manuscripts) he points out that work is essential to
human self-realisation:

> The end of man, whatever his place in the scale of humanity, is
> the free and integral development of his physical, intellectual and
> moral faculties. Society, established in the interests of all, ought
> to give him the means to attain this end. The first of these means
> is work.

In 1853 he became vice-president of the Central Statistical
Bureau which he had helped to set up in 1841. With his
Budget Studies of 1855 he can be said to have introduced the
practical methodology into Catholic social studies which
later characterised Belgian socio-economic and educational
programmes.

In the 1840s the liberal atmosphere of Belgium made it a
refuge for political exiles from other countries. Among
Catholics who had contacts with foreign social reformers
was Adolph Bartels (1802–62), one-time travelling salesman
turned professional journalist and founder-editor of an
influential journal, the *Débat Social*. Bartels was a devout
Catholic convert. In 1842 he wrote his *Essai sur l'organisation
du travail* in which he propounds an eclectic but elegant and
somewhat austere form of corporativism, to be achieved by
gradual and partial expropriation of superfluous wealth
through a heavy, progressive tax. In 1847 he helped found
the radical but rancorous Democratic Association (of which
Marx was vice-president), but retired the following year, a
defeated man.

Third of this first generation of progressive Catholic
intellectuals was a Frenchman, Francois Huet (1814–69).
Author of *Le Régne Social du Christianisme*, Huet lived in

Belgium for 15 years and must be counted part of the scene of this time. Professor of Philosophy at Ghent, his ideas, which reconciled Christian principles with those of the French Revolution were spread through his teaching and by the men of influence who had been his students. He was expelled from Belgium in 1848.

The 'Year of Revolutions' was marked by some half-hearted demonstrations, but the Liberals and Catholics sank their differences in the face of danger, and besides, the liberties demanded by the republicans in France were already guaranteed by the constitution. A wave of reaction spread none the less. From now on the main vehicle for Catholic activity was the development of the workers' circles, or 'oeuvres'.

The earliest of these were beginning to appear in the 1830s, though the movement received its main impetus later from Charles Perin. Essentially an instrument of edification and pacification, the 'oeuvres' served both liberal bourgeois society and the Church while at the same time partially meeting a need. From 1850 there was a proliferation of these associations. The Archiconfrérie de St Francois Xavier, the most important of them, was founded in 1854 by the Jesuit Louis van Caloen and a group of workers.

In the 1850s progressive Catholicism was given a new impetus by a group of young men, the 'First Young Right', led by Prosper de Haulleville, a disciple of Lacordaire. Their proposals included an enlargement of the franchise, democracy, a free economy on the American pattern, and legalised trade unions on the English. It was a synthesis of Liberal and Catholic principles but found favour with neither party, though the Young Right aroused the awareness of the Catholic lay bourgeoisie of their role and responsibilities in the social question. Continuity to the Second Young Right was ensured by some members of the group, notably A. Nothomb.

With de Haulleville and the other young Progressists and with the support of an Assembly General of German Catholics at Louvain, Ducpétiaux brought about the first of the three large congresses at Malines, opened in 1863 by the Baron de Gerlache and attended by Montalembert who spoke out for 'a free Church in a free State'. Here Ducpétiaux expounded his Theory of Independence of the worker, 'free and responsible of his essence. From this freedom and this responsibility devolve his rights and his duties'.[26] However the progressive measures he suggested were defeated by the supporters of Charles Perin, Professor of Economy at Louvain from 1845 to 1881. Perin was a reactionary conservative and supported the role of charity and private initiative as against State intervention in social matters. He wrote *De la richesse dans les sociétés chrétiennes* and had a considerable following. The congresses did however achieve the creation of the Fédération des Sociétés Ouvrières Catholiques in 1868 to co-ordinate Catholic activity in the social sphere. Ducpétiaux retired before the third congress having achieved at least the beginning of his dream, the proper independence of the Christian working man and his family. The Catholic party came to power in 1870 with a new coherence.

In the 1870s Belgium began to be affected by the corporativist ideas of La Tour du Pin and other French reformers whom we shall consider presently. In 1878 Georges Helleputte (1852–1925), whose ideas at this time were imbued with the nostalgia typical of the Belgian traditionalists for the old corporations, started a guild at Louvain which was copied in a number of other towns. Helleputte and other Belgians were involved in the Union of Fribourg, founded in 1884 by Cardinal Mermillod of Geneva, and the advantages of corporativism were canvassed there.[27]

No less important, in 1879 the Catholic writer J. Dauby, a self-educated typographer, in *Des grèves ouvrières* proposed a careful and challenging itemisation of the components of a just wage. It should include:

1. What is needed to keep the workman and his family in a style appropriate to his trade.
2. Compensation for risks, including unemployment, sickness and death.
3. The maintenance of the capital represented by his tools, and interest on any loans he has needed to acquire them.
4. Amortisation of the capital spent on his education and apprenticeship, no less than the full amount of which he has a duty to restore to his children.

5. A net profit, to enable him to participate in the general progress of society.[28]

As well as several articles of practical advice for workmen, and analytic studies in the manner of Ducpétiaux, Dauby wrote a popular handbook, *Le livre de l'ouvrier*,[29] which anticipated a similar work of Léon Harmel, *Manuel d'une corporation chrétienne*, written in 1877.

The year of the publication of *Des grèves ouvrières* witnessed the presence in Belgium of a social worker better known for work of a different kind. Protestantism had been virtually extinguished by the *furia español* but a small community had managed to hold together since 1785 in the Borinage, and it was here that Vincent Van Gogh came in 1879, fresh from the new training school for Evangelists in Brussels. In the village of Paturage he taught, visited the sick and practiced bible reading among the miners' families. However the extremes of misery he encountered persuaded him that bible texts were less important than the practical work of nursing the sick and wounded, and he gave away all his belongings and went to live in a miner's hut. This literal zeal found little favour with his superiors and he was dismissed.

Dubbed the Year of Strikes, 1886 saw a number of new developments. In a series of congresses in Liége (1886, 1887, 1890 and one in Malines in 1891) there were debates similar to those which had occurred in Germany between corporativists and meliorists. They marked the Church's break with Liberalism, if not with the conservatism which attached to it. Corporativism had an extraordinary success during these years, especially in Flanders, and its main protagonist was Helleputte. As a result of the 1886 congress the Abbé Mellaerts, seconded by Helleputte and F. Schollaert, founded the 'Boerenbond' or Farmers' Union. Intended for the benefit of the peasantry, this still plays an important part in Flemish agriculture. Helleputte, who is credited with the expression 'Christian Democracy', eventually shed his corporativist bias in favour of the meliorist strategy of social legislation and unmixed unions defended by the school of Liége, which had emerged from the social teaching and activities of the Abbé Pottier (1849–1923). Six weeks before the publication of *Rerum Novarum* the Belgian Democratic League was founded, with Helleputte as President, to take over the functions of the Fédération des Sociétés Ouvrières Catholiques. It was to co-ordinate all Catholic democratic institutions, including the unions, and represent them politically after the elections of 1894.

Among those most active at the congresses were Pottier and Arthur Verhaegen (1847–1914) who later succeeded Helleputte as president of the Democratic League. One-time traditionalist, Verhaegen became committed after the second congress to an independent Catholic workers' association Vrede (Freedom). As early as 1857 another workers' association had been founded by the spinners and weavers of Ghent. Initially neutral, if Christian in character, it gradually became dominated by a socialist faction which formed the successful co-operative society Vooruit (Forward). Eventually the Catholic unions formed their own society in direct competition. This rivalry proved fruitful – indeed in general the Catholic workers' movement profited from the stimulus provided by commonsense Belgian socialism. In 1891 the two Catholic groups united as a federation under the presidency of Verhaegen forming a complex of associations, economic, educational and religious, which generated the important co-operatives Het volk (reorganised finally on the Rochdale model) and La Durme.

The same year saw the federation in the Liége district of the many independent economic associations and co-operatives whose transformation from charitable societies had been engineered by Pottier. Through seminars and in his *École Professionelle Leo XIII*, economic skills were propagated among the workers alongside democratic ideals. Similar educational projects were undertaken in other districts and similar federations formed. The young Catholic unions developed parallel with other social organisations, often with the help of the clergy. By the turn of the century, in spite of the loyalty of his bishop Mgr Doutreloux and the support of the Vatican, Pottier's vigorous political career was extinguished by alarmed conservative Catholics. He was forced to retire to Rome whence he exercised his influence on Belgian affairs from a distance.

THE NETHERLANDS

Although Belgium and the Netherlands were united for long

parts of their history, from our point of view they differ in two important ways. The main impact of industrialisation came early, as we have seen, to Belgium, whereas in the Netherlands it was not experienced until 1890–1910. And Belgium was a Catholic country whereas Catholics were persecuted in the Netherlands from 1580 until the French overran the country in 1795.

In the Netherlands as in Belgium Catholics worked with the Liberals during the period immediately following the separation of the two countries. They supported J. R. Thorbecke's Liberal government in 1848–53, and obtained the restoration of their hierarchy. The alliance, however, did not last. Catholics were mistrusted, especially after the publication of the *Syllabus Errorum*, and the Liberals became identified with laissez-faire policies when an industrial proletariat began to appear in the 1870s.

At about this time the Calvinist minister Abraham Kuyper (1837–1920) started an exclusively Protestant movement which was theologically reactionary, but which represented the small man and the worker against the liberals of the Right.

In 1874 Kuyper was elected to Parliament, in 1877 he founded a mixed association for workers and employers, and in 1878 he launched the Anti-revolutionary Party. The Catholics followed suit. The priest Herman Schaepman (1844–1903) was elected to Parliament in 1880. He seems to have wished to merge with Kuyper and have an inter-confessional party comparable with the German Centre Party. Kuyper preferred to remain independent, but Catholics and Protestants of his persuasion (he had his own Reformed Church as well as his own party) generally supported one another on social legislation. At the end of the 1880s a Catholic tobacconist W. C. Pastoors (1856–1916) and a priest A. Ariens (1860–1928) began founding unions: for workers and employers together, for workers alone, and even, in the case of Unitas, for Catholic and Protestant workers in concert. Before 1891 this activity could be described as rudimentary. After that year it developed in a similar way to the Belgian Democratic League. A Catholic political party under Schaepman's leadership came into being in 1896. In the twentieth century Dutch Catholics like

Belgian Catholics have aimed at comprehensive social provision independently of the State.

THE ENGLISH-SPEAKING WORLD

In English-speaking countries Catholics were a minority, and clergy and laity alike were slow to raise voices against the economic order of things (outside Ireland, at least) or propose reforms. In 1883 Charles Devas, a Catholic acquainted with Continental Catholic economists like Le Play, published his *Groundwork of Economics* which reinforces George's attack on Malthusianism. But the chief contribution of the Church before 1891, apart from works of charity, was to show sympathy with organised labour. In England Bishop Bagshawe of Nottingham drew attention in his pastorals (reissued in pamphlet form in 1885 under the title *Mercy and Justice to the Poor*) to the 'desperate condition' of industrial workers in towns. Besides calling for State intervention and referring to the French Oeuvre des Cercles he says of strikes: 'Bad as they are, they are certainly a better remedy than none.'

In 1889 Cardinal Manning won the confidence of the strikers in the London Dockers' Strike. The following year in Australia Cardinal Moran intervened in a similar fashion in Sydney. In the United States there was a more considerable connection between the Catholic Church and the Knights of Labour.

Industrialisation came early to the northern United States, and although its effects were mitigated by the availability of unoccupied land for development, trade union militancy against capital began to appear in the 1820s and 1830s. This ceased, or was suppressed, after the financial crisis of 1837, and for the next 20 years opponents of capitalism looked less to strike action than to various forms of co-operation. After the Civil War, however, combinations of employees against employers re-emerged. In order that their members might not be penalised by employers, they surrounded themselves with secrecy; and they had much ceremonial of the masonic type and took imposing names like the Knights of St Crispin and the Knights of Pythias.

The Knights of Labour was founded by Uriah Stephens, a Baptist and a Mason, in 1869. It differed from other working men's associations in accepting members whatever their trade, or whether, indeed, they had a trade or not. It included unskilled labourers and a few (very few) Protestant ministers. The Knights of St Crispin, in contrast, had been founded in 1867 to fight the introduction of machinery that could be worked by untrained men, and the regular unions at that time represented the skilled workers rather than the working class as a whole. After a slow start, the Knights of Labour grew steadily between 1872 and 1885. A successful railway strike was then followed by a rush from all sides to join, and by 1886 the Knights was the strongest body of working men in America, with 700,000 members. The membership of the regular trade unions was only about 250,000.

Of these 700,000 Knights, 500,000 were Catholics, mostly Irish. From 1879 to 1893 the president of the organisation, the Grand Master Workman as he was called, was also a Catholic, Terence Powderly. The attitude of the Catholic clergy was initially one of suspicion. That was partly because at least until 1882 the Knights was a secret society, and although in the eighteenth century Catholics had belonged to secret societies – Daniel O'Connell was a Freemason for many years – without ecclesiastical censure, in the nineteenth century this was severely forbidden. A further consideration was that in the 1860s and 1870s a secret society of largely Irish membership, popularly known as the Molly Maguires, had terrorised mining districts in Pennsylvania. The history of this body and its romantic destruction by a Pinkerton's detective is probably best known to English readers from Conan Doyle's *The Valley of Fear*. The secrecy of the Knights made it possible for the hierarchy to fear in them a revival of the Mollies.

In 1881 branches of the Knights appeared in Canada, and there too the high proportion of Catholics caught the eye of the hierarchy. The English-speaking Archbishop Lynch of Toronto was sympathetic, but the senior see of Quebec was occupied by the French-speaking Archbishop Taschereau whom a visiting fellow of Balliol College, Oxford (J. E. C. Bodley) described as belonging rather to the eighteenth than to the nineteenth century. Taschereau procured a condemnation of the Knights from Rome and tried to enforce it in 1884. South of the border he was followed by the Bishop of

Portland, Maine, but the United States bishops were for the most part undecided. Powderly displayed tireless diplomacy in trying to reassure them. Several bishops admitted the need for working men to combine, and Archbishop Gibbons of Baltimore persuaded the hierarchy, instead of denouncing the Knights, to preserve a 'masterly inactivity'.

By 1886 appeals were being made to Rome, and in 1887 two bishops, closely followed by Gibbons and Taschereau themselves, went to Rome to try to obtain a definitive statement on the labour question. Gibbons submitted a long statement of reasons against condemning the Knights, and secured the influence on his side of Manning. Gibbons acquired the reputation, especially outside America, of being a good friend to the working man. In his diocese there had been activity on behalf of working class families by immigrant German Catholics since the foundation of their Central-Verein in 1855. The chief arguments he employed, however, were, as H. J. Browne has shown,[30] those of realism: there was no stopping the labour movement, and to condemn it would simply be to alienate the working class. These considerations prevailed. Catholics were told they could belong to law-abiding labour organisations, and the Church in America was saved from a blunder which might have been hardly less serious than Pius VI's condemnation of the Rights of Man. The gain, however, was less than might have been hoped.

Already in 1887 the Knights were losing members. Employers discriminated savagely against them, and at the same time they fell out with the trade unions. The reason was that the Knights wished to change the whole economic order, while the unions wished to work for the best possible terms for their members within it. When they struck in 1886 for an eight-hour day, Powderly advised against the strike, and the Knights were blamed for its failure. By 1890 the membership of the Knights had fallen to 100,000, and from being industrial and working class in character it was becoming middle class and agricultural. In 1893 Powderly was unseated from the presidency, and although the Knights were not disbanded until 1917 they did not again have a chance of influencing the course of social history.

'To talk of reducing the hours of labour' said Powderly in

his *Thirty Years of Labor* (1889) 'without reducing the power of machinery to oppress instead of to benefit, is a waste of energy.' Powderly and his supporters in the leadership could look back to the attempts at producers' co-operatives in the 1850s and 1860s. The preamble to the constitution of the Knights, agreed in 1878, laid down as 'first principles' the fundamental aims of workers' solidarity, education and 'the establishment of co-operative institutions, productive and distributive'. In the 1880s more than 130 producers' co-operatives were in fact established, mining and cooperage being the most favoured trades. One can sympathise with the desire of the leaders, when they were at their strongest to go for the big prize: 'the establishment' in Powderly's words 'of a just and humane system of land ownership, control of machinery, railroads and telegraph, as well as an equitable currency system.[31]

At the same time one can see that the gamble was unlikely to succeed. By the 1880s the tide of working class thought was setting in the direction of State socialism, while the radical 'first principles' of the Knights were what chiefly alarmed the Catholic clergy. Collective bargaining, even supported by judicious strikes, was understandable, but Powderly's programme raised the twin spectres of Marx's atheism and Fourier's sexual licence.

FRANCE 1871–1891

In August 1870 France embarked on a war with Germany. Within a month the army had been defeated, the Emperor Louis Napoleon, who accompanied the army, had been taken prisoner, and the Third Republic was declared in Paris. There followed the siege of Paris by the Prussians (19 September 1870 to 30 January 1871), the rise of the Paris Commune against the Republic (18 March) and the siege of Paris by the French (2 April to 21 May).

Count Albert de Mun (1841–1914) and Count René de La Tour du Pin (1834–1925), subsequently Marquis de La Charce, were prisoners of war in Germany and took part in the second siege of Paris. These experiences, and the work and writings of Ketteler, with which they became acquainted in Germany, led them to dedicate themselves to two objectives: reversing the de-Christianisation of the workers, and overcoming the existing divisions and hostility between classes.

In December they and a few friends set up a committee to organise what were called 'Cercles Catholiques d'Ouvriers', Catholic working men's clubs. These were societies which brought together rich and poor for social and religious activities. A typical Sunday would comprise Mass, a committee meeting, a visit to people in need, an educational meeting, sports, a lottery, a concert and evening prayers. Gambling was forbidden, and so were arguments about politics and religion. Cercles were set up in different districts of Paris and throughout the country. In 1880 the Jesuit Antonio Vincent started clubs modelled on them in Spain, and in 1889 M. F. da Fonseca did the same in Portugal. Apart from straightforward works of charity, these were the only Catholic moves to deal with the social problems in these countries before 1891.

In France by 1878 there were about 350 Cercles with about 45,000 members, of whom perhaps 37,000 were working class. The rest (who did pretty well all the organisation) came mostly from old and military families, though with an admixture of the bourgeoisie. They tended to be reactionary. Many were monarchists, and the founders had started by sending Pius IX a declaration of unreserved loyalty to the teaching of the *Syllabus Errorum*. They were not lacking, however, in energy. In 1886 they founded the Catholic Association for French Youth (ACJF), a prototype for similar bodies in other countries, which drew its membership chiefly from the student class. Albert de Mun was considered one of the best French orators of the nineteenth century. He and Emile Keller, another of the founders of the *Oeuvre*, as it was called, *des Cercles*, belonged to the Chamber of Deputies, and from 1880 onwards tried to introduce legislation to shorten working hours in factories and to encourage various kinds of workers' associations. De Mun's first preference was for corporative associations, but in 1886 a Catholic workers' union of silk workers came into being at Lyons, and in 1887 the Christian Brothers in Paris encouraged the foundation of the unmixed Syndicat des Employés du Commerce et de l'Industrie. This was the germ from which eventually developed the Catholic confederation, the CFTC.

The Catholic reformers met with opposition from both left and right. In 1884–5 they tried to found a Catholic party on the lines of the German Centre Party. It was impossible, however, to secure agreement among leading Catholics or to detach the programme of social reform from designs to restore the monarchy, and towards the end of 1885 Leo XIII asked de Mun to abandon the attempt.

Besides the Cercles themselves, the Oeuvre organised studies of political and economic problems, and from 1876 had a journal, *L'Association Catholique*. The leader in this part of its activities was La Tour du Pin. Though he professed himself a pupil of Le Play, from 1877 to 1881 he was military attaché in Vienna, and he may have been influenced by the Austrian corporativists. In 1883 he contributed an article to *L'Association Catholique* on 'The Corporative Regime' in which he laid down as conditions for a corporation:

1. Funds should be subscribed by members.
2. Managers should hold professional qualifications, and workers should be given opportunities to acquire skills.
3. There should be representatives of the three interests capital, management and labour – though in a trade like tailoring, customers might take the place of capital.

A further article, 'De l'essence des droits et de l'organisation des intérêts économiques', published in July 1891 but written before *Rerum Novarum*, gives fuller details. In trades where a corporation exists, there should be a council consisting of delegates from capital and labour in equal numbers. In other cases recourse should be had to 'corporative chambers' composed of delegates from what associations there are. The functions of these bodies are to oversee rates of pay, to police the keeping of rules, to make welfare arrangements, and to represent the trade in its dealings with people outside. Measures they recommend should be referred to all persons active in the trade, and if approved should be sanctioned by the government.

Wider proposals are contained in La Tour du Pin's article on 'Capitalism' (1889). The first step to dismantling the capitalist system is to pay off the national debt. For this purpose expenditure on the army must be reduced and heavy taxes imposed on items of luxury and foreign imports. The laws of inheritance which split up estates into small units which were uneconomic should be repealed. Laws should be passed penalising absentee landowners and encouraging agricultural co-operatives. In industry, a switch from family to co-operative ownership should be encouraged by changes in the laws limiting the liabilities of entrepreneurs. Wage-earning employees should be encouraged to become co-proprietors of the plant. One way in which this might happen is indicated by a scheme for dividing profits set out in the 1891 article. The share of capital should be to that of labour as the cost of amortisation or replacement to what is needed to maintain the workforce and cover schooling, holidays, sickness, retirement, etc.

La Tour du Pin's form of corporativism appealed to many Catholics at the time, and remarks like this still read well:

> Capital is not the only form of property . . . The possession of a career or a trade can also invest itself with the character of property when it is guaranteed by law.[32]

The social studies of the Oeuvre attracted the favourable attention of Leo XIII and probably contributed to his setting up a Committee for Social Studies in Rome in 1882. Perhaps even more influential, however, was the industrialist Léon Harmel (1829–1915). The Harmels were a strongly religious family from the Ardennes whose attempts to apply Christian principles within their factory near Reims will be described in Chapter Eight. Léon Harmel met de Mun by accident when some workers he was leading on a pilgrimage disrupted by excessively jolly music a more dignified procession by the local Cercle. The meeting resulted in his becoming one of the chief figures in the Oeuvre. In contrast with de Mun and La Tour du Pin, he insisted that what was done for the workers must also be done by them. He opposed paternalism and corporativism, and favoured worker-only unions. He and de Mun were influential guests at the Belgian congresses of the 1880s.

A project peculiar to Harmel was to take working people to Rome to see the Pope. These pilgrimages had several ends: to make people aware of the unsatisfactory condition of the Popes after the loss of Rome in 1870; to elicit from Leo XIII directives on social issues; and to make working people look to the Papacy rather than to the enemies of religion for the redemption of the world of work (so Felix Harmel in his address at the Audience of 9 November, 1889). The first pilgrimage took place in 1885. Although it had been very carefully prepared, and there was a grand reception by the Pope and ten cardinals, no working men were induced to take part: Harmel was accompanied only by 100 industrialists. In 1887 he tried again. This time he managed to bring 1,800 companions, including 1,400 workers. Leo XIII was extremely pleased – it should be remembered that in 1887 the prestige of the Papacy was at a low ebb – and Harmel promised to return in two years with 10,000 pilgrims. The promise was fulfilled. It was necessary to charter 17 trains, and since Rome in those days could not hold such an influx, the pilgrims came in successive batches, and the whole affair lasted six weeks. The pressure for some formal response from the Pope was irresistible. It came with the Encyclical *Rerum Novarum*, which Leo declared (address of 19 September 1891) was the 'reward for the pilgrimages of the French workers'.

CHAPTER SIX

Official Catholic Teaching and Action After 1891

RERUM NOVARUM (15 May 1891)

Workers have been handed over, alone and helpless, to the inhumanity of employers and the greed of unbridled competition. The evil has been increased by devouring usury, the undertaking of contracts and the conduct of all trade is concentrated in the hands of a few; with the result that a small number of extremely rich men have imposed on the great mass of the proletariat a yoke like that of slavery. (Section 2.)

The document which contains this indictment of industrial capitalism is the encyclical *Rerum Novarum*. A Papal encyclical is a kind of lengthy circular letter. According to the *Enciclopedia Cattolica* it is addressed by the Pope 'in virtue of his official and universal authority to teach, to the whole of Christendom, for the preservation and advancement of the spiritual life'. Although encyclicals appear above a Pope's signature, they are normally by several hands (*Rerum Novarum* went through a succession of drafts by different theologians), and make no claim to the controversial property of Infallibility. At least one fairly recent Papal statement (23 June 1964) seems to imply that their teaching can be revised when revision is opportune. On the other hand they have considerable binding force on Catholics by virtue of proceeding from what is called the 'ordinary magisterium'. In this phrase 'magisterium' means 'teaching authority' and 'ordinary' means not 'usual' but 'official and undelegated'. In the last hundred years encyclicals have become the main vehicle for official teaching. They are referred to by the opening words of their original, usually Latin, texts.

Rerum Novarum calls for careful study because it is the

foundation of subsequent Catholic teaching on several central issues: on property, the mutual responsibilities of capital and labour, the role of the State, a just wage, and workers' associations. The first question about property is whether men have any right at all to appropriate land and means of production, as distinct from food and what they need for immediate use. Leo defends a general right to appropriate in two ways. First, we are able to plan ahead and provide for the future: without property we cannot exercise this capacity, and our lives will be brutish. Secondly, we have a right to marry and provide for our children; a man 'can do this in no other way than by the possession of productive property which he can bequeath to his children'. (Section 10.) There is a strand in traditional Christian thought that by natural law all things are common, and appropriation is due at best to human convention, at worse to avarice. Leo says, however:

> Man is senior to the State; hence he ought by nature to have the right of providing for his life and body before any State is formed. (Section 9.)

Moreover the family is 'a true society, and one more ancient than any State'; if the State attacks its rights it becomes 'an object of detestation rather than of desire'. On how property can justly be acquired, Leo follows in the liberal tradition that goes back to Locke, and ignores difficulties raised by more recent thinkers like Proudhon. A man . . .

> . . . attaches to himself that part of the natural world which he has cultivated, and on which he has, so to speak, impressed the form of his personality. (Section 7.)

This gives a right to appropriate; but once a man has supplied the requirements of his household and 'what he needs to keep up what befits him in his station . . . it is a duty to give to the poor from what remains over'. (Section 19.) This duty, indeed, is not one of justice 'except in extreme cases' but of charity. Nevertheless Leo quotes Aquinas's statement of an austerer Christian ideal:

> Man should not consider his material possessions as his own, but as common to all, so as to share them without hesitation when others are in need.

Between capital and labour there is no necessity for conflict. They need each other, and harmony will emerge if each recognises certain obligations to the other. Workers should do what work they have undertaken to do, and refrain from violence in defending their cause. Employers should treat their workforce with respect, recognising that it is not disgraceful but creditable to work for gain. They must allow their employees time off for religious duties, have regard, in assigning work, to age and sex, pay a just wage, and 'refrain from cutting down the workmen's earnings, whether by force, by fraud or by usurious dealings'. (Sections 16–17.) (Workers were often required to buy on credit, at exorbitant prices and rates of interest, from shops belonging to their employers.)

In 'Action by the State' (sections 23–35) Leo is keenly alert to the danger of 'undue interference' (section 34) by the State:

> To hold that the civil power should penetrate as it pleases into the private life of the home is a great and pernicious error. (Section 11.)

Nevertheless the State has a duty to protect both proprietors and property-less employees:

> The first thing of all is to rescue unhappy working people from the cruelty of avaricious men, who use human beings as instruments for making money. To exact so much work that the mind is stupefied and the body is worn out is what neither justice nor humanity will bear. (Section 33.)

This entails making the State responsible for ensuring that workers are paid a just wage. Leo does not say in precise terms what the minimum wage should be, though suggests (section 35) that it should enable a workman, besides supporting his family, to make savings. But he challenges the laissez-faire opinion, still held by most Catholics of the richer classes, that any wage is just which is freely agreed between employer and employee. A man's labour, he argues, has two aspects. It is personal, in that it proceeds from his individual free will, and it is practically necessary, in that without its results he cannot live. Insofar as it is personal, he has the right to work for a low wage, or for none at all. But insofar as he is obliged to work in order to live, he does not have this right, any more than he has the right to 'assent to any treatment which is calculated to defeat the end and purpose of his being'. (Section 32.) It follows that the fixing of wages is not the exclusive concern of employer and employee.

> If the worker, driven by necessity or by the fear of a worse evil, accepts a harder condition which he would have to accept even against his will because the employer or contractor imposes it, he is the victim of violence and injustice. (Section 34.)

The State is then bound to intervene – unless, what Leo would prefer, the matter can be settled by some kind of trade union or syndicalist organisation.

Trade unions and other kinds of association are discussed (sections 36–44) and Leo confirms the right of workers to enter into association of any type they please. He shows some preference, however, for mixed associations over those for workers alone, and he warns Christians against joining unions with secret or anti-Christian leaders. This warning was to lead to the questionable policy of insisting on separate, confessional trade unions.

Rerum Novarum made social responsibility part of the official teaching of Catholicism. While some people (like Henry George, who addressed Leo a book-length open letter on the subject) thought it did not go far enough, many Catholics thought it went too far. In 1896 Bishop Francisco Venegas Galván of Querétaro addressed an audience of Mexican landowners in words that proved to be prophetic:

> Wealthy gentlemen, there is no other way: you must either open your hearts to charity and tear them apart from worldly riches as the Catholic Church commands you, and learn to consider your servants as brothers and children of God, lightening their burdens, shortening their hours of work and raising their pay in accord with the precepts of Leo XIII, or you will reap in a not too distant day the fruits of accumulated hatred and venom, when the stormy winds of socialism sweep over Mexico raising mighty waves that will bury your wealth and yourselves.[1]

There were Catholics in Italy and France, however, who needed no such admonitions.

In 1894 Giuseppe Toniolo (1845–1918), who presided over

the Intransigents' institute for social studies, produced a programme at the Congress of Milan which could have been the basis for a Catholic Social party. It called, among other things, for agricultural co-operatives and for sharing by workers in the profits and capital of industry. More radical Intransigents, calling themselves 'Young Christian Democrats' grouped themselves round the priest Romolo Murri and in 1899 demanded a complete transformation of society, starting with a corporative state. The first article of their programme ran: 'We desire the gradual organisation of society in associations which are vocational, corporative, autonomous, general and official.' They also desired proportional representation of parties in government, decentralisation, referendums, enlarged suffrage, laws to protect workers' welfare, producers' co-operatives, and reduction in expenditure on arms and bureaucracy. Riots followed, the priest-journalist Davide Albertario was sentenced to prison for 20 years (he benefited later from an amnesty), and all political associations were, for the time being, dissolved by the government.

In France a party aiming at Christian Democracy emerged from workers' study groups started by Harmel. The name 'Christian Democracy' did not then have the conservative overtones it has acquired since 1945; rather it suggested a dangerously radical republicanism, though the aim was to have a party of the centre. Centre parties are exposed to strong centrifugal forces, and it proved impossible to hold the various French Catholic interests together. Harmel insisted that the party should be working class in character, and thereby alienated the paternalistic employers of the north-east. Although the party was supported by the so-called 'democratic abbés', men like Lemire, Gayraud and Six, several of whom became deputies, mostly practising French Catholics remained monarchists. The party was also divided over the Dreyfus affair and over the Jewish issue generally. It did badly in the elections of 1898, and received the *coup de grace* in 1901 from Leo's Encyclical *Graves de Communi*. This forbade Catholics to use the expression 'Christian Democracy' except for social action which was strictly non-political and amounted, therefore, to a ban on Catholic political parties.

Leo's action seems to have had various motives. He was doubtless alarmed by the extremism of the Italian Democrats and by the Government's reaction to it. He was also persuaded by enemies of the French democrats that their political ideas were inextricably bound up with the theological position, abhorrent to the Vatican, called 'modernism'. In any case this retrograde policy of his last years was continued by Pius X (1903–14). Although he slightly relaxed the *non expedit* in *Fermo Proposito* (11 June 1905) in 1906 he suppressed Romolo Murri's National Democratic League, and in 1909 Murri was excommunicated. In 1910 he suppressed the radical Catholic movement led by Marc Sangnier which chiefly represented Christian Democratic thought in France after *Graves de Communi*. Local bishops followed suit. In 1913 the Bishop of Leeds stopped an attempt by Henry Somerville to start a Catholic Socialist party in his diocese. At about the same time A. Hlinka (1864–1938), the Czech popular leader, and Lemire, who was elected Mayor of Hazebrouck in 1914, underwent periods of suspension from their priesthood.

Even under Pius X, however, the embargo on political activity was not complete. Belgium, Holland, Germany and Austria retained Catholic parties. Hungary was remote from the sources of industrialisation and in 1900 only about 5 per cent of its workforce was employed in industry. Nevertheless a Catholic Popular Party was founded there in 1895 by Count Nador Zichy (1829–1911). A number of churchmen entered public life, Bishop Ottokar Prohaska (1858–1927) being perhaps the most prominent. In 1916 he proposed a law limiting land-holdings to 10,000 acres, but despite his offer to have the law applied first to the episcopal holding of his own diocese, the law was rejected.

The approach, moreover, of Pius X to the social question was by no means wholly negative. In place of political solutions he proposed what came to be known as Catholic Action. This term applies to organisations and activities of lay people the aims of which are rather moral and spiritual than political or economic, and which are co-ordinated and directed by the hierarchy. Such organisations and activities already existed in 1903 in several countries; under encouragement from Rome they increased very considerably in the next 30 years, and in some countries they have in fact provided a solution to the problems attendant on industrial-isation.

The degree of hierarchical control over Catholic Action has varied in different countries and at different times, and has generally varied inversely with political engagement. It was at the authoritarian end of the spectrum in Italy under Pius X and Pius XI, and has been at the opposite end in Belgium.

After 1891 the growth of Catholic unionism in Belgium accelerated and in 1903 Fr Rutten (1875–1952), who had studied the German movement, founded the Secretariat Général des Unions Professionels Chrétiens, superseded in 1908 by the Confédération des Syndicats Chrétiens et Libres, an independent body which now included the Flemish and neutral unions. In 1912 with a membership close on 100,000 this became the Confédération des Syndicats Chrétiens, the modern CSC. By 1939 membership trailed that of the CGTB by 200,000; by 1970 it was 100,000 ahead. Flemish industry developed late and the Church was ready for it.

One notable Catholic movement to operate outside the Democratic League was the popular Flemish Christene Volkspartij, created in 1893 by the Abbé Daens (1839–1907). With a programme of reform similar to that of the pottierists in most respects it was briefly affiliated, but Daens himself was a character so uncompromising that he antagonised all but his own followers.

The Volkspartij did not long survive as a serious political party after Daens's suspension in 1899, though daensisme lingered on. Like Pottier, Daens had fallen foul of the ascendant conservative Catholic factions.

It was not until after the Congress of Malines of 1909, dominated by Désiré Joseph Mercier (Archbishop of Malines from 1906 to 1926), that conservative attitudes began to weaken. At about the same time a scandal in the Congo enabled progressive Catholics to come to power with Schollaert as prime minister. The progressives had a vigorous ally in Mgr Mercier, but the peculiar success of Catholic social organisations in Belgium cannot be unconnected with the fact that, notwithstanding the strength and adventurousness of Catholic leadership, they were not primarily created from the top but formed independently of each other at a local level. In

1921 the Democratic League became the League of Christian Workers and in 1945 it assumed its present form as the Mouvement Ouvrier Chrétien (MOC).

The part of the MOC which has been exported most successfully to other countries is the Young Christian Workers (Jeunesse Ouvrière Chrétienne, or JOC). This was originally created not by the institutional Church but by a young parish priest, Joseph Cardijn, and its foundation will therefore be described in Chapter Eight. In 1925, however, it received the approval of Pius XI, it quickly spread to France, and by 1935 it had 80,000 members in Belgium and 50,000 in France. It differed from other Catholic Action organisations in that although it had priests as chaplains, the administrative offices were all held by laymen. Moreover unlike the longer established youth associations inspired by de Mun, its membership was solidly working class. For these reasons, and also because it started with study groups aiming at quite specific improvements in working and living conditions, JOC was able to engage more closely than other forms of Catholic Action with the difficulties of working class life between the wars, and it can hardly be doubted that the strength of the MOC after 1945 was due to the presence of an elite formed in the JOC before 1939.

The Netherlands has followed the same Catholic Action strategy as Belgium. From the 1890s on Catholics developed their own insurance funds, housing associations, organisations to fight tuberculosis and alcoholism, consumer co-operatives and cultural centres. In 1907–9 the hierarchy acted against a tendency which was emerging towards inter-confessional Catholic and Protestant trade unions, and thereafter it was a peculiarity of the Netherlands that social provision was triplicated by the two main religions and the non-religious. From the beginning of the century until 1939 the Catholics and Protestants between them had a majority in the Dutch Parliament. Although they did not enter into a formal alliance except over the issue of religious schools, they achieved a creditable record of legislation on social issues. The Catholic organisation was particularly effective in the mining district round Limburg. The mining industry there did not develop until after 1900, and the Church was ready for it. Thanks especially to the energy of the priest H. A.

Poels (1868–1948) the transition was negotiated without either distress or de-Christianisation.

Germany, Austria and France had Christian trade unions and proceeded some way down the same path as Belgium and Holland, but their organisations were not so comprehensive or well supported. In France the initiative was taken by the Jesuits. H. J. Leroy had started a union combining employers and employees as far back as in 1890. In 1903 he set up Action Populaire, which still exists under the acronym CERAS (Centre for Social Research and Action). This gave support in their hour of need to Marc Sangnier and to the worker-priests; it also, under the lead of Gustav Debuquois, encouraged the development of Catholic unions. The Syndicat des Employés du Commerce et de l'Industrie was joined by other unions from 1905 onwards and itself grew to have 9,000 members by 1919. In that year the CFTC (Confederation Francaise des Travailleurs Chrétiens) was founded. In 1920 it had over 300,000 members and took part in an international Christian congress representing 3,500,000 workers, mostly Catholic but with some Protestants from Holland. At that time Italy and Germany had the greatest numerical strength, but in those countries the Christian unions were taken over by the Fascists and Nazis, the process perhaps being eased by the fact that the unions had been organised in an authoritarian way from the top downwards. In France, however, the CFTC continued to grow, though its growth was greatly outstripped by the socialist – and later Communist – dominated CGT (Confederation Generale de Travail). This was founded in 1895, later than the first Catholic unions, and the Catholics might have done best to enter it at the start and use the advantage of their experience to influence its development.

Pius X was succeeded by Benedict XV (1914–21) and Pius XI (1921–39). Benedict relaxed the checks on Catholic political activity. In 1919 the Sicilian priest Don Luigi Sturzo was allowed to found the Italian Popular Party, and it got off to a good start with the support of 4,000 co-operatives, winning a fifth of the seats in the Chamber of Deputies. Of party leaders about this time who were priests one might mention W. H. Nolens (1860–1931) in Holland, Hlinka and Sramek (1870–1956) in Czechoslovakia, Seipel (1876–1932) in

Austria, Korosech (1872–1940) in Jugoslavia, Kaas (1881–1952) in Germany.

Unfortunately by the end of the 1930s most of these parties had been suppressed, notably the Italian Popular Party in 1926 and the Germany Centre Party in 1933. Under Seipel's successor Dollfuss in 1934 the Austrian party put through a new constitution to make Austria into a corporative state. This was a fatal mistake for which Dollfuss paid with his life within a few months. The new regime was Fascist in character and fell to Hitler in 1938.

QUADRAGESIMO ANNO (15 May 1931)

Meanwhile in 1931 Pius XI marked the fortieth anniversary of *Rerum Novarum* with a new encyclical on social issues, *Quadragesimo Anno*. Passages of historical retrospect and moral exhortation make this read less forcefully than Leo's original document, but on several points there is a real advance.

Leo had said that the policy of the State should be 'to induce as many as possible of the people to become owners' (section 35), but he had imagined this happening through workers making savings and investing them in land. Pius perceived that this is unrealistic and proposes instead . . .

> . . . that the wage-contract should, when possible, be modified somewhat by a contract of partnership . . . In this way wage-earners and other employees become associated in ownership and management, or participate in some proportion of the profits. (Section 69.)

Pius is careful to say that this modification is not an obligation of justice. (Section 64.) In a similar spirit he denies that 'all products and profits, excepting those required to repair and replace capital, belong by every right to the workers'. (Sections 55, 57.) Nevertheless the idea that some form of co-partnership should be introduced where possible is new in papal teaching, and we shall see it acquiring more and more prominence under later Popes.

On the topic of wages, Pius makes the fresh point that they should be at a level to maximise employment. (Section 74.) This addition is not prompted merely by Europe's experience of unemployment after the First World War. It comes from a changed view of the relationship between the individual and society. Leo so far retained the liberal preconceptions of his age as to write as if families could exist and act without States, and even individuals without families, much as they exist and act now. Pius points out (section 69) that labour, especially in industry, has a social as well as an individual aspect: it is essentially the work of members of a society who co-operate.

If men cannot exist, or at least cannot lead human lives, except in an organised society, it is tempting to infer that the interests of individuals should be subordinated to those of society as a whole. That inference, however, is invalid, and the Church has never accepted it. Pius introduces a principle which has been used by later Catholic thinkers to set a theoretical limit to State encroachment:

> Just as it is wrong to take away from individuals what they can do by their own exertions and industry, and entrust this to the community, so to hand over to a larger and higher society things which can be accomplished and provided by smaller and lower societies is an injustice, a grave harm and a disturbance of public order. (Section 79.)

The principle that functions should be reserved to the smallest society that can discharge them is called 'the principle of subsidiarity'. French and English liberals, following Rousseau and Mill, have always held that State interference should be restricted to actions which affect persons other than the doer: freedom is the right to do as you like so long as you do not injure others. The principle of subsidiarity does not compete with this, but can be a useful complement to it. Not only is the liberal principle powerless to adjudicate between States and intermediate societies like the family; acts do not, in fact, divide into those which affect only the agent and those which also affect others. Rather, every action has a self-regarding and an other-regarding aspect. Hence there is hardly any State encroachment the liberal principle by itself cannot be used to justify. Mill himself invokes it to prohibit nudity, if that is what 'offences against decency'[2] means.

Pius commends mixed unions or corporative vocational

groups. (Section 83.) This teaching was used to justify the
authoritarian corporative states set up in Portugal and
Austria. Pius himself has been censured for making a
concordat with Mussolini in 1929 and collaborating with the
Fascist government between 1931 and 1939. In fairness to
him it should be remembered that he condemned Fascism in
1931 and National Socialism in 1937. Sturzo, whom according to some he abandoned, considered adequate these
remarks on the Italian system in *Quadragesimo Anno* itself:

> To our knowledge there are some who fear the State is
> substituting itself in the place of private initiative, instead of
> limiting itself to necessary and sufficient help and assistance. It is
> feared that the new syndical and corporative institution possesses
> an excessively bureaucratic and political character and that,
> notwithstanding the general advantages referred to above, it
> risks serving political aims rather than contributing to the
> initiation of a better social order. (Section 95, Sturzo's transla-
> tion.)

A final point: though Pius declares that 'socialism' (that is,
Marxism) is so bound up with materialism that it can never
be compatible with Christianity (section 117), he concedes
that:

> Certain forms of property must be reserved to the State, since
> they carry with them a power too great to be left to private
> individuals without injury to the community at large. (Section
> 114.)

This gives non-Marxist socialists all they desire.

Since *Quadragesimo Anno* it has become papal practice to
refer to social and economic questions on each tenth
anniversary of *Rerum Novarum*. Partly, no doubt, because
Europe was at war, Pius XII (1939–58) did not issue an
encyclical in 1941. On 1 June, however, he made a radio
broadcast, and he recurred to the subject in a number of
addresses throughout his pontificate.[3]

During the Second World War an important initiative was
taken by the French hierarchy: they trained and sent out what
came to be known as worker-priests. In 1943 800,000 French
workers had been conscripted to work in armaments

factories in Germany. The German authorities would not allow any French clergy to attend them, so the bishops sent 25 priests disguised as ordinary workers. Of these priests (who were chosen from 200 volunteers) some were secular and some regular. They owed part of their inspiration to two lay persons who will be discussed in Chapter VIII, Emmanuel Mounier and Simone Weil. Three of them have left records of their experience: the Dominican Jean Doyen and the Jesuits Victor Dillard (who died at Dachau) and Henri Perrin, whose book, *Journal d'un prêtre ouvrier en Allemagne*,[4] established the term worker-priest ('prêtre ouvrier'). These priests on the mission to Germany were at once appalled by the alienation of the workers from Christianity, and convinced that they could not be brought to the Church but the Church must be brought to them.

The same message was contained in a report,[5] published also in 1943, by two JOC priests, Henri Godin and Yvan Daniel. The hierarchy accepted it and immediately began training a small number of carefully selected volunteers to infiltrate the working class. They were to take full-time employment in factories and live on their earnings; they were to wear ordinary clothes and lodge not in religious houses but in working class accommodation; and they were to regard the step they were taking as committing them irrevocably for life. At the same time they were to remain priests and keep in touch with each other and the hierarchy through regular meetings and retreats. There were worker-priests in a number of cities throughout France, also a few in Belgium, but the most famous mission was in Paris, where seven priests under the Abbé Hollande started work in the Communist stronghold known as the banlieu rouge ('the red outer sector') in January 1944.

The original aim was rather religious than political or social. The priests found, however, that to become workers they had to engage in political action. Nearly all of them joined not the Catholic CFTC but the Communist CGT. They became union activists, leaders of strikes and demonstrations, activists even in the Communist Party.

In the nine years which followed, the worker-priests were completely successful in the first step of their strategy: they turned into and were accepted as members of the working class without ceasing to be priests. They did not cause a flow of workers into churches on Sunday, but to that they refused to attach a high priority. What was important was that through them the Church should have a presence – the word 'incarnation' was sometimes used – in the working class. The best proof that they were right is that although they numbered barely a hundred throughout the whole of France and Belgium, they aroused consternation among hardline Marxists. Harmless in empty churches, their trained minds and personal dedication became infinitely dangerous on Party committees. But unfortunately conservative Catholics were alarmed too. The bishops who appointed them, especially the Archbishop of Paris Cardinal Suhard, were conspicuously loyal and defended them as well as they could. But accusations of selling out to the Communists, spiced with hints at sexual irregularity, were sent to Rome, and Rome, in a series of directives in 1953–4, brought the experiment to a halt. In particular there were to be no more priests in full-time employment.

On questions of politics and economics the worker-priests tended to take the Communist view, rather as their Protestant equivalents in England tended to side with the Labour left. Where they were original was on the religious side: in their recognition of how deeply middle class Catholicism had become, and in their efforts to develop a form of it which would be both authentic and acclimatised to the industrial world. In the 1950s it looked as if those efforts were being effectively extinguished by the Holy Office, and the Anglican Bishop E. R. Wickham could argue that because of the differences between the French and the English working classes, full-time working priests would never have a large role in England. But the story was not destined to end in the 1950s. As in the case of Lamennais, the Belgians were able to pretend that the Vatican rulings did not apply to them. In 1967 the Cardijn Seminary opened specifically for the training of worker-priests, and the first of its students was ordained in 1973. In 1967 also the French hierarchy voted unanimously for reinstating worker-priests. In 1975 for the first time a worker-priest was made a bishop. At present there are about a thousand French priests with employment of one kind or another, though perhaps not much over half are full-time workers in factories. How the number of industrial chaplains in England has increased, we have seen in Chapter Four.

After the war the Catholic workers' organisations in Holland, Belgium and France which had been suppressed under German occupation were revived. It is only in Belgium, however, that the strategy of comprehensive Catholic provision has been persevered in and succeeded. The Belgian MOC today is a federation of bodies which reaches like an octopus into every department of life. Besides the JOC it includes the Confederation of Christian Trades Unions, to which half the industrial workers of Belgium at present belong; full scale savings and insurance schemes to cover sickness, retirement and unemployment; chains of consumer co-operatives providing everything one might need or desire from food to foreign travel; a women's organisation; organisations for cultural and spiritual development; and a daily newspaper.

The drawbacks to keeping the French CFTC an exclusively Catholic body had been pointed out by Simone Weil in 1937; they were acknowledged in 1964 when the bulk of its membership went over, not indeed to the CGT, but to the neutral Confédération Democratique de Travail. The CFTC still exists but has only about 150,000 members. The Catholic co-operatives of France, which for a while retained a separate identity, have now similarly joined the non-religious co-operative union.

Catholic workers' associations were stronger in the Netherlands than in France, and the system of threefold provision by Catholics, Protestants and Socialists continued until fairly recently. In the last five years, however, partly for reasons of ecumenism, the Catholics have given up their confessional unions and merged with the socialists and Protestants.

In Western Germany Christian unions were not revived after the war. The Catholic workers' organisation (Katholische Arbeiter Bewegung) or KAB had, however, survived under the Nazi government by presenting itself as purely religious. The Secretary General, Mgr H. J. Schmitt, was sent to a concentration camp, but after his release in 1945 he was able, with the help of Cardinal Frings of Cologne, to lead the KAB back into the field of economic life. Today it has about 300,000 members, all from the workers', as distinct from the managerial, side of industry. Some 25–30 members of the Bundestag belong to it. It is backed up by the Catholic Social Institute at Bad Honnef which provides courses of various lengths and kinds, and corresponds in some measure to Plater College at Oxford. There is a separate institute for Bavaria, and an office at Munchengladbach to advise the hierarchy on social questions.

German Catholics have not, like the Belgians, aimed at social provision independent of the State; neither is there much support of the idea of co-operatives. Rather, they have concentrated on giving workers more say within the factory. Since as early as 1848 Germany has had Catholic conventions, Katholikentage. Suppressed by the Nazis, they restarted after the war and in 1949 the convention at Bochum passed strong resolutions calling for sharing of responsibility and co-determination. More recent conventions have had the character more of a popular religious fiesta than of a forum for serious discussion of social problems, but the Bochum conference almost certainly contributed to the legislation by which workers are now represented on boards of management throughout the coal and steel industries and in any firm which has more than 1,000 employees.

MATER ET MAGISTRA (15 May 1961)

The next encyclical devoted formally to social issues is *Mater et Magistra* by John XXIII (1958–63). In layout this follows *Quadragesimo Anno*, but there are strong differences in emphasis.

In the first place, by 1961 extremes of poverty and injustice had disappeared from the technologically advanced West. This improvement, however, had been effected by a multiplication of State rules and institutions which conspire to 'make it difficult for the individual to think for himself independently of external influences, act on his own initiative, perform his functions as he should and develop his mental and moral potentialities'. (Section 62.) Accordingly John says:

> Justice must be observed not only in how the produce of labour is divided, but in the conditions under which men produce. For

it is a need of human nature that the man who effects something by his action should have a share in the decision-taking, and perfect himself thereby. It follows that if an economic system is such that the human dignity of the workers is impaired, their sense of responsibility is weakened, and the opportunity of exercising initiative is removed from them, we hold the system to be unjust, no matter how great the quantity of goods produced or how justly and fairly they are distributed. (Sections 82–3.)

Secondly, *Rerum Novarum* envisages a system in which capitalist enterprises are run by their owners – in which there are only two parties, the master and his family, and the hired hands. In 1931 the scene had changed, and Pius XI notes that now:

Immense power and despotic economic domination are concentrated in the hands of a few who are, for the most part, not the owners, but only the trustees and directors, of invested funds.[6]

By 1961 the norm was a system of three parties, the shareholders, the workforce and the management, and of these the first, although they were in fact the owners, were by far the least important. Because of this, and because social security had removed the need for private sources of income:

Today men desire proficiency in some vocation more than the possession of property; and they rate more highly an income which derives from work and its rights than one which derives from property and its rights. (Section 106.)

As a result of these changes, much of the positive teaching of the encyclical[7] is a development of the suggestions about co-operation and co-partnership of Pius XI and Pius XII.
    Pius XII had said:

The small and average-sized undertakings in agriculture, in the arts and crafts, in commerce and industry, should be safe-guarded and fostered by granting them the benefits of a larger firm by means of co-operative unions.[8]

John observes that small industrial enterprises will have to be able to adapt themselves quickly, and recommends, therefore, government aid in the provision of technical education and credit. (Sections 87–8.) In agriculture he hopes the family farm will survive, but observes that families will not make enough to live in reasonable comfort without some association or co-operation. (Sections 143, 146.)

In medium and large concerns, workers should participate in decision-taking and direction. (Sections 91–6.) Where firms expand by self-financing, 'workers should be allocated shares'. (Section 75.) And John does not stop there. Noting that what happens in the economic field is increasingly determined not by individual firms but by the State, he says:

> It is therefore high time that the State authorities and public institutions . . . should co-opt the assistance of workers or of those whose function it is to look after workers' rights, needs and aspirations. (Section 99.)

These recommendations apply within particular economic sectors in places like Western Europe and North America. *Mater et Magistra* breaks new ground by considering relations between whole sectors – it calls attention to the depressed state of agriculture *vis à vis* industry and public services – and still more between developed and developing countries. The injustices which have been eliminated from Western Europe still exist in other countries where millions of workers are 'condemned through the inadequacy of their wages to live with their families in utterly sub-human conditions'. (Section 68.) John also notes the predilection of the richer nations for . . .

> . . . giving technical and financial aid with a view to gaining control over the political situation in the poorer countries . . . Let us be quite clear on this point. A nation which acted from these motives would in fact be trying to establish a new form of colonial control. (Sections 171–2.)

As a solution to the problems of developing countries, the encyclical is predictably averse to attacking the birth rate. Instead, advanced countries with food surpluses should give emergency aid to countries suffering from famine (sections 161–2); they should also remove the causes of famine by making available scientific, technical and professional training and the necessary capital for speeding up development. (Section 163.) At the same time:

> Everything must be done to ensure that social progress keeps pace with economic progress. (Section 168.)

In order that this whole, ambitious programme may be translated into reality, John recommends 'compulsory courses' in Catholic social teaching in schools of all kinds, in seminaries and in ordinary parishes (sections 221–33) – a recommendation which cannot yet be said to have been fully carried out.

GAUDIUM ET SPES (7 December 1965)

Social questions were on the agenda of the Second Vatican Council (1962–5). In the 1950s and 1960s certain early writings of Marx which are more consonant than the standard ideology of the Soviet Union with Christian thinking were coming to be studied by Catholics, and there were those who held that the Church could or even should support quasi-Marxist solutions. In England this view was taken by the clergy and laity of the Slant group; the *Slant Manifesto* by Adrian Cunningham and others (1966) contains a provocative statement of it by Martin Redfern. Although the Council did not endorse it – in particular it reiterated the value of 'property and other forms of private ownership' – the constitution *Gaudium et Spes*, issued at the end of 1965, does contain a section on social and economic life which gives some of the more progressive Papal teaching the stamp of approval of the whole Church. It is also possible to detect a couple of developments. *Mater et Magistra* had declared that:

> Work, which proceeds directly from a human person, is to be placed above any abundance of external goods, which are by nature instrumental. (Section 107.)

The Council goes a step further:

> The whole process of productive labour should be geared to the personal needs and way of life of whoever is doing it. (Section 67.)[9]

It is a natural consequence of this that 'investments should be aimed at providing opportunities for work' (section 70), and that:

> In economies which are in a phase of transition, for example . . . in which automation is on the increase, it will be necessary to see that enough and suitable work as well as adequate technical and professional training is provided. (Section 66.)

Secondly, the Council gives further attention to the developing countries. It restates in fuller detail the obligations of the richer nations; and its adds some recommendations addressed to the developing countries themselves:

> In many under-developed regions there are large, even vast, country estates, poorly cultivated or for reasons of gain left uncultivated, while the majority of people have no land or only the smallest plots – all this, when an increase in productivity is evidently urgent. (Section 71.)

Among the remedies is:

> The redistribution of insufficiently cultivated estates among those able to make them productive.

The Council does not envisage this redistribution being carried out without compensation; but that it approves it at all shows how far official teaching had travelled since *Rerum Novarum*.

In 1967 Paul VI (1963–78) set up a Pontifical Commission for Justice and Peace to further the recommendations of *Gaudium et Spes* and the Catholic social programme generally. Local Commissions for Justice and Peace now have responsibility for doing this in particular countries. It is a matter of opinion how galvanic in various countries they have actually been.

The United States is the country to which, today, one might look first for a lead. The first draft of a long promised Pastoral Letter on 'Catholic Social Teaching and the U.S. Economy' appeared in November 1984. It contains strongly-worded condemnations of censorious attitudes towards the poor and the unemployed, of the inequalities of income and wealth in the United States, and of United States policies in relation to developing countries. Critics have already appeared who complain that it looks for salvation too much to federal government action, and even that it is 'overwhelmingly on the side of the Democratic Party' (Robert Spaeth in *The Tablet* 12 January 1985). The draft does not in fact mention the Democratic Party, and that its recommendations are nearer to one political party's policies than to the other's might be thought a natural consequence of their being more than pious commonplaces. The measure of government intervention called for is very moderate by European standards, and the bishops defend it by saying that a great deal of intervention in the play of market forces already exists and is here to stay. The kind of laissez-faire liberalism, however, which started to decline in Europe a hundred years ago is still strong in America, and it is hard to predict how far the draft will be modified before it appears with the backing of the whole hierarchy.

Before this draft, not much had been written by United States bishops about economics; but the Catholic Church has taken some action in concert with other Christian denominations to bring its investment portfolios under regular review and to try to influence the policies of companies in which it invests. The American National Council of Churches has drawn up guidelines for investors which list points about a company which ought to be considered. The points fall under five main heads: the company's effect on the environment; its employment policies; the nature and extent of its dependence on military activity; its behaviour abroad – special attention has been paid to operations in Latin America and South Africa; and its dealings with the consumer. In the 1970s the Council of Churches provided a centre for supplying information about companies, from where there developed an advisory and co-ordinatory body called the Interface Center in Corporate Responsibility.

Although the Catholic Church in America has been active in developing this approach to the forces of industrial capitalism, in England Christian action of this kind has been confined to the Protestant churches; or been taken by voluntary secular bodies like the recently established EIRIS (Ethical Investment Research Information Services), an initiative for which various Rowntree Trusts have been chiefly responsible. A Catholic working party on Church investment was set up, and reported in 1978, but its recommendations were not accepted, or even made public. The statement by the Bishops of England and Wales after the Pastoral Congress of 1980 contained the following discouraging comments:

> At the Congress relatively little attention seems to have been paid to the basic economic and ethical principles which are at the heart of social justice . . . Little emerged in the reports on the major questions posed by such matters as industrial relations, the breakdown of trade agreements, the influence and role of employers' associations and trade unions, the economic and party-political considerations often relevant in wage-negotiations, and the consequences to the rest of the community of strikes and other restrictive practices.[10]

POPULORUM PROGRESSIO (26 March 1967)

It would seem that in Rome after 1960, as in the Church of England, attention was often directed away from the economic scene in Europe and North America to the poorer countries of the world. On 26 March 1967 Paul VI issued the encyclical *Populorum Progressio* which chiefly spells out what the Council had said about these countries. Paul appears, in fact, to have felt that the live issues of social justice concerned relations between economic sectors, regions and whole nations more than between employers and employees. It is characteristic that he applies Leo XIII's reasoning about wage contracts to trading agreements between developed and developing countries.[11]

A similar assessment of the situation is reflected in *Octagesima Adveniens*, the Apostolic Letter to the Chairman of the Commission for Justice and Peace, issued on 15 May 1971 to mark the eightieth anniversary of *Rerum Novarum*. It is only in John Paul II's *Laborem Exercens* that we are brought back to specific questions about labour, capital and the individual worker.

LABOREM EXERCENS (14 September 1981)

This encyclical builds on the conception of the intrinsic value of human work which we have seen emerging in *Mater et Magistra* and *Gaudium et Spes*. There is, of course, an ancient tradition, Christian and indeed pre-Christian, that work is in itself an evil, which exists only for the sake of leisure and the enjoying of the good things it has produced. John Paul disarms this view, however, by distinguishing between work proper, which the theist should see as nothing less than a sharing in God's creative activity, and toil, which does have to be counted, along with pain and disease, among evils inherent in life here and now. Even if theological considerations are left aside, work as distinct from toil is intrinsically good, not only because it is enjoyable, but because it is 'worthy; that is, something conformable to the worthiness of man, which declares that worthiness and increases it'. (Section 9.)

The fundamental doctrine of the encyclical is 'the precedence of labour over capital'. (Section 12.) John Paul says that this has 'always' been taught by the Church, but 'always' seems to be an exaggeration. Leo XIII and Pius XI, at least, speak of capital and labour as if, being interdependent, they were on a level. It is just this view, that they are two co-ordinate 'production factors', which John Paul stigmatises as 'the error of economism'. (Section 13.)

The principle that capital should be subordinated to labour he defends by several considerations, of which the most striking is that a period of work may be regarded from two angles: we can consider what results from it; or the person who does it. From the former angle the value of the work is proportional to the use-value of the product. In classical economic theory the worker's time is also (indeed primarily) valued at the cost of his subsistence for that time. John Paul wishes to replace this narrowly economic conception by a broader moral one:

> The basis on which the importance and value of human work are to be established is not the nature of the work done but the fact that it is done by a person. (Section 6.)

He also claims that all work is in the first instance for the sake of the individual who executes it:

> 'The target [*scopus*] of any work a man does . . . is always the man himself'. (Section 6.)

These are substantial and controversial claims. It is typical of the encyclical form that no formal arguments are offered for them. Perhaps, however, John Paul would appeal in the end to the idea which is also, for him, the basis of the rights of workers: work is a universal human duty. (Section 16.)

The subordination of capital to labour leads to a fresh treatment of property. Earlier popes, as we have seen, are careful to distinguish the right to possess means of production from the right to use them as one pleases or even to leave them idle. John Paul goes beyond this distinction when he says:

> The one legitimate reason for possessing means of production, whether in the form of private or in the form of public or collective ownership, is *that they should serve labour*. Hence while they are in use, they ought to advance the fulfilment of the primary principle of this order, namely that goods are destined for all, and all have a right to use them. (Section 14.)

Unlike his predecessors John Paul refrains from condemning, on that ground alone, regimes where private ownership has been abolished:

> We cannot exclude, under appropriate conditions, the bringing together of the means of production under socialist common ownership. (Section 14.)

On the other hand, a person who works desires not only a wage but the knowledge that he is working 'for himself'. (Section 15.) Even in a fully socialist State 'every effort must be made' to meet this desire, though just how it can be met we are not told. In a capitalist society, and not least in many countries which have only lately gained self-determination, the right to private property should undergo 'a fruitful revision' with the result that:

> Each man on the basis of his own work has the full right to consider himself at the same time a co-owner of that great workshop in which he works along with everyone else. Progress can be made towards this goal, if so far as is feasible, work is combined with ownership of capital, and if there is a maximum variety of intermediate bodies pursuing social and cultural as well as economic ends. (Section 14.)

As regards trade unions John Paul says (section 20) that although they should not have 'too close links' with political parties, they can and should . . .

> . . . try for the common good of society as a whole to correct defects in the ownership of the means of protection or in the way in which they are managed.

Presumably these words were written with an eye rather to the Polish union Solidarity than to the British National Union of Mineworkers.

A final point of novelty in the encyclical is the use John Paul makes of a distinction between direct and indirect employers. The direct employer of a workman is the individual or institution that enters directly into a wage-contract with him; the indirect employer is any factor which has an influence either on the wage-contract or on any other economic arrangement. The concept includes, then, not only persons but also principles, collective contracts and entire politico-economic systems. It is through viewing the whole of society as an employer that John Paul is able to say:

> It is the observance of the objective rights of the worker – whether manual or intellectual, industrial or agricultural – that should form the appropriate and principal criterion for an economic system, whether within the limits of a particular society or State, or within the whole ambit of the world's economy. (Section 17.)

Laborem Exercens will not be the Vatican's final word on social problems. It is safe to predict that there will be a major encyclical in 1991, the centenary of *Rerum Novarum*, if not before. Less predictable are its contents. Will it continue the shift of emphasis from individual to various kinds of shared or collective ownership? Will it revert to a preoccupation with relations between richer and poorer nations? However that may be, one further document has come from Rome since *Laborem Exercens* which calls for mention here.

The new *Code of Canon Law* retains and tightens up restrictions on clerical participation in political and economic life:

Clerics are forbidden to assume public office wherever it means sharing in the exercise of civil power. (Section 285: 3.)

Clerics are forbidden to practise commerce or trade, either personally or through another, for their own or another's profit, except with the permission of the lawful ecclesiastical authority. (Section 286.)

They are not to play an active role in political parties, or in directing trade unions, unless, in the judgement of the competent ecclesiastical authority, this is required for the defence of the rights of the Church or to promote the common good. (Section 287: 2.)

It is true that Canon 288 states that these rules do not apply to permanent deacons. The fact remains that, except in three countries, the United States, West Germany and Belgium, the permanent diaconate is virtually non-existent. Those countries account for 7,068 out of the world's 9,794 deacons; in the remaining countries deacons are rarer on the ground than bishops.[12]

CHAPTER SEVEN

Non-Christians

It is impossible to form a just estimate of the Christian response to social problems so long as Christians are considered on their own. In the present chapter we shall try to see what responses, down to the end of the nineteenth century, came from thinkers who rejected Christian beliefs, and how Christians and non-Christians influenced one another. Our excuse for not carrying the survey beyond 1900 is that by then the most dynamic and instructive interplay of Christian and non-Christian ideas was over. That non-Christian tradition which goes back to Marx and Bakunin had established itself in a position of hostility to Christianity; with other non-Christians, such as those in the tradition of liberal humanism, Christians had come to co-operate at least on broad issues of social reform. These days there seems to be no significant division between approaches to these issues on Christian-humanist lines.

BRITAIN

The principal non-Christian pioneers of social reform in Britain can be put into two groups, social liberals and socialists. The former believe in free trade and competition as mechanisms for increasing the general happiness, and uphold individual ownership of the means of production, but look to legislation and hence to a measure of State intervention for reforms in areas of social and economic life. The socialists emphasise co-operation against competition, and advocate collective or State ownership of the means of production.

Among the social liberals, we have already suggested that Thomas Paine (1737–1809) should be considered the first. He is chiefly remembered as a scourge of hereditary systems of government and a champion of the institutions of representative democracy. But for our purposes it is his radical proposals for welfare arrangements which are mainly of interest. They are contained in the long final chapter of Part II of *The Rights of Man*.

In the absence of any official statistics, Paine employs a characteristically rough and ready method of his own to estimate that the population of England contains approximately 70,000 persons needing support between the ages of 50 and 60, and the same number over 60. He then proposes that the former should be paid £6 annually, and the latter £10. Reckoning that there will be a total of 630,000 children under the age of 14 in the families of the poor, he proposes:

> To pay . . . to every poor family . . . four pounds a year for every child under fourteen years of age; enjoining the parents of such children to send them to school, to learn reading and writing and common arithmetic; the ministers of every parish, of every denomination, to certify jointly to an office, for that purpose, that this duty is performed.

Families which 'though not properly of the class of the poor, yet find it difficult to give education to their children', will receive 10 shillings per child. In addition there are to be donations of £1 at each birth and marriage, and allowances 'for the funeral expenses of persons travelling for work, and dying at a distance from their friends.'

Paine claimed that these payments could be provided out of central government funds, and would make it possible to abolish the hated poor rates. However doubtful his arithmetic, the proposals are important because they are set not within the framework of some imaginary Utopia, but in the familiar existing world of eighteenth-century Britain. By virtue of his Welfare State proposals Paine is an undoubted social liberal and a man in this respect almost a century before his time. He is also exceptional in that he emerged from an artisan background – he was originally a stay-maker by trade – and not from an intellectual one.

The British liberal economists form a small and closely united group. James Mill (1772–1823) and his son John Stuart Mill lived next door to Jeremy Bentham (1748–1832) in London, and spent many months staying with him in the country and with his brother Sir Samuel Bentham in France. David Ricardo (1772–1823) was a close friend and to some extent a protégé of James Mill; and Thomas Malthus was on terms of warm personal friendship with both Ricardo and the Mills. Malthus was a clergyman of the Church of England, and Ricardo was probably by conviction a Jew, although he conformed to the Church of England in order to enter Parliament for an Irish borough. Bentham, however, and the Mills rejected all religious beliefs. Their moral philosophy rested on the principle that laws, institutions and individual actions are good insofar, and only insofar, as they promote 'the greatest happiness of the greatest number', a phrase Bentham borrowed from Joseph Priestley. Although these five men are the leading British exponents of laissez-faire, Bentham and especially J. S. Mill in later life can be thought of as social rather than as straight liberals. They all and their friends supported, in the first place, extension of the franchise: they took it that parliamentary democracy is the indispensable basis for everything else. Bentham throughout his life was advocating a wide range of legal and administrative reforms. Perhaps most relevant to the problems arising from industrialisation was the plan in the 1790s to replace the existing parochial work-houses by a national system of self-supporting 'houses of industry' which would hold 2,000 paupers each.[1] Chronologically these establishments stand between Bellers's 'colleges of industry' and Owen's 'villages of industry'; but they contrast with both in being compulsory and sounding extremely austere and dismal. They were based on a plan worked out by Samuel Bentham for a circular prison building which would enable prisoners to be kept by a minimal staff of warders under continuous surveillance.

We have seen in Chapter Four how J. S. Mill brought together the liberal and socialist traditions. His *Principles of Political Economy* is the culmination of laissez-faire economics, but the ink on it was hardly dry before he and his future wife Harriet Taylor were converted to 'a qualified socialism'. The extent of Mill's conversion is still the subject of lively debate, and Pedro Schwarz in *The New Political Economy of J. S. Mill*[2] argues in effect that Mill never really separated himself from straight laissez-faire economics or recanted his famous wages fund doctrine. It is beyond our scope to explore these issues; but both *Principles*[3] and the *Autobiography*[4] show that the Mills, husband and wife, were deeply influenced by events and writers in France. The economic system to which they look forward contains a certain amount of profit sharing, but the predominant form of ownership will be the kind of producers' co-operatives described by H. Feugueray, from whom Mill quotes extensively.[5]

Bentham and Mill identify the good with pleasure and see their philosophy as opposed above all to what they call 'asceticism'. As Halevy points out, however, in practice they advocate something almost indistinguishable from Weber's work-ethic of ascetic Protestantism. They lay on us the duty . . .

> . . . in virtue of the natural conditions to which life is subject, to sacrifice present pleasure to the hope of future pleasure, and to purchase happiness at the cost of labour and suffering.[6]

It is significant that in the *Autobiography*[7] Mill is more eager to see the rich working than the poor at leisure. His claim that some pleasures, without being pleasanter, are higher and better than others, is formally inconsistent with his ethical hedonism, but none the less for that it speaks straight to the English conscience. He shows himself the son of the James Mill who started life as a preacher in Scotland when he declares that the emancipation of the workers ceased to be in doubt . . .

> . . . when dissenting preachers were allowed to go among them, and appeal to their faculties and feelings in opposition to the creeds professed and countenanced by their superiors.[8]

The socialist tradition begins with Thomas Spence (1750–1814). In 1775 he proposed that land should be owned by parishes and let out in small holdings under short leases. The details of this scheme seems to have been inspired partly by the American Revolution and partly by the arrangements governing the Town Moor at Newcastle-upon-Tyne. Spence also said that all the expenses of government could be met from these rents. He is therefore the pioneer of the Single Tax idea, the best known exponent of which was Henry George.

Spence had a certain working class following (which included some committed Christians), but a far more influential writer among the educated classes was William Godwin (1756–1836), the husband of Mary Wollstonecraft and the father of the author of *Frankenstein*. Godwin started life as a Sandemanian minister, and although the philosophical arguments of the Enlightenment convinced him that Christianity was false, his social thinking retains a more Christian character than that of Bentham and Mill, and his *Enquiry concerning Political Justice* (1793) does not scorn the support of biblical texts. Its more recent authorities are Mably and Wallace.

Godwin denies that we have any active rights, any right to do as we please, over anything whatever. Justice requires us always to use things in the way most beneficial to mankind as a whole. He distinguishes three kinds of property. First, food, shelter and clothes are needed for subsistence; we have the strongest rights to these. Next, a man has a fairly strong right to the produce of his labour. Thirdly, existing societies recognise or confer 'a faculty of disposing of the produce of another man's industry'.[9] This conflicts with the second kind of property-right, and Godwin holds that accumulated property of the third kind is a great evil. The system which he regards as ideal, and which he calls 'a system of equality' is one in which it would not exist. For the rest, he may be regarded as the father of the anarchist tradition. The ideal society will have no coercive bodies. Godwin is opposed even to co-operation, chiefly on the ground that it is irksome for people to have to adjust to one another. His fear of State encroachment leads him to particularly eloquent warnings against letting it take over education. We are lucky that what he says about State-financed universities no longer applies: they . . .

> . . . have long been remarked for formal dullness . . . The knowledge taught there is a century behind the knowledge which exists among the unshackled and unprejudiced members of the same political community.[10]

Godwin's communistic society is agricultural. The first English writer to deal specifically with the problems of industrialisation is Charles Hall (*circa* 1740–1820). Unfortunately his *Effects of Civilization* (1805), which contains extremely acute criticism of Hume, Adam Smith and Paley, attracted hardly any attention. The man who first set people in Britain thinking seriously about alternatives to industrial capitalism was Robert Owen (1771–1858).

Owen acquired the reputation of being an atheist, but in fact he was a deist with spiritualistic leanings – leanings shared, it may be noticed, by others who were attracted to Communism, for example the Shakers. His social thinking has the same Christian character as Godwin's. Like Godwin, also, he took an optimistic view of human nature, though in his case this view was based on the belief that there is nothing that cannot be achieved by education:

> Any character, from the best to the worst . . . may be given to any community . . . Children are, without exception, passive and wonderfully contrived compounds who, by due preparation and accurate attention, may be formed collectively into any human character.[11]

Owen's criticism of capitalism gains authority from the fact that he was himself a brilliantly successful capitalist. Starting with nothing, by the age of 30 he had married the daughter and taken over the four spinning mills of David Dale of New Lanark. Between 1800 and 1813 he not only abolished child labour in these factories and greatly improved living conditions for a workforce of 2,500; he also increased profitability. He then launched his famous educational experiments. In these he was aided not only by the Quakers but also by Jeremy Bentham.

After the Napoleonic wars England suffered from grave unemployment, and Parliament set up a committee to consider the problem. Owen laid before it a very bold plan. Instead of going to poor relief the poor rates should be used to acquire land for 'villages of industry'. These should have a population, ideally, of about 1,200 persons. They should be mainly agricultural, but should also have workshops, and although families would have their own sleeping quarters, meals and recreation would be communal. In the next quarter century Owen elaborated these schemes, and devoted the whole of his considerable savings to getting such communities set up. Where did the idea of them come from?

His biographers say, from New Lanark. Another possible source is Bentham's 'houses of industry'. But it is arguable that Owen's main sources were Christian. His villages closely resemble Bellers's 'colleges'. Owen even proposes, like Bellers, a labour-currency. In the same year in which Owen published his villages scheme (1817) he reprinted Bellers's *Proposals for raising a College of Industry*. He also reprinted an account (by Spence's disciple Evans) of Rapp's community at New Harmony.

In 1824 Owen left New Lanark for America to put his community scheme into practice. He bought New Harmony from Rapp, and by autumn 1825, 900 colonists had assembled there to attempt communal life. They were not, however, well prepared for it, whisky flowed too freely, and Owen returned to England before order was established. When he returned in 1826 the experiment was unsavable. Communal production was abandoned in 1827, though the educational department of the venture survived, and some of Owen's family remained on the site.

While Owen was absorbed in this American project, an important development was taking place in England. The repeal of the Combination Acts in 1826 was followed by the formation of the trade unions. Just before this time William Thompson (1775–1833) had been converted from Benthamism to Owenism. In 1824, in his *Inquiry into the Distribution of Wealth*, he argued that since labour alone creates value it ought in justice to receive 'the whole product of its exertions'. In *Labour Rewarded* (1825) he explains how this could be brought about. It is not enough for the trade unions to bargain for high wages; they should use their funds to set up factories for their members. The capital should then be divided into as many shares as the enterprise could employ workers, and the workers (male and female alike; like Owen and in opposition to James Mill, Thompson was an early champion of the rights of women) should be encouraged each to buy a share. As an insurance against industrial recessions, these manufacturing co-operatives should acquire land as well, and train members for both industry and agriculture.

When Owen returned from America he took up these projects, but the trade union movement was not yet strong enough to challenge the forces of capitalism, and Owen's unorthodox religious views were a source of disunity. By the end of 1834 it was clear that the unions were not to be the means of transforming society along Owenite lines. From then onwards the unions and Owen went different ways, and Owen's way led him increasingly into realms of ethical and metaphysical speculation. The co-operative ball, however, which he had set rolling did not come to a stop as soon as he took his eye off it.

Noyes mentions nine or ten short-lived communities started in America under the influence of Owen's first visits. Owen's visits continued into the 1840s, and he was in touch with the Fourierist and Protestant communities of that decade. Two communities were attempted in Britain, one of which lasted six years (1839–45), impressed Engels, and had Owen himself as a governor long enough to consume the remains of his fortune. The leading French socialists were critical of his form of socialism, but Etienne Cabet (1788–1856) sent 69 colonists to Red River, Texas, to found a society which can be classed as Owenite in 1848. They had the fates against them. They suffered from yellow fever, one man was struck by lightning, and the doctor went mad. In spite of these misfortunes, several changes of settlement, and constant internal quarrels, they survived until 1895, achieving a far longer life than any other non-religious community.

These experiments aimed at communal life. Owen also inspired some more modest initiatives which were destined to be much more important and on which, in fact, his place in history chiefly rests. While he was away from England in the 1820s, some of his working class followers, with the encouragement of William King, tried to put his ideas into practice piecemeal by starting consumer co-operatives. Owen himself is said to have been unenthusiastic about them, but they nevertheless continued, and in 1844 the Rochdale Pioneers started the store from which, it may be said, all modern co-operatives are descended.

FRANCE

The most celebrated French response to industrial capitalism is what Marx and Engels have taught us to call 'Utopian socialism'. This could be traced back to Rabelais's Abbey of Thélème and beyond, but in modern times starts with the works of Morelly. Hardly anything is known about the author of these books; it is disputed even if they are by a single hand; but they appeared between 1743 and 1755. Morelly held that men are naturally sociable. He blamed human misery on private property, and rejected the liberal doctrine that this is inseparable from organised society. In an exotic fantasy, the *Basiliad* (1753), he depicts a society which is organised – it has a king – but in which there is no private property and no coercion, and this ideal is expounded more directly in the *Code of Nature* (1755).

The Utopian tradition was continued by two thinkers who are commonly grouped together, although personally they were very different, Count Henri de Saint-Simon (1760–1825) and Charles Fourier (1772–1837). One was a nobleman who signalled his commitment to liberty and change by fighting for the Americans in their War of Independence and participating in the French Revolution until he was imprisoned by Robespierre in 1794. The other was a bourgeois and a shy recluse.

Saint-Simon professed himself the follower of the eighteenth century Marquis de Condorcet. In his *Exquisse d'un tableau historique des progrés de l'esprit humain* (1793) Condorcet maintains that thanks to the progress of the social and political sciences, man will proceed indefinitely in the direction of greater happiness and perfection. Saint-Simon agrees; but while Condorcet proposes to improve the condition of the poor only by education and life insurance, Saint-Simon advocates radical constitutional reform. The main lines of his thinking are laid down in *Letters from an Inhabitant of Geneva* (1802–3). Education, general legislation and moral leadership should be in the hands of a small group of scientists and artists; executive power and the drawing up of financial legislation are entrusted to the leading 'industriels', a word he uses to cover farmers, manufacturers, merchants and bankers. Saint-Simon deplored accumulations of hereditary wealth in the hands of *rentiers*, but he did not recommend forceful appropriation, still less State ownership of the means of production. In an article of 1818 he states what is, in fact, the traditional Christian view:

> The individual right to property can only be based on the
> common and general utility of the exercise of that right, a utility
> which can vary from one age to the next.

Saint-Simon believed that moral and intellectual leadership
had passed from the Church to the lay intelligentsia, but he
was not for doing away with religion altogether. In his *Letters*
he proposed an entirely new religion based on the cult of Sir
Isaac Newton. This would be lightly equipped with dogma,
though Saint-Simon retained a Hell for the accommodation
of his persecutor Robespierre. In his last work *The New
Christianity* he gives up the idea of a totally new religion, but
advocates a simplified form of Christianity. The essential
message of Christ had been 'Men should treat one another as
brothers'. Adapted to the conditions of 1825, this became:
'Men should direct all their work and all their activity
towards the aim of improving as quickly as possible the
moral and physical condition of the most numerous class'
(First Dialogue). Saint-Simon denounces both the Catholic
Church and the Lutherans for swerving from the original
Christian mission. Of the Catholic Church he complains,
among other things, that it gives 'a bad education to
seminarists'; priests are taught nothing but theology, and in
all knowledge which is useful for life in the present world
they are far behind the laity. This criticism was to bear more
fruit than Saint-Simon himself may have anticipated.

After Saint-Simon's death his disciples continued to
develop his ideas. They added a commitment to the
emancipation of women, and in 1829 started a Saint-Simonist
Church with its own hierarchy of Supreme Fathers, Apostles
and so forth. This was open to charges of absurdity, and the
feminist programme looked like abolishing marriage. In
1831, by which time their numbers had risen to about 40,000,
they split. It is clear that many young people who were
becoming aware of the problems resulting from industrialisation were impressed by Saint-Simon's strictures on the
Catholic Church. Some of these now returned to the
Catholic fold with the idea of reforming the Church from
within. Frederick Ozanam is a conspicuous example. The
development of Catholic social thinking after 1830 which
was surveyed in Chapter Five certainly owes something to

Saint-Simon. Those who stayed in the Saint-Simonist Church achieved less. In 1832 a party of missionaries attempted to evangelise England, but despite a sympathetic hearing from Mill and Carlyle they were unsuccessful. Perhaps they put people off by wearing fancy dress, including waistcoats which buttoned up the back and could therefore be put on and taken off only through co-operative efforts. The same year the Supreme Fathers were sentenced to a year in prison for undermining French morals. Thereafter the torch of amateur reformism passed to the Fourierists.

Fourier's system is amazing and comprehensive. It embraces man, God, the planets, the universe, and not only the universe but the biniverse, the triniverse, and other cosmological innovations. In this system physical events are explained by gravitational attraction, and psychological events, including the voluntary actions of human beings, by a kind of emotional attraction according to principles of which Fourier believed himself to be the discoverer. All that concerns us here is his scheme for reorganising human society.

More alert than Saint-Simon to the abuses which capitalism permits, Fourier rejects individual ownership of land or factories. Whereas Saint-Simon hoped to change society from the top, Fourier concentrates on what, for him, is the lowest social unit above the individual, the phalanx: once phalanxes get going, constitutional change will follow automatically. A Fourierist phalanx consists of between 1,600 and 2,000 persons who live together (in decorous but complete sexual promiscuity) in a single large building called a 'phalanstery'. The means of production used by a phalanx are owned collectively, but Fourier's society is not egalitarian. He envisaged rich men bringing money into a phalanx and receiving capital shares. Remuneration, though it is conceived rather as a dividend that as wages, is to have three components: these represent capital, talent and labour, the reward for labour, naturally, being greater where the labour is more disagreeable. Life in a phalanstery is strenuous.[12] Only five hours a day are allowed for sleep, and no time at all seems to be reserved for sitting about doing nothing. Life is pleasant, nonetheless, because people do only things they want to do – each individual works out his own timetable for the day – and because they never work at the same task for more than a couple of hours. The tasks to be done are distributed among small groups which are ordered in series according to Fourier's art of bringing the various passions of man into harmony. Since each individual will belong to some 30 or 40 different series, there is no risk of monotony. Fourier is an eloquent and perceptive champion of women's rights, and a complete equality of the sexes is a conspicuous feature of phalanstery life.

Mill declared that Fourier's scheme deserved a trial.[13] It received one, though perhaps not a fair one, in the United States. In 1840 Albert Brisbane, an American who had travelled in Europe, introduced Fourier to his compatriots in *The Social Destiny of Man*. New England was appalled by Fourier's ideas about sex, but these were represented as detachable from the rest of the system, and not only did America develop a version of Fourierism which Christians could accept, but men of the strongest Christian convictions, Horace Greeley and W. H. Channing, became its most active prophets.

In the next five years between 30 and 40 phalanxes were started at sites from New York to Wisconsin. The general principle on which they were organised was that of an ordinary joint-stock company in which members took shares, and they were mainly agricultural, though they tried to meet as many needs as possible with their own manufactures. The largest, with over 400 members, was at Clarkson on Lake Ontario, and it is regrettable that very little information about it survives. A member, John Greig, reported that it failed only because its constitution had been badly drafted by the lawyers, and it could neither draw on its own capital nor obtain credit. Noyes, however, whose *History of American Socialism* is the fullest account of Fourierism in America, gives reasons for thinking there were other troubles which Grieg glosses over.

The best documented phalanxes are the North American, which lasted from 1843 to 1855, and Brook Farm. Brook Farm was founded not as a Fourierist but simply as a Christian community in 1841. In its pre-Fourierist period Hawthorne belonged to it, and it provides the setting for his novel *The Blithesdale Romance*. In 1844 it turned itself into a phalanx and became the propaganda centre for Fourierism. Although Hawthorne writes about it condescendingly, it seems to have suffered less from internal quarrelling than any other phalanx, and the immediate causes of its dissolution in 1847 were visitations of smallpox and fire.

These American experiments were all far below what Fourier considered the minimum viable size, but they are interesting because of the attempt to Christianise Fourierism. The American Fourierists were all influenced by existing Christian communities. There were the establishments at Brook Farm and Hopedale, and Brisbane appealed to the success of the Inspirationists, whom he visited in 1845. Fourierism, in turn, influenced religion in America. Many Fourierists also embraced spiritualism or Swedenborgianism, and it may not be too fanciful to see Fourier's hand in some of the more exotic religious communities of the later nineteenth century, such as those of Thomas L. Harris. But other Fourierists were more orthodox. Of these, Greeley is a fair representative. When phalanxes failed to catch on, he used his paper the *New York Tribune* to preach profit sharing and producers' co-operatives, and the founding in 1870 of Greeley in Colorado, now a thriving city, was a co-operative venture organised by him and a one-time leader of the Trumbull Phalanx, N. C. Meeker.

There was a similar feedback from Fourierism to Christianity in France. Between 1832 and 1850 Victor Considérant and others ran two journals for the dissemination of Fourier's ideas, *La Phalange* and *Democratie Pacifique*. Ducpétiaux acknowledged that his ideas about workers sharing in profits are borrowed from the first, and J. B. Duroselle counts the second as the chief source for Catholic social thought between 1843 and 1851.[14] Fourier himself, of course, though far from being an orthodox Christian, was no atheist either. Every Fourierist phalanx was to have its church and its priest, even if the precise nature of the deity to be served did not bear very close scrutiny.

A system of communal ownership rather different from Fourier's was proposed by Louis Blanc (1811–82). A journalist and historian, Blanc became concerned at the condition of French industrial workers in the 1830s, and in 1839–40 published a series of articles which subsequently appeared in book form under the title *Organisation of Work*. The government, he said, should raise a loan and establish 'social workshops', 'ateliers sociaux' in the main branches of industry. Wages should, if possible, be equal. After the first year, the management would be elected by the workforce. Profits would be divided into three, not necessarily equal, parts. One would be distributed among the workers in equal shares; one would go to an insurance fund for the old and sick and for other associations in times of adversity; the rest would be added to the capital assets, which would be inalienable. Subordinate trades should be grouped round a principal one, so that each workshop was carrying on several different kinds of work. Blanc hoped that a 'life in common' would ensue naturally, and yield big savings. Initially the social workshops would compete with conventional capitalist firms. The State, however, would ensure that they alone benefited from new inventions, and Blanc thought that in time they would prevail over their competitors and absorb them. Investors might put in money and receive interest, but should have no share in the profits without becoming members.

Louis Blanc's proposals are not Utopian, and they are often spoken of as original. They are so similar, however, to those put forward in *L'Européen* in 1831–2 that it is impossible to doubt that his ideas derive, directly or via the tradesmen who produced *L'Atelier*, from Buchez. Buchez (*Revue nationale*, April 1848) and Feugueray (*Association Ouvrière*) criticise him on points of detail, but his solution to the social problem is substantially the same as theirs. His importance is that thanks to his brilliance as a writer, he gave that solution more publicity than they had been able to give it.

P. J. Proudhon (1809–64) was the self-educated son of a small craftsman, matters which Marx characteristically uses as grounds for dismissing him (letter to Schweizer, 24 January 1865). In 1840 Proudhon published a concise but powerful attack on the existing order entitled *What is Property?* His famous answer 'It is theft' ('C'est le vol') is derived from a short essay by J. P. Brissot de Warville, *Philosophical Inquiry into the Rights of Property and into Theft*

(1780). In the next few years Proudhon became closely acquainted with Marx and Bakunin. His *Philosophie de la misère*, however, contains a long critique of Communism leading up to the conclusion that it is 'la religion de la misère', and Marx retorted in 1847 with the full length attack on him entitled, a little obviously, *Misère de la philosophie*. Thereafter, though Proudhon had a comfortable spell of political imprisonment under Louis Napoleon (during which he edited a radical journal and got married), he and the revolutionary socialists of Germany and Russia moved further and further apart.

In politics Proudhon is an anarchist. Anarchy, however, for him means life without rulers, not without rules or principles.[15] The ideal society would be orderly, but have no apparatus for coercion – all Proudhon's thought is coloured by an intense love of freedom. The Seventh Study in *General Idea of the Revolution in the Nineteenth Century* (1851) contains a fairly full, positive description: contracts, made by individuals, towns or industrial associations take the place of legislation, and arbitration and commercial tribunals replace policing and criminal courts.

Proudhon's theory of property rests on the distinction (taken from Rousseau[16]) between ownership, the right to use and abuse so long as you do not break the law, and possession, which is a matter of fact rather than right. Tenants and usufructuaries have possession but not ownership. Proudhon's main thesis is that we should abolish ownership while retaining possession. With an eloquence hard to resist he argues that there is no coherent moral justification for ownership. The inadequacy of Locke's theory is easily shown. Proudhon remarks in this connection[17] that agricultural labourers not only improve land but maintain it. He notes among other ways in which workers suffer injustice, that their wages are proportional only to what a single person could produce if he were working alone. In fact, ten men working together can produce more in a single day than one man can produce in ten days; they can lift things, for example, that a single man could never lift at all. The surplus value produced, the difference between what the workers could do singly and what they do together, is unjustly appropriated by the employer. Since it is 'social property', the produce of co-operation, no individual can rightly own it.

Although private ownership is an injustice, Communism is 'oppression and slavery'.[18] Neither has association any great merit in itself. Believing (unlike most anarchists) in indissoluble matrimony, Proudhon is not attracted to Fourier's phalanxes, and he blames Louis Blanc[19] for pinning all his hopes on producers' co-operatives. Co-operation may be necessary for certain projects, but in general Proudhon prefers 'mutuality', with producers keeping their independence while freely exchanging goods and services.

Proudhon fiercely attacks Christianity for preaching resignation to the poor and giving the imprimatur of Divine Providence to liberal economic theory. But as H. de Lubac shows in *The Unmarxian Socialist*, Proudhon cannot be classed as an atheist or even as an enemy of religion generally. He constantly refers to the Bible and in a letter to J. A. Langois (August 1848) names it as the first 'of my real masters, those who have called fertile ideas to spring up in my mind'. Avant-garde Christians of today can perhaps come closer to Proudhon than to any other non-Christian writer of his time.

None of the thinkers we have considered up to the present was a revolutionary. Le Play recalls hearing Blanc say:

> Let us avoid revolutions: experience teaches us that after them the people has never gained anything; on the contrary it is always less happy and less free.[20]

A man of very different stamp was Francois Noel Babeuf (1760–96). Having started life as a provincial lawyer, in the French Revolution Babeuf gathered experience and skill working on committees and was secretary to the Paris Food Administration in 1793. At the same time he ran a series of inflammatory and more or less underground journals, and had spells in prison in 1790, 1793–4 and 1795, during the last of which his daughter died of starvation. Originally he had campaigned only for redistributing land among the peasants; hence his calling himself Gracchus after the agrarian reformers of the Roman Republic. Now, however, he adopted a more radical programme, and in the winter of 1795–6 started conspiring to force it through by violent revolution. Property was to be abolished altogether, and production and distribution organised by the government. Buonarroti, one of the conspirators, later admitted the bureaucratic implications: 'public functions' would have been 'very much multiplied' and 'magistrates' would have been 'fort nombreux'.[21] The first step was to be a bloodbath. It would be followed by a period of dictatorship by the 'insurrectionary Committee of Public Safety' in which the powers of the police would be strengthened and prison camps set up on offshore islands and elsewhere. Only when the existing order had been totally smashed would power be returned to the people through a mixture of representative government and government by referendum. By this time there would have been a moral transformation of society, and although food rationing might be expected to continue indefinitely, idleness would be the only crime in need of punishment.

The coup nearly succeeded. There were sympathisers in the army and the police, and the conspirators had a realistic plan for seizing the government signalling terminals and the Paris arsenals.[22] The Day of the People was fixed for 19 May 1796. On 28 April there was a mutiny in the Police Legion. The conspirators were unready, and the opportunity was missed. A couple of days later they were betrayed, and Babeuf and other leaders were arrested on 10 May.

In the nineteenth century Auguste Blanqui (not to be confused with his brother Adolphe, the conservative economist) tried to imitate Babeuf, and as a result spent just about half of a fair-lengthed life (1805–81) in prison. Blanqui was a true destroyer. 'I have no programme' he told The Times in an interview published 28 April 1879. No programme, that was, on the positive side; for on the negative:

> First and foremost, France must be dechristianised. She must be rid, not only of Catholicism, but of Christianity.

Blanqui was Babeuf's sole French successor of note, but the seed Babeuf sowed was to bear fruit in other countries. He is the only one of Marx's predecessors of whom Marx has nothing but good to say; and history has proved that (except, of course, for the transfer of power to the people) his formula for revolution is fatally capable of being put into practice.

GERMANY

The thinking of the English and French socialists and anarchists was compatible, and reacted fruitfully, with Christianity. But the forms of socialism and anarchism which prevailed at the end of the nineteenth century, and which the words 'socialism' and 'anarchism' chiefly signify today, are not English or French but German or Russian, and derive from Hegel (1770–1831). The 'tremendous effect' of Hegel's writings 'in the philosophy-tinged atmosphere of Germany' is well described by Engels.[23]

Hegel was not a highly original thinker, but at his death his pupils were planted out all through the German university system. No one who approached social problems from a theoretical standpoint, either in Germany or in Russia which in the early nineteenth century was an intellectual dependency of Germany, escaped his influence.

We have seen that the concept of the corporative State goes back at least to Fichte. Hegel develops it. He distinguishes the State proper, fully mature civil society, from organised groups generally. The latter exist for the benefit of the members, but in the former, this relationship is reversed. According to the Introduction of his *Philosophy of History*, the State proper is 'the realisation of freedom . . ., the idea of God as it exists on earth . . . All the value a man has, and all his spiritual actuality, he has through the State'. Hence man's 'supreme duty is to be a member of the State'.[24] In his main treatment of political and social questions, *The Philosophy of Right* (1821), Hegel sees corporations, that is, guild-like organisations of masters of various trades, not only as regulating commercial practice, but also[25] as sending deputies to a lower legislative chamber. These corporations, however, are to be under the control of the central government,[26] and more important than the organisation of industry into guilds is the organisation of the whole State into three 'stände': agriculturalists or nobles, industrialists or commons, and bureaucrats.[27] The appearance of bureaucrats where Müller had spoken of the clergy is doubtless due to the fact that Hegel's own country, Prussia, had a vigorous civil service; but Hegel's idealisation of them as 'the universal class', having 'for its task the universal interests of the community', and deserving therefore, 'to be relieved of direct labour' is one of three elements in his thought which had a profound effect on the subsequent history of socialism.

A second is the theory that history proceeds by virtue of an inner necessity, more or less independently of the choices of individuals. To those who accept it and infer that history is on their side, this theory can give boundless courage, ruthlessness and fanaticism. In Hegel's own system it is balanced by an exaltation of speculative thought at the expense of practical behaviour. The whole of history is seen, in fact, as leading up to nineteenth-century German philosophy. Among his pupils, however, was Count August von Cieszkowski (1814–94), a Pole and a Catholic. In *Prolegomena to Historiosophy* (1838) Cieszkowski introduces the notion of what he calls 'praxis'. Instead of coming to rest in Hegelian metaphysics, history is entering on a new phase in which philosophical thought will be applied in practice. Praxis is this application, and Cieszkowski is strikingly insistent that it can take place only in society: man must become a truly social individual. For Cieszkowski personally, praxis turned out to involve founding an agricultural college (subsequently suppressed by Bismarck), and Cieszkowski lived long enough to read and be delighted by *Rerum Novarum*; but the praxis of other Hegelians was more revolutionary.

Cieszkowski had some unorthodox theological ideas, but was not hostile to religion. Neither was Hegel; but Hegel's view that a State ought to be united by a national religion implied a subordination of religion to the State in a way as threatening to Christianity as the most militant atheism. Although some of his followers developed a Christian variety of socialism, others were attacking the foundations of Christianity within a few years of his death, and it is to this third element in his thinking that both the two most vigorous forms of German socialism, Marxism and Nazism, owe their strongly anti-Christian character.

The first of Hegel's successors to develop the socialistic tendency in his thought was the Swedish-German economist Karl Rodbertus (1805–75). Rodbertus held that under capitalism, the wages of workers can never rise much above subsistence. Known as the 'Iron Law of Wages' this principle goes back, as we have seen, to Turgot and Hume. He further maintained that as productive techniques advance, the proporton of a nation's wealth which falls to labour diminishes. As an immediate remedy, the State should freeze the proportion which is distributed in wages. This measure should be accompanied by the introduction of a currency of labour-notes, a proposal Rodbertus seems to have reached independently of Owen. In the long term Rodbertus desired State ownership of all means of production. This was to be effected peacefully, and not without compensation of the dispossessed; but State ownership was preferable to distribution among producers' co-operatives.

Rodbertus may claim to have been the father of State socialism. He was the inspiration of Bismarck's monarchical socialism and was looked on as a prophet both by Lassalle, the founder of what later became the Social Democratic Party, and by the conservative 'Kathedersozialisten', the 'socialists of the professorial chair'. Two of the leading professors were Adolf Wagner (1835–1917) of Berlin and Albert Schäffle (1831–1903) of Tübingen. They jointly edited a *Journal of Political Science*, and the foundation in 1872 of the Union for Social Politics was largely the work of Wagner.

The professors favoured corporative institutions of the Hegelian type. What is more important for our purposes, they were friendly to Christianity. Schäffle supported the efforts of the Centre Party to legislate against employing mothers in factories; he also argued for the compatibility of State socialism with Christianity (in *The Quintessence of Socialism*, 1874) and declared that international agreements for the protection of workers were 'a universal demand of humanity, morality and religion, especially from the standpoint of the Church'.[28] Wagner helped Pastor Adolf Stöcker (1835–1909) to found the Christian Socialist Party in 1878, and succeeded him as chairman of it.

Stöcker commended the English Christian Socialists in his article 'Christlich-social, evangelisch-social, kirklich-social' of 1904, but he was very different both in his thinking and in his career from Maurice and Kingsley. In 1874 he had been appointed by Wilhelm I to an important benefice in Berlin. He sat in the Reichstag from 1881 to 1893 and from 1898 to

1908. He and his friends backed Bismarck's welfare proposals, and it may have been through Schäffle's influence that
the Insurance Law of 1884 took the corporativist form of
involving groups of employees and employers instead of
being administered solely through the central bureaucracy.
The Christian Socialists opposed, at least for the foreseeable
future, State ownership of the means of production. Instead
they desired a corporative structure with vocational groups
consisting of elected representatives of employers and employees at the bottom, and higher bodies such as courts or
arbitration and perhaps ultimately a labour Parliament, filled
not by popular election but from the lower bodies. It was not
proposed, however, to give employees a share in the actual
running of businesses, as distinct from the organisation of
welfare and the like. So far as management went, Stöcker
advocated a patriarchal system in which the employer acted
as 'housefather' and the workers were his extended family.

This vision failed to captivate the working class, and the
party never established itself in the Reichstag. Its greatest
success was at the beginning, when a combined list of
Christian Socialist and Conservative candidates obtained
72,000 votes in Berlin. By focusing attention on the so-called
Jewish question Stöcker gained some anti-Semitic supporters
from the lower middle classes, but these soon found more
aggressive leaders. Stöcker's anti-Semitism was the chief
factor which led to his being deprived of his benefice in 1891,
and after that his party disintegrated. A young pastor,
Friedrich Naumann, tried to form a party out of the less
rigidly conservative members, but (in spite of some support
from Max Weber) it was not successful, and Naumann later
moved away from socialism towards liberalism.

Unfortunately for his reputation, Stöcker's anti-Semitism
attracted the approving attention of Hitler. Evalyn Clark in a
long article on Adolf Wagner in the *Political Science Quarterly*
of 1940,[29] accuses Stöcker and Wagner of being the precur-
sors, if not actually the authors, of Hitler's National
Socialism. That is a severe judgement, and does not take
account of the fact that Stöcker was sufficiently respected
outside Germany in 1891 to be invited to describe the
German experience to the Protestant Société Chrétienne
d'Économie Sociale in Switzerland. Stöcker seems to have

been led to enter politics by genuine concern at the state of the poor – before going to Berlin he was pastor of the industrial parish of Hammersleben in Saxony – and after losing his Berlin post he devoted himself to charitable work with the Inner Mission and with the Evangelical Social Congress which had been started largely by his efforts.

Stöcker's Christian Socialism was a genuine product of Hegelianism, but a small and untypical one. To find the main course of development we must go back to those of Hegel's immediate heirs who are known as the Young Hegelians. In 1835 D. F. Strauss published his *Life of Jesus*, the first serious attempt to prove that the New Testament accounts of the life of Christ are largely false. Bruno Bauer supported him in works published in 1840–41, and in 1841 Ludwig Feuerbach's *Essence of Christianity* argued that man's idea of God is really an idea of himself (or of his self-awareness), misconstrued as an idea of something separate from himself. Religion is an alienation of ourselves from ourselves. This challenge to Christianity was seen both as a symbol and as a central part of an intellectual revolution extending through politics, ethics and eventually economics. Arnold Ruge (1802–80), Moses Hess (1812–75), Marx and Bauer all made atheism the basis of their political and social programme. As Marx put it: 'The criticism of religion is the presupposition of all criticism'.[30]

Karl Marx (1818–83) emigrated from Germany in 1843. He lived in Paris with a group of young Hegelians until 1845; between 1845 and 1848 he was in Brussels; and then, after being briefly in Paris and Germany again during the revolutionary months of 1848–9, he settled in London. During his first stay in Paris he made the only friend he did not afterwards come to hate and abuse, Friedrich Engels (1820–95). He also, soon after his arrival, met Cieszkowski, and he became closely acquainted with Proudhon and Bakunin.

From 1844 there survive some fragmentary drafts known as the Paris Manuscripts. In one of these Marx declares that industrial capitalism alienates the worker not only from the product of his labour and from the capitalist who appropriates it, but also from his labour itself, which becomes compulsory, mindless and hateful, and from his own nature as a member of the human race. Marx's development of this theme employs two related ideas. One is that the good for man is not pleasure, as the liberals held, but the activity distinctive of the human species. The other is that this distinctive activity is not just intelligent behaviour but productive work.

These thoughts are eminently compatible with Christianity. The notion of alienation is borrowed from Feuerbach, but Marx's use of it, unlike Feuerbach's, is theologically unexceptionable. The view about the good for man goes back to Aristotle, is endorsed by Christian philosophers of the Middle Ages, and may have reached Marx through Cieszkowski. Christians might deny that a distinctively human life must consist solely in productive work, and even that productive work must be an essential part of it for everyone (Marx himself seems not to have done much of it); but they would concede that it will be a central part for most people. Hence it has been possible to claim on the basis of the Paris Manuscripts that Marx points the way to a truly Christian response to the problems of industrialisation. Without disputing this claim we should note that these Manuscripts were not published until 1932 and that the writings published before then, which alone could exercise an influence on events, are different in character.

In 1847–8 Marx and Engels composed *The Communist Manifesto*. In this they accept Hegel's idea that history proceeds by an inner necessity, and identify class warfare as the chief mechanism by which this necessity works. The present class struggle will inevitably end with the victory of the proletariat, but those who wish to be on the side of history must strive by all available means to accelerate that victory. Exactly what would constitute the proletariat's winning is not spelt out, but universal male suffrage would probably have sufficed. The proletariat will then use its political supremacy to put through a programme of which the *Manifesto* contains only a half-page summary. The main items are: free education in State schools and 'the abolition of children's factory labour in its present form'; a heavy income tax and the abolition of inheritance; nationalisation of land, banks and means of transport and communication; and, more vaguely, 'industrial armies, especially for agriculture', and 'combination of agriculture and industry'. In a separate manifesto drafted for Germany in 1848 Marx adds 'national workshops', but presumably that was just in order not to be outbid by the new republican government in Paris. These measures are proposed as transitional, not permanent, but it is notorious that Marx and Engels never describe the kind of society towards which there is to be transition. It will have no coercive machinery; but how the 'fort nombreux' officials of the transitional period are to be eradicated is a problem which still awaits solution.

Between 1849 and 1864 Marx supported himself in London by writing for Greeley's *Tribune*, and devoted his main efforts more to theoretical economics than to practical politics. He kept in touch with German socialists on the Continent like Lassalle, but when Lassalle lavished hospitality on him during a visit to Germany and tried to help him get a passport, Marx's arrogance could not stand the strain, and he withdrew to London complaining (letter to Engels, 30 July 1862) that Lassalle was a 'Jewish nigger'. Marx himself, of course, was of Jewish descent, but his ancestors, unlike Lassalle's, were aristocratic rabbis famous for their learning.

Ferdinand Lassalle (1825–64) represents a third way of developing Hegelianism. Like Rodbertus, whom he admired, he wanted State socialism, but whereas Rodbertus refused to take any part in politics, Lassalle, like Marx, was a political activist. The earlier part of his career was like that of other Young Hegelians. He went to Paris in 1845, took part in resistance to the German government in 1848–9, and for this received a short prison sentence. For the next ten years he was away from political action. In 1849 Herman Schulze (1808–83; commonly known by his territorial style as Schulze-Delitsch) started a system of credit associations. This was hailed with enthusiasm by laissez-faire liberals, though Schulze was marginally anticipated by the Evangelical Raiffeissen, and credit associations for landowners had existed in Prussia since the eighteenth century. Schulze's institutions multiplied until by 1883 there were 3,500 of them with a capital of £10,000,000 but to industrial workers on subsistence wages they were of small use. When Lassalle returned to active politics in 1862 he pointed this out. In his *Open Reply to the Leipzig Working Men's Association* (1863) he proposed producers' co-operatives financed by the State. To bring this about, the workers should form a political party and demand universal suffrage. The debate which followed between Lassalle and those liberals who favoured 'self-help' for workers along Schulze's lines without State intervention, was the occasion for Ketteler's important book on 'the labour question' *Die Arbeiterfrage und das Christenthum*. Ketteler and Lassalle seem to have been personally on friendly terms.

Lassalle's sources for the idea of producers' co-operatives, as revealed in the *Open Reply*, are the shortlived but successful Rochdale textile co-operative of 1858–61, and the Parisian Association of Masons which was founded in 1848, probably under Buchezian influence. His correspondence with Rodbertus has led some readers to suspect that he used co-operatives only as a bait to draw workers into a political party. It is hard to detect any insincerity in the vigorous argument of the *Open Reply*, but the correspondence and the treatise *Acquired Rights* (1861) do confirm that Lassalle's ideal was to have all means of production under the control of the State.

In 1863, Lassalle founded the Universal German Workers' Association. At that moment he was the leader of German socialism. In August 1864, however, he was killed in a duel, and the leadership passed to Marx in London. In September a number of skilled English workers convened the first meeting of the International Working Men's Association (the 'First International'). Marx was invited and immediately obtained an ascendancy. Implacably committed to class conflict and the destruction of the existing capitalist order, he soon drove out the naturally peace-loving English workers and foreign moderates like Mazzini, and the International became a central agency for revolutionary activity. If there is any time which was decisive for the breach between Christian social reformers and the radical Continental left, it was probably the end of 1864. While Marx was taking over the infant International, the Vatican was denouncing social-ism in the encyclical *Quanta Cura* (8 December) and rounding it off with the *Syllabus Errorum*. It was about now also that anarchism, which under Proudhon's leadership had been merely anti-clerical, became anti-religious through the con-version to atheism of Bakunin.

Mikhail Bakunin (1814–76) in 1835 gave up a military

career in Russia to study philosophy, and in the next five years graduated from Kant to Fichte and from Fichte to Hegel. In 1840 he emigrated to Germany, and by 1842 he was an active Young Hegelian with a special interest in Strauss and Feuerbach. He then, however, came under French influence. He read with great enthusiasm some political essays by Lamennais, and on a visit to Switzerland in 1843 became acquainted with Wilhelm Weitling (1808–71). Although Weitling was a German, he had lived in Paris for some time in the 1830s, and he was able to tell Bakunin about Saint-Simon and Fourier. Like Saint-Simon he wanted a revival of religion on idealised early Christian lines. He found Bakunin receptive, and it is significant that Bakunin, when he was in Belgium in 1847–8, lived, on his own admission, with the Merodes and Montalembert 'in the very centre of Jesuit propaganda'. It was not until 1864, under the influence of anti-clerical Italian freemasons, that he arrived at his famous dilemma:

> God exists: hence man is a slave.
> Man is intelligent, just and free: hence God does not exist.
> And now let all choose.

In 1868 Bakunin and his followers, who included the principal opponents of private property in Italy and Spain, joined the International. Bakunin had no original positive economic programme, but he was able to contribute some practical expertise in conspiracy and violence. His protégé Nechaev provided the idea for Dostoevski's novel *The Possessed*. In the International, thanks, presumably, to the influence of Lamennais and Proudhon, he opposed Marx's immediate aim of State socialism with a strong central government. He wished to abolish the State straightaway and have a federation of minimally organised productive communes. In 1872 the struggle between these strategies was resolved by his expulsion from the International. This was disastrous for the International, since it split into a Marxist and a Bakuninist faction. The Marxist faction retained the name but removed to America, and was wound up in 1876. In Europe, however, the anarchists were not left long in possession of the field. Aileen Kelly in a recent biography[31] points out that Bakunin was not a consistent enemy of collectivism, and that in temperament he was fully as authoritarian as Marx. Nevertheless he wished to dispense with an organised political party; as agents of revolutionary change he preferred to rely on spontaneous eruptions of popular violence and such randomly acting forces as brigandry. In any contest between those who believe in organised parties and party-political action and those who do not, the former will always prevail.

The way in which Marx's plan of class warfare leading to State ownership of the means of production came in England to replace the French and native English varieties of socialism, has been described in Chapter Four. In Germany in 1875 followers of Marx and Lassalle came together to work out a programme for what was to be the Social Democratic Party. Although Marx himself disowned the programme, the party was rather Marxist than anarchist in character. When the Second International was founded in 1889, it was predominantly Marxist, and thereafter opposition to Marxism from within the left came from people like Bernstein whose tendencies were towards liberalism and working within the existing system rather than towards anarchism.

But there remains one anarchist to whom, after considering Marx and Bakunin, it is a relief to turn. Prince Peter Kropotkin (1842–1921) was converted to anarchism in 1872 when on a visit to Switzerland he met some watchmakers who were followers of Bakunin. He was activist enough to be twice imprisoned and to be obliged to live in exile from Russia (mostly in England) for some 40 years. Nevertheless he condemned both freelance terrorism and State bloodbaths of the Babeuf–Lenin type. His nobility of character is acclaimed by allies and opponents alike.

In Chapter Two it was noted that laissez-faire thinking drew new strength from Darwin's theory of evolution. T. H. Huxley and Herbert Spencer among others used it to justify unlimited cut-throat competition. In 1890–6 (in articles later published under the title *Mutual Aid*) Kropotkin argued that co-operation too must be recognised as an instrument of biological progress. Competition, particularly between members of the same species, is exceptional and more injurious than beneficial. Not only are animals generally sociable and disposed to help one another; they are also playful and disposed to engage in pleasurable activities for their own sake.

Kropotkin's social thinking is based on his biology. Society is older than man, and the fundamentally social nature of man at once explains why we recognise duties towards one another, and enables us to discharge those duties without duty-enforcing coercive institutions. Kropotkin does not, however, insist on communal living. Certain communal arrangements may lighten the housework which men regularly try to load off onto women; but human beings desire privacy, and he seems to envisage families of a traditional kind living in separate households.

An anarchist society is one of freely federated communes and productive associations. To prove that a strong, central-ised authority is not essential for efficiency, Kropotkin appeals to the international postal and railway systems, and to organisations like the Red Cross and the English Lifeboat Association. He also dwells at length on guilds and other types of association in medieval towns. Historians often write as if Europe in the Middle Ages was so dominated by religion that to commend anything medieval is automatically to praise the Catholic Church. Kropotkin, in contrast, blames the Church for the ruin of medieval urban and village life:

> While early Christianity, like all other religions, was an appeal to the broadly human feelings of mutual aid and sympathy, the Christian Church has aided the State in wrecking all standing institutions of mutual aid and support which were anterior to it or developed outside of it. [32]

Kropotkin addresses himself most positively to social problems in *Fields, Factories and Workshops* (1888–90). He first tries to establish two points: the greater part, even of industry which uses highly sophisticated machinery, can be carried out in small economic units away from urban centres; and rural industries decline not because they are not competitive but because of rural depopulation and migration, especially by farmworkers, to big towns. He then urges distributing industry as far as possible through the country: 'Have the factory and the workshop at the gates of your fields and gardens, and work in them.'[33] This would benefit agriculture as well as industrial workers, since it would repopulate the country and provide labour for agriculture at times of special need, like harvest-time.

The assumption here is that the same individuals will engage in both agriculture and industry. Kropotkin thought this a further advantage; pushed to extremes, the division of labour is dehumanising. For a population that can manage both industry and agriculture he looks to education. Everyone of average ability should be educated at least to the age of 18 or 19. Academic and technical education should proceed together. As regards the former, 'apparatus used to illustrate the fundamental laws of nature ought to be made by the children themselves.'[34] For the latter it is not enough to send children to ordinary, commercial workshops: technical skills should be taught in the same way as laboratory work at universities, and pupils should learn not just one skill but a whole range, starting with drawing and working up through carpentry to mechanical engineering. These reforms are as necessary for the arts and sciences themselves as for the people who are to acquire them. Good art can be produced only when artists are also craftsmen, and good science only by scientists who are also mechanics.

Although Kropotkin believed that science and theism cannot both be true, there is none of his practical proposals that Christians cannot accept. Tolstoy advocates a kind of blend of Christianity and Kropotkinian anarchism and we shall see his opinions on small rural industries, on guilds and on the arts being advanced by the English Distributists (some of whom may have known him personally) and Simone Weil.

CHAPTER EIGHT

Applications and Individuals

In Chapters Three to Six we traced the emergence of official lines of Christian teaching and action on social questions. We shall now look at some attempts to put Christian principles into practice, and also at some proposals and initiatives by individuals who stood outside the main stream of development.

These proposals are no less part of the Christian response for being unofficial, and sometimes they were influential and fruitful.

EARLY CO-OPERATIVES

We saw that from the 1830s onwards Christian thinkers have preached the setting up of producers' co-operatives. Although the efforts of the preachers themselves, such as Buchez and the English Christian Socialists, were mostly unsuccessful, by the 1850s more successful co-operatives were beginning to appear in many parts of Europe. The movement was more agricultural than industrial, but it deserves mention as part of the reaction against laissez-faire individualism, and a part in which there was substantial Christian involvement.

The movement starts with Robert Owen, or perhaps rather with men like William King who were inspired by him but who winnowed out the idea of co-operation from his views on religion and his enthusiasm for Communism. The Rochdale Pioneers opened their store in 1844. In the next couple of years consumers' co-operatives and agricultural credit associations were started in Czechoslovakia by Samuel Jurkovič and in Germany by F. W. Raiffeissen. Raiffeissen was a committed Evangelical Protestant who intended his credit organisations to have moral and educational as well as economic value.

J. M. Kirschbaum says that:

The development of co-operatives in Slovakia owes its origin to a great degree to the activities of the Catholic clergy in the period of the Enlightenment, and later also of the Protestant clergy, educated at German universities.'[1]

These countries were followed by Italy and Austria in the 1850s, and Poland in the 1870s. In Poland the rural parish priests seem to have been active from the beginning. In Italy, where the movement gathered momentum in the 1880s, Catholic participation was stimulated by the Congresses. The greatest zeal was displayed by the most intransigent of the Intransigents; they preferred this strategy for dealing with the social problem to one which relied on trade unions. Co-operation thrived and still thrives in Italy more than in any other European country. It is not clear exactly what proportion of co-operatives was founded under Catholic inspiration. When, however, in 1919 the movement to the left of the main federation of Italian co-operatives, the Lega, led to the foundation of a separate Catholic confederation, more than a quarter of the Lega co-operatives joined it. Co-operation has been less limited to agriculture in Italy than in other countries; it is particularly strong in the building trade; but it has to be noted that the Catholic co-operatives are mostly agricultural or located in rural areas.

In Austria and what is now Yugoslavia, Catholic involvement was precipitated by *Rerum Novarum*. The year after the encyclical there was a Catholic congress at Vienna which commended this type of economic structure. From 1902 to 1916 the Catholic co-operative movement was led by the priest Janez Krek.

Meanwhile in 1866 Hans Christian Sonne, a Lutheran pastor at Thisted in Jutland, introduced co-operation into Denmark. He started with a co-operative grocery on the model of Rochdale. It was joined in 1882 by a co-operative dairy. The proximate source for this idea was probably America where there had been agricultural co-operatives, also derived indirectly from Rochdale, at least since 1865. Farmers sent their milk to a factory of which they owned the share capital. Besides a fixed interest on this, each received a share of the profits proportional to the value of the milk he had sent in.

The benefit of this system to the Danish farmers, who had formerly been among the poorest in Europe, attracted attention in England and Ireland. In 1894 Horace, later Sir Horace, Plunkett, founded the Irish Agricultural Organisation Society, which had a propaganda magazine, *The Irish Homestead*. Among his associates were clergy as well as laymen, and in 1901 a correspondent of *The Western Mail* (7 November) reported that:

> The Roman Catholic priest and his inveterate enemy the Protestant minister . . . were now quite frequently seen on the same platform, actively co-operating for the material advancement of their flocks.

The movement spread to England, and was marked by a similar spirit there. William Charleton, who had worked with Plunkett in Ireland, was the principal agent in setting up the British Agricultural Organisation Society in 1899. He and his cousin Hugh Fairfax-Cholmeley, who directed the movement in Yorkshire, came from families noted for their attachment to Catholicism. They were supported by the Anglican Bishop of Hereford, and the Rev G. F. Eyre started a producers' co-operative in his parish in Worcestershire. The Catholic clergy, however, unlike their Irish confreres, kept off the platforms. They also omitted, for the most part, to call the attention of their flock to *Rerum Novarum*. It seems to have been largely through ignorance that there was any Catholic social teaching that Charleton and Fairfax-Cholmeley eventually defected from their families' religious allegiance.

Agricultural co-operation in England had to contend with constitutional reluctance to co-operate on the part of small farmers, and with severe financial difficulties after 1918. An experiment of Charleton's in Norfolk, however, deserves to be remembered. A 98-acre farm was divided into small-holdings. One division was run as a model by a Danish agriculturalist. The rest of the land could be leased at low rates by persons who wished to learn small-holding. It was possible to start with one acre (for which the deposit was 15/–) and gradually acquire more. There was provision for building cottages. The farm as a whole belonged to an association of the tenants, and if anyone wanted to leave, the association would buy back his lease at a price which reflected the value of improvements. Charleton hoped that there would be a steady turnover of tenants, with people selling out and thus obtaining capital for larger holdings of their own once they had acquired agricultural expertise. This plan was disrupted by the First World War, and one particularly efficient tenant came to dominate and eventually to own the whole enterprise.

At about the same time as when these attempts at agricultural co-operatives were taking place in Europe, in 1900, the French Canadian journalist Alphonse Desjardins started the first 'caisses populaires' in the province of Quebec. These were co-operative savings and loan societies. Sources of credit were of course essential for any kind of producers' co-operatives, and these 'caisses populaires' were the forerunners of the Nova Scotia co-operatives we shall consider later in this chapter.

CHRISTIAN CAPITALISTS

The Christian who is also an industrial capitalist may take one of three views. He may think that his religion has nothing to do with his business life; or that they are incompatible, in which case one or the other must be sacrificed; or that they can be reconciled by an application of the principles of the first in the second. We shall here consider two famous but strongly contrasting families which took the third view: the Catholic Harmels in France, and the Quaker Rowntrees in England.

Jean-Jacques Harmel was a descendant of a family of craftsmen in the Ardennes. In 1841 he built a spinning factory at Warmeriville near Reims on a site he named Val des Bois. To get to know his employees he made a point of paying them individually in person, and he and his family adopted a modest style of living in a house beside the factory. In 1842 he set up a savings scheme and in 1846 an insurance scheme or 'caisse de secours'. This was administered by workers elected by their fellows, and paid members half wages during sickness as well as the full cost of medical attention, drugs, and, at a later date, burial. When the Harmels wished to enlarge their workforce – the factory came to employ between four and five hundred persons – they tried to persuade whole families to move into the neighbourhood and settle. In the 1860s they brought in about 50 families averaging ten members each.

Leon Harmel was not the oldest child of Jean-Jacques, but he was the most interested in the business, which he saw as giving him the opportunity of an apostolate to the working class, and the rest of the family gradually conceded to him the leadership. In 1862 he put up a chapel next to the factory, and he also placed a statue of the Virgin within the factory itself, but he had the patience to wait many years for the first workers to go to Mass. Meanwhile, in fidelity to the principle that what is done for the workers must also be done by them, he got going as many as 40 standing committees dealing with every aspect of work and life. All these were run by the workers. The most important was the Factory Council, started in 1883, which was responsible for good relations generally between the Harmel family and the workforce. It consisted of workers elected by workers, and met a member of the family once a fortnight. It discussed pay, discipline, safety, hygiene and apprenticing; communicated the demands of the workers; adjudicated between workers and foremen; and considered ways of making the work easier and more profitable. Attached to the factory were a school, co-operative shops, including a bakery, and Harmel tried to work out a scheme by which workers could acquire their own houses at Val des Bois, but failed to find a way round all the difficulties, particularly that of preventing houses from being alienated from the whole enterprise when workers moved away.

While Leon was alive, he and his family devoted endless time and heroic patience to cajoling the employees into taking responsibility and running these various activities. This required a degree of dedication few industrialists could be expected to match. Leon died in 1915. His heirs preserved the Christian tradition, and kept the factory going until 1980. No one emerged, however, who could take his place: who could unite the community, give it new directions, or, as conditions for the textile industry became more exacting, maintain profitability. (Today the factory belongs to a co-operative which numbers only a quarter of the former workforce, and when visited in spring 1984 was struggling to survive.)

Fairly remote from Reims, both geographically and culturally, is York, where the Rowntrees, who had previously owned a grocery shop, acquired a modest cocoa and chocolate making works from another Quaker family, the Tukes, in 1862. At that time the numbers employed were no more than a dozen and the business was constituted as a family partnership. It was transformed into a limited company in 1897 when Joseph became the first chairman. In 1923, two years before his death, he handed over the reins to his son Seebohm, who had for many years been Labour Director. Seebohm remained Chairman till 1941, though he had relinquished his executive responsibilities five years earlier. The close and direct family links effectively came to an end with his death in 1954.

As manufacturers of cocoa, chocolate and confectionery, the Rowntrees employed a large proportion of semi-skilled female workers. A full account of their industrial betterment policies would take us beyond the scope of this book, but one of the first steps, almost if not quite unprecedented when it was taken in 1891, was the appointment of a full-time woman welfare worker to take responsibility for the health and other individual and social needs of the female part of the workforce. This first post was quickly expanded into a team of posts. Later, in 1904, there were two similar initiatives in rapid succession. First, a works doctor, and then a works dentist was appointed. The services of these professionals were available free of charge to all employees in the cocoa works. Much later, in 1922, a works psychologist was added. The appointment is described by Asa Briggs[2] as a 'landmark in British industrial history'. Meanwhile in 1906 the Rowntree pension scheme was introduced. It predates by two years the Old Age Pensions Act of 1908 and was decidedly more generous. Based, like most of today's schemes, on contributions from both employee and employer, the amount of the Rowntree pension was fixed at roughly 50 per cent of the employee's average wages over the last five years before retirement, a formula which agrees with the Harmels's sickness benefit and compares not unfavourably with what many pensioners are receiving today.

As well as pioneering pensions, Rowntrees was probably the first major British industrial company to introduce its own supplementary unemployment benefit arrangements:

> Benefits were paid to unemployed workers dismissed as 'redundant', the scale being designed so that with State and trade union benefits the dismissed worker would receive at least half of his previous average earnings. Additional benefit (10 per cent of average earnings) was paid to a dependent wife and 5 per cent for each child under 16.[3]

These arrangements may seem more paternalistic than those at the Val des Bois. Briggs, however, quotes from an unpublished paper by Joseph Rowntree of 1916 in which:

> The point of departure was the need to foster 'a sense of right independence' among 'workers of average power with no special ability'. In using the words 'right independence' he explained: 'I have in mind the statement that in many places "the normal wage earner finds himself spending his whole time in subjection to the arbitrary orders, even to the irresponsible caprices, of the employers and their agents".'[4]

Joseph speaks with the same voice as Leon Harmel when he says:

> Labour will never achieve an industrial constitution worthy of the name of Democracy, till workmen boldly claim the problems of working conditions and processes of industry as *their* problems, and treat attempts to meet them . . . not as something imposed from above but as their own concern, on which they should be consulted as a matter of right.[5]

During the First World War a Works Council was set up, which Seebohm could later claim incorporated in the firm the four essential elements of democracy:

> First, people's right to make their own laws; second their right to have a say (though often an indirect one) in the administration of the laws; third, their right to protection by impartial courts of justice; and fourth, freedom to criticise the Government either by word of mouth or in writing.[6]

The activities of the Rowntrees were not confined within the bounds of the factory. In 1901 Seebohm published his first study of poverty in York, which earned him (from Lady Megan Lloyd-George) the title of 'the Einstein of the Welfare State'. His later studies of 1936 and 1950 are hardly less valuable to the social historian. As early as 1903 Joseph had transferred 56 per cent of the firm's share capital away from the family into three trusts. They, and especially the Joseph Rowntree Social Service Trust (which is *not* a charity), are probably more important today than the company itself in promoting his own progressive ideas and those of his son Seebohm. The actual Rowntree business was merged with Mackintosh in 1969, and the three trusts are now at most small minority shareholders in the combined undertaking.

It may not be improper to add a personal note. For some years the Social Service Trust has been supporting Job Ownership Limited, a small unit directed by one of the present writers for the promotion of production co-operatives and employee ownership in other forms. The Rowntrees themselves were sceptical about production co-operatives and placed much more reliance in trade unions and State intervention. At the end of his life, however, Seebohm wrote:

> I think the Labour Party is making a great mistake in nationalising so many industries. If we get everything national-ised we shall find that England has become a totalitarian State.[7]

PARIS, LE SILLON AND ITS HEIRS

At the turn of the century the leaders of the French Catholics were brought to a halt by divisions over the issues of monarchy and republicanism, the Dreyfus affair, and the formation of a political party. From Catholics outside the leadership, however, Paris saw considerable activity.

In the last years of the nineteenth century the Abbé Rudynski, a descendant of an old Polish family, was appointed to a Parisian parish in which there were many unemployed youths. He devoted two years to learning a trade as a motor mechanic and repairer, and in 1901 opened a workshop to teach apprentices. He soon had 90 pupils taking a three-year course. He tried to finance it by the work the apprentices did, and although the ends never quite met, he was able to carry on until 1914.[8]

At about the same time there appeared a new kind of Catholic thinking on the left. Poet and philosopher, Dreyfusard and patriot who died fighting in the first weeks of the First World War, Charles Péguy was an unorthodox socialist who became a Catholic in 1908. In 1900 he started *Cahiers de le Quinzaine*, a serial which ran until 1914 and which was the main inspiration for the Christian humanism or personalism of Jacques Maritain and Emmanuel Mounier.

More important for our purpose than either Rudynski or Péguy was Marc Sangnier (1873–1950). Sangnier's interest in social questions developed during the 1890s in informal discussions with friends. In 1899 he started writing in a minor periodical called *Le Sillon*, which gave its name to his movement. This movement was held together by his personality. He disliked formal organisation, but had great personal magnetism, and having also some private means he was able to dispense with the machinery of subscriptions, officers and formal membership. By 1900 he had 21 study groups meeting in Paris once a month. They would read and discuss a passage with a social orientation from the New Testament, and then turn to topics of the present day. The movement spread beyond Paris, and by 1904 Sangnier had perhaps 20,000 supporters.[9] At this time the anti-clerical party was pushing forward the campaign which culminated in 1905 in the separation of Church and State and the Church's loss of its property and revenues. Sillonists were harassed in the streets, and Sangnier started the 'Young Guard', a corps of vigilantes who had been trained at a gymnasium and were admitted by a long initiation ceremony like that for medieval knights.

Le Sillon was deeply committed in theory to co-operative enterprises, and several attempts were made to put these ideas into force. They met with mixed success. 'L'Effort Démocratique', a co-operative grocery which lasted from 1904 to 1909, was a complete failure. So was 'Le Pain du Jour', a bakery intended to provide a model for better working conditions. There were three clothing firms, 'L'Aune', 'La Perce-Neige' and 'La Semeuse', which were designed to benefit women clothes-makers. Since the women who were to work in them had no savings, loan-stock holders put up the capital. The takings, after interest and amortisation, were divided between the women and various social projects, mostly run by Le Sillon. It was possible to pay the workers considerably more than women in the same work received elsewhere, and this in itself was a valuable achievement. 'La Perce-Neige' lasted until 1973. It had specialised in clerical dress, and perhaps because of a dwindling market, it did not recruit new members as the old ones retired.

'La Fraternelle', a consumers' co-operative grocery at Quimper, did well enough for a second shop to be opened in 1908. 'Chez Nous' was a producers' co-operative making shoes. Shoes appear to lend themselves to co-operative production. 'Chez Nous' was started in 1907 by the Abbé Chesnais with workers who were experiencing a lockout, survived the First World War, and in 1920 had a turnover of 3,000,000 Francs. Still more successful were restaurants in Paris. One was opened in 1905, a second in 1908, and a large complex including a hotel was about to be begun in 1910 when the whole Le Sillon movement was terminated in a way we shall see shortly. Last, and in some ways most interesting, there was La Démocratie, a daily newspaper. The capital for this, 275,000 Francs, was put up by the subscribers, and it lasted from 1910–14, when it had 9,000 subscribers and was printing 50,000 copies.

As time went on Le Sillon was increasingly active in politics. Its position was unpopular. Its republicanism anta-gonised many Catholics, its Catholicism many republicans. The Catholics were the more dangerous enemies. In 1906 the Bishop of Quimper, and in 1908 some 30 French bishops and archbishops, forbade their clergy to take part in the move-ment. It is to be feared that what some bishops found objectionable were things which would now be considered particularly creditable: Sangnier's ecumenism, his friendship with Jews and atheists, his encouraging workers to join the non-Christian though not yet Marxist CGT. The charges actually brought were that Le Sillon was teaching that democracy was the only form of government permissible to Christians, and that it was committed to Modernism. These charges, particularly the second, were unfounded. Nevertheless in August 1910 Pius X issued a letter condemning the movement. Sangnier submitted, and *Le Sillon* ceased to appear.

Although Sangnier's personal activities terminated then, they continued to bear fruit for the next 30 years. Almost every development in Catholic social thinking up to 1939 can be seen as radiating from him.

An English Jesuit student named Charles Plater met Sangnier on a visit to Paris in 1904. As a result partly of this meeting and partly of reading biographies of Ketteler, he formed the projects of starting study groups in England for working men and women, and also a Catholic college for adult education along the lines of Ruskin College (then Ruskin Hall). The study group plan was launched as the Catholic Social Guild with strong episcopal backing in 1909; this seems to have been the first imaginative attempt to bring home to Catholic working people in England that the Church had any social teaching. By 1914 the Guild had 1,500 members in 100 groups. The college was founded as a memorial to Plater after his death in 1921, and still exists.

Another clerical student who visited Sangnier was the Fleming Joseph Cardijn (1882–1967). Cardijn had a working class background and was led to study for the priesthood by seeing how his contemporaries lost their faith and became brutalised on entering working life. As a student he visited Germany, France and England. In England he met the trade union leaders Tom Mann and Ben Tillett, and was deeply impressed by their Christian outlook and way of life (Godinne lectures of 1948). Starting work in Brussels in 1913 he was given responsibility for a Catholic social club for young working girls. Under his influence this grew into a chain of groups called the Women's Christian Workers' League. Groups had a weekly study session in which they considered how they could improve the quality of their lives in every respect from conditions at work to private spiritual development. There were also general study days and days of spiritual recollection. A comparable organisation for young men soon followed. Cardijn attended meetings of Emile Vandervelde and never discouraged interest in the socialist movement among his groups whom he took to socialist rallies, and indeed sometimes spoke himself from the platform.

Although Cardijn was imprisoned by the Germans twice in the First World War he managed to keep his organisations going, and after the Armistice they developed rapidly. In 1924 conservative Catholics, considering that his young workers were politically too far to the left, obtained a veto on his activities from the local hierarchy, but Cardijn appealed to Rome, and in a personal interview with Pius XI in 1925, converted him decisively to his side. The result was the setting up of JOC, described in Chapter Six. In the Second World War Cardijn was again arrested by the Germans, and two of the three original founder members of JOC died at Dachau, but the organisations again survived, and now have spread through over 100 countries. In 1965 Paul VI made Cardijn a Cardinal.

Although Cardijn's supporters have always pressed for reforms within the guidelines laid down in the encyclicals, they have never committed themselves to any detailed system of economic arrangements. Their ultimate objectives confessedly transcend the material conditions of working life. In 1949 Cardijn said:

> The worker's tool stands in his hand as the chalice and the paten in the hands of the priest. Just as the priest offers the Body and Blood of Christ on the paten and in the chalice, so the worker-apostle must learn to offer . . ., in and with his tools, the sufferings of Christ, the tiredness and weariness of Christ, with which he is united as part of the Mystical Body.[10]

Among those who actually took part in the *Le Sillon* movement was Peter Maurin (1877–1949). He came from a Languedoc peasant family which, according to his biographer Arthur Sheehan[11] had owned its farm for 1,500 years. He himself once told a socialist group he was addressing: 'I am the son of a peasant and so pre-capitalist.' He trained and taught as a Christian Brother in Paris for ten years, but without taking his final vows, and in 1903, when the anti-clerical ministry was in the process of suppressing confessional schools, he left the Brothers and worked for five years with Sangnier and the Sillonists. He came to hear of them and become interested in social questions through one of the study groups of the Oeuvre des Cercles which was still surviving at the turn of the century. In 1908 he found himself drifting away from *Le Sillon*. One point of difference was that Sangnier wished to transform industry through workers' unions, whereas Maurin wanted a return to agriculture and crafts. He spent a year travelling round country districts in France and studying the viability of small enterprises, and then migrated to Canada where he started farming on a small grant of land in Saskatchewan.

There followed a period in which he passed through many jobs, mostly manual, in Canada and the United States; he himself said of this period, 'I was out of the Church for ten years'. In 1925, however, his life underwent a change. He ceased to accept money, lived entirely without possessions or thought for the next meal or night's lodging, and devoted himself to teaching on social matters both orally and in writings of a form peculiar to himself. They were something like short prose poems, and he originally called them that, though later he gave them the name *Easy Essays*. These are partly critical of existing ideas and institutions. To give a couple of illustrations:

> To make the present different
> one must give up old habits
> and start to construct new habits.
> But to give up old habits
> and start to construct new habits
> one must be a fanatic.
> And liberals are so liberal about everything
> that they cannot become fanatics.

And:

> The training of social workers
> enables them to help people
> to adjust themselves
> to the existing environment.
> The training of social workers
> does not enable them
> to help people
> to change the environment.

But Maurin was not purely negative. He had a simple three-point programme: study meetings and open discussions between people of different views; shelters or 'houses of hospitality' for the destitute; and 'farm colonies or agronomic universities'. These were to be models or pilot schemes with a view to a general resettlement on the land of the industrial unemployed, who in America at that time numbered over 10,000,000.

Still in the United States in 1932, Maurin met Dorothy Day (1897–1980), a militant radical who had recently become a Catholic. They took to each other and formed an extremely dynamic team. Since Dorothy Day was a journalist, Maurin urged her to start a paper, and the result was the *Catholic Worker*. According to its first editorial in May 1933, its aim was to provide a 'Catholic paper printed for the unemployed'; to prove that it was 'possible to be radical without being atheistic', and to popularise and make known the Church's social teaching. Starting with 2,500 copies distributed free, the paper soon built up a large readership. At the same time Maurin and Dorothy Day proceeded with the three-point programme. Before the end of 1933 they had started public meetings and opened the first house of hospitality. The meetings were successful and the houses of hospitality multiplied through the northern half of the United States. On the agricultural side, however, progress was poor.

In 1935 a start was made with a garden on Staten Island. In 1936 a 28-acre farm was bought at Easton, Pennsylvania. This served as a holiday centre in summer, and was visited by priests who had set up agricultural co-operatives elsewhere in North America, Fathers Tompkins and McGoey from Canada, Mgr Luigi Ligutti from Iowa; but partly repeating the experience of the Fourierists a century earlier, it suffered from personality clashes and was not a successful farm. In 1944 farming was abandoned and the place was used for retreats. Other farms were started in Pennsylvania, Michigan, Massachusetts, Vermont, Missouri and Ohio, but they were mostly small and ran into difficulties. The most robust seems to have been Upton, Montana, reported as still functioning in 1959.

Maurin favoured a system in which families participating in a commune should each have its own house and a very small garden, but everything else should be in common. Provided that there was a good balance of agriculture and crafts, he looked forward to communes so large as to have a thousand families.

The personalism of Emmanuel Mounier (1905–50) should probably be reckoned among the products of *Le Sillon*, although Mounier himself spoke of the Sillonists as too benign to be effective, and the proximate influences on him were those of Maritain and Péguy. Mounier qualified as a philosopher at the Sorbonne, but partly as a result of working on Péguy in 1928–31 he became dissatisfied with academic life, and in 1932 he founded *Esprit*, a journal which, in the tradition of *Le Sillon* and *L'Avenir*, became a symbol and a mouthpiece for the radical Catholic left.

Like the Distributists, Mounier was implacably opposed to capitalism, and called for a complete transformation of society on Christian lines. In some respects he was more realistic than they. In his *Personalist Manifesto* (1936) he dissociates himself from hostility to mechanisation as such and nostalgia for the craftsmen of the Middle Ages.

The economic theory of personalism[12] starts from the real needs of the consumer, which are divided into two classes: things we need for living, which include not only necessities but such luxuries as 'inventiveness produces and conscience approves'; and things we need for 'creative enjoyment', that is, for enjoyable intelligent activity. Production is to be regulated with an eye to these needs, not to the maximisation of profit or wealth. Mounier does not advocate nationalisation, and recommends that State planning of the economy should be limited to ensuring that everyone has a necessary minimum of goods and services; beyond that there should be freedom and may be competition. On the other hand shareholders who are not actively engaged in an enterprise should have no control over it. Labour, Mounier insists, anticipating the encyclical *Laborem exercens*, has an inalienable priority over capital.

The management of enterprises should be democratic, but Mounier does not favour the principle of 'one man, one vote'. He warns against 'carrying over into this economic regime all the sins of parliamentary democracy'. Every worker should have 'the ownership of his own vital wage and a share in the returns' and, 'The most elementary form of ownership should be that of one's trade or craft, and society has the duty to ensure it for everyone, and under all circumstances.' But for management, an elite is needed, and a worker should not have a share in it before he is properly informed. The managers should be chosen by workers 'who have given proof of their competence, personal worth and loyalty to the enterprise'. For those who do not satisfy these conditions, Mounier envisages some kind of union organisa- tion and non-managerial functions: notably exercising vigi- lance to prevent the emergence of an elite managerial caste, and participating in arrangements concerning safety, hygiene, and welfare.

Mounier was forceful both as a personality and as a writer, and he could have had far more influence than the Distributists or even the Sillonists ever had on events. When *Esprit* first started it was the journal of a lively political movement, led by friends of Mounier, which hoped to become a political party. Mounier appears to have had a strong personal aversion to organised political action, and renounced the connection in 1933. In 1943 Gilbert Dru, who was influenced by him and shared his general aims, tried to persuade leading Christian Democrats to found a party which would unite both Christians and Communists. Collaboration in the Resistance had produced an opportunity which had not existed in France since 1791 to form a broadly based party committed to radical reforms. If Dru had succeeded, France might just conceivably have become a 'personalist' society. Although Mounier had great authority, again he failed to take a lead. He told Dru: 'You are going to inherit the Catholic masses, who tend to be conservative, and you will be their prisoners'.[13] This sombre prophecy was fulfilled. A massive party did come into being in 1944, but it was the conservative Mouvement Républicain Populaire.

Mounier's aversion to political parties was a reflection of his view[14] that we must not use the same means as the corrupt society we are trying to replace. His preferred strategy was that we should first aim at a personal conversion of individuals. We should then plant, as seeds, at selected points in the social fabric, 'organic communities formed about an embryonic personalist inspiration' such as business enterprises run on non-capitalist lines, credit unions and study groups. A number of groups of 'friends of *Esprit*' were in fact formed, and today the Association of Friends has 500 members, issues a six-monthly Bulletin, and holds conferences. Like *Esprit* itself, however, which prints 10,000 copies and is in a thriving condition, it is concerned with political, religious and cultural issues generally, and neither gives any special attention to socio-economic problems or industry.

SMALL IS BEAUTIFUL

The Distributists, Simone Weil, and E. F. Schumacher do not stand by any means in a line of continuous succession; rather they are examples of individual thinkers outside any stream of development. They are united, however, by their hostility to large-scale industry.

The origins of Distributism can be traced back to 1906 when Arthur J. Penty broke away from the mainstream of English socialism and became convinced that the evils of industrialism could be remedied only be restoring guilds on the medieval model to regulate production and fix just prices and wages. Penty's guilds were to be primarily regulative, not productive. Penty thought that producers' co-operatives, besides being very hard to establish, did not in fact suit the majority of working people.[15] Between 1908 and 1920 a number of people followed Eric Gill to Ditchling in Sussex, and in 1920 there was formally established the Guild of St Joseph and St Dominic. This consisted of a number of craftsmen and their families who from a legal point of view remained independent, but who shared some buildings and a chapel. They attempted small-holding, but their main interests lay in stone-cutting, weaving, wood-engraving and the like. Meanwhile Hilaire Belloc published bitter attacks on the existing capitalist system in *The Servile State* and *Economics for Helen*, and Distributist ideas were put forward in a series of journals run by him and the Chestertons: the *Eye Witness*, *New Witness* and *G.K.'s Weekly*.

Perhaps the most formal statement of Distributist thinking is Penty's *Distributism: A Manifesto*, published in 1937 when his death and G. K. Chesterton's had brought the movement to a halt by depriving it of its principal leaders. The movement was Christian in inspiration, though not exclusively Christian in membership. Its fundamental principle was that 'without private property there can be no economic freedom, initiative or sense of personal responsibility'.[16] That being so, the main objective was that property should be widely distributed, that as many people as possible should have some. Distributists believed that society must be rebuilt on agriculture,[17] that every country should produce at least 80% of its food.[18] This part of its programme was much stressed by the Dominican Vincent McNabb, and was summarised in the phrase 'three acres and a cow'. In the industrial sector most of the Distributists regarded mechanisation as an evil, and wished to restrict the use of machinery. They also opposed free trade, and called for fixing of wages, prices and rents. The instrument for achieving these ends, as we have seen, was to be guilds.

These ideas attracted enough interest for the Distributist League to be founded in London in 1926. Although, however, there were some country branches, it remained a group of friends rather than a political force. One or two Members of Parliament, most notably Sir Henry Slessor, sympathised with Distributist aims, but the great majority of Englishmen of the 1930s who felt social concern were mistrustful on account of the high proportion of Catholics involved, the controversial praising of medieval guilds, and the failure of prominent Distributists to denounce Fascism adequately.

The Ditchling experiment at putting Distributism into practice received a set-back in 1924 from Eric Gill's withdrawal from it. In spite of this, and of the fact that the original members are now all dead or retired, there still is a Ditchling community.

After leaving Ditchling, Gill gathered communities round him in Wales and, subsequently, at Piggots in Buckinghamshire. Plans by Graham Carey, who popularised Gill's ideas in America, to start something of the kind in Vermont were disrupted by the Second World War.

Although Simone Weil (1907–43) did not found any movement or organisation, she must be classed with those who were not content with armchair speculation. The child of Jewish parents settled in Paris, she was attracted while still at school to the politics of the radical left. She studied

Philosophy at the École Normale and passed into the State educational system; but in 1934–5 she obtained leave to spend nine months working in factories. In 1936 she spent two months with anarchist troops in the Spanish Civil War. Although this *curriculum vitae* may not sound likely to bring her close to the Catholic Church, in March 1937 she wrote to Mounier in the hope that *Esprit* might persuade the CFTC to join the CGT. Though not herself a Catholic, she said, she found the 'Christian idea', which 'one cannot renounce without becoming degraded', compatible with the spirit of the CGT. In 1938 she experienced some kind of conversion, and although she refused ever to accept baptism, she has to be counted as an influence on Catholic thinking from within. Her experience as a factory worker paved the way for the worker-priests. When France was occupied by Germany, after a period working on the land in the south she accompanied her family to America. In 1942, however, she returned to England to work with the Free French there. She died in 1943 mainly as a result of not taking enough food. In the earlier part of her illness she refused to eat more than the rations current at that time in France. Simone Pétrement's biography[19] shows, however, that at the end she was trying to eat; she did not, as an unintelligent inquest declared, commit suicide by starvation.

By the early 1930s Simone Weil had rejected the Stalinist solution to the problems of modern civilisation. Her religious conversion led her also to condemn economic liberalism and utilitarianism. She regarded these as intellectually dishonest attempts to paper over the fundamental irreconcilability of a mechanistic metaphysics with a humanistic theory of morals. Many non-Christians, of course, deny that mechanism and humanism really are incompatible, and some Christians have not been satisfied with the way in which Simone Weil hoped to resolve the tension between them, but these are philosophical issues we need not consider here. In 1943 she wrote *The Need for Roots* which had the practical purpose of showing how society might be restructured in France after an Allied victory. She proposes both specific reforms and ways of getting them implemented. As was remarked earlier, France let the opportunity of 1944–5 slip. This does not, however, invalidate Simone Weil's ideas.

A human being [she writes] has roots by virtue of his real, active and natural participation in the life of a community which preserves in living shape certain particular treasures of the past and certain particular expectations for the future. This participation is a natural one, in the sense that it is automatically brought about by place, conditions of birth, profession and social surroundings. Every human being needs to have multiple roots. It is necessary for him to draw wellnigh the whole of his moral, intellectual and spiritual life by way of the environment of which he forms a natural part.[20]

The need for roots in this sense is, of course, precisely what the classical liberal tradition denies, and acceptance of it justifies the value Simone Weil places on such notions as obedience, order and patriotism. She sees uprootedness, inability to draw life (except at the most material level) from the environment, as affecting the whole of modern civilised society and not just the industrial working class. It is her proposals, however, for the industrial sector which chiefly concern us here.

Large factories, she said, should be abolished. Large concerns, on the other hand, she thought made an appeal to the imagination of those who belonged to them, and should therefore be retained, but in the form of federations.

A big concern would be composed of an assembly shop connected with a number of little workshops, each containing one or more workmen, dispersed throughout the country.[21]

These workshops would belong to the people working in them, individually or collectively, and it would be these workmen who, in turns, worked in the central assembly shop. Turns of work at the centre would provide opportunities for meeting other members of the concern and learning about overall policy and the people using its products in other countries. Ideally the centres would be sited near universities or centres of research. Children were to be encouraged to frequent workshops while still at school, and the teaching of theoretical subjects like mathematics was to be combined with exercises in their application. School-leavers were to be encouraged to travel widely as journeymen. On marrying, and subject to a proficiency test, a man would be given a house, a garden and a machine or a share in a workshop. This scheme was to be administered by boards composed of representatives from the legislature, the executive, the owners or managers, and the trade unions. Large personal fortunes should disappear, and the State would provide capital for new ventures to entrepreneurs of competence and honesty. Those who failed to reach the level of proficiency required for any kind of ownership of the means of production should be employed as wage-earners, but where possible in providing services rather than in production. Along with these changes in social organisation should go technological changes. In particular the primary consideration in designing machinery should no longer be profit or even the needs and means of the consumer, but the good of the workers who are to use it.

Simone Weil acknowledges debts to Marx and Proudhon, but her ideas on education and on the organisation of production will be recognised to bring her closer to Kropotkin. She differs from all these thinkers in insisting on the role of religion. Lack of religious inspiration, she says, is one of the four main obstacles that 'separate us from a form of civilisation likely to be worth something'.[22] Work had been sanctified in some pre-Christian religions (though not in that of classical antiquity) and it was significant that Christ himself was a working man.[23] Simone Weil clearly believed that without religion of some kind we have no hope of accomplishing what she called the 'particular mission' of our age: 'the creation of a civilisation founded upon the spiritual nature of work'. We have seen how this idea is developed by John Paul II.

E. F. Schumacher's background, like Simone Weil's was Jewish. He married a Lutheran, however, and late in life became a Catholic, so he can be claimed as a Christian thinker. He came to Britain first as a Rhodes scholar and later as one of that distinguished band of German intellectuals who sought refuge in the years before the Second World War. In 1950 he joined the National Coal Board, and held the position of its Economic Adviser from then to 1970. *Small is Beautiful* was first published in 1973, though the chapter (entitled 'A Question of Size') which suggested that famous slogan began as a lecture, delivered as early as 1968.

The slogan itself, of course, is entirely consonant with the Christian principle of subsidiarity. For that principle implicitly values the small more highly than the large as well as insisting that, in large scale organisations, decisions should be reached at as low a level as possible.

Schumacher's ideas about ownership start from the important distinction highlighted by Tawney in *The Acquisitive Society*.

> As regards private property, the first and most basic distinction is between (a) property that is an aid to creative work, and (b) property that is an alternative to it. There is something natural and healthy about the former – the private property of the working proprietor; and there is something unnatural and unhealthy about the latter – the private property of the passive owner who lives parasitically on the work of others. This basic distinction was clearly seen by Tawney.[24]

It is scarcely surprising, given their identical starting points, that Schumacher's conclusions should be closely similar to Tawney's. Both men favour private ownership for the really small scale business. Both men reject it for the larger. Schumacher's position differs from Tawney's, if at all, only in that he recommends Scott Bader's arrangements when he discusses the ownership of undertakings of an intermediate size. He summarises his position on those issues succinctly enough:

> (a) In a small scale enterprise, private ownership is natural, fruitful and just.
> (b) In medium scale enterprise, private ownership is already to a large extent functionally unnecessary. The idea of property becomes strained, untrustful and unjust. If there is only one owner or a small group of owners, there can be, and should be, a voluntary surrender of privilege to the wider group of actual workers, as in the case of Scott Bader & Co. Ltd.
> (c) In large scale enterprise, private ownership is a fiction for the purposes of enabling functionless owners to live parasitically on the labour of others. It is not only unjust but also an irrational element which distorts all relationships within the enterprise.[25]

In large-scale businesses, he argues at the end of *Small is Beautiful*, the State should take a holding of 50 per cent: that would reflect the reality of what is contributed to the success of a business by the community as a whole. Transfers of ownership to the work-force at Scott Bader and elsewhere will be described below. But it is not only because of its ownership arrangements that Schumacher favours Scott Bader:

> Its merit lies precisely in the attainment of objectives which lie outside the commercial standards, of *human* objectives which are generally assigned a second place or altogether neglected by ordinary commercial practice.[26]

For example he quotes the requirement that not more than 20 per cent of the company's net profits may be paid 'as bonuses to those working within the operating company', and the adjoining obligation to devote 'to charitable purposes outside the Scott Bader organisation' a sum equal to whatever is paid out in bonuses.

LATER CO-OPERATIVES

Maurin, Mounier and the Distributists, it might be said, were more productive of thoughts and words than effective of substantial changes in their economic environments. Roughly contemporaneous with them, and in touch at least with the Catholic Worker movement, was a movement in Canada with the opposite emphasis.

Nova Scotia is a province with an inhospitable climate which by the end of the nineteenth century had a sparse population of Scots, Irish and French. Life was hard, living standards were low, and in the first quarter of the twentieth century conditions were made worse by increasing unemployment. A policy for dealing with the economic troubles of the province was worked out and set in operation very largely by two priests, James Tompkins (1870–1953) and Moses Coady (1882–1959). These priests were cousins, and came from farming stock in a remote valley in Cape Breton Island. They were educated at the St Francis Xavier University in Antigonish, a university where Henry Somerville taught sociology. They completed their clerical studies

in Rome, and after ordination took up positions in St Francis
Xavier University, Tompkins teaching Greek and Mathematics, and Coady Philosophy. Both were men of dynamic
personality; the older cousin, Tompkins, was the intellectual
pioneer, but Coady was the better publicist and the abler at
getting their ideas put into practice. In 1920 Tompkins
became convinced that the key to improving conditions in
Nova Scotia was adult education, and the following year he
started the first People's School for this purpose. He was also
impressed by the 'caisses populaires' of Alphonse Desjardins
and began to advocate co-operation. As a result of discussion
between academics, parish priests and farmers, in 1928 the
University set up its so called Extension Department for
adult education with a practical orientation. Coady was
appointed director and held the post until he reached retiring
age in 1952.

The procedure of the Department was first for Coady and
his colleagues to travel round depressed areas holding public
meetings. A public meeting, if successful, would be followed
by the formation of small study groups. Once the groups
were established, they joined together into larger federations,
and conferences were organised both for particular vocations
like farming and fishing, and for all comers. The movement
depended on good local leadership. Between 1933 and 1939
the Extension Department trained more than 700 local
leaders (including a notable proportion of priests) in four-
week courses. During the Second World War, when it was
difficult for people to be away from home for so long, the
Department laid on four-day courses in local centres.

Tompkins and Coady were emphatic that education and
prolonged study of local circumstances were essential pre-
liminaries to any action. The next step was the setting up of
credit unions and consumers' co-operatives. These were
founded on the Rochdale principles of moderate interest,
dividends on purchases, and one member one vote. The first
form of productive co-operation they recommended (after
the formation of trade unions, which they viewed as co-
operatives for selling labour) was co-operative selling of
agricultural produce and fish. The real basis for progress,
however, should be the gradual taking over by co-operatives
of . . .

. . . stores, wholesales, banks and service institutions . . . When the people own, co-operatively, enough of these institutions and when the volume of demand grows, they can federate into wholesales and either build or take over the manufacturing plants in the distant industrial centres.[27]

In the long term Coady looked forward to a mixed economy in which there would 'individual ownership of farms' (he never abandoned, however much he enlarged, the outlook of a farmer's son); 'a large measure of co-operative ownership in all the economic processes'; 'a measure, perhaps a very large measure, of socialism' to cover welfare, communications and services like electricity; and 'an area of private-profit enterprise'.[28]

It is now more than 50 years since the setting up of the Extension Department, and the Antigonish movement must be judged at least a *qualified* success. The qualification is necessary because the dreams of James Tompkins and Moses Coady have not really been fulfilled: though agricultural and fishing co-operatives still survive, the former are now co-operatives in little more than name, and the latter scarcely extend beyond a few tiny groups of lobster pot fishermen. Even Coady's credit unions are now little more than personal savings and loan societies and their membership is by all accounts mainly middle class. On the other hand the movement played a major part in bringing Nova Scotia through the depression between the wars, and St Francis Xavier University now runs courses to train people from developing countries all over the world in adult education and co-operative production.

In England since 1945 the phenomenon has appeared of firms changing from having a capitalist structure to being owned by the workforce in common. Although instances of this transformation are few, they are relevant to this study because they have often been motivated, at least in part, by a wish to put Christian ideas into practice.

We have reported Schumacher's admiration for Scott Bader. With a labour force of 250, this manufactures a range of intermediate chemical products, chiefly polyester resins, outside Wellingborough in Northamptonshire. Ernest Bader, the original capitalist owner, was a Swiss by birth and a Quaker throughout his long life. In two stages, in 1951 and

1963, he transferred the ownership of the firm from his family to the workforce. The legal entity through which his employees own it, the Scott Bader Commonwealth, finances the Industrial Common Ownership Movement and Industrial Common Ownership Finance. These in turn unite, support and have in some cases helped to fund a number of other co-operatives, of which the largest, Bewley's Cafes in Dublin, also belonged originally to a Quaker family and was made over to the employees for idealistic reasons.

But by far the most important initiatives in co-operative production in recent years have been taken not in any English-speaking country but in the Basque province of northern Spain. The co-operatives of Mondragon are mainly in industry, and industry, moreover, which is technically quite advanced. They have already been described in considerable detail by one of the present writers (Robert Oakeshott: *The Case for Workers' Co-ops*) and we shall not repeat the description here; it will be enough to recall certain points.

Mondragon sent three battalions to fight against Franco in the Spanish Civil War, and was over-run by his troops in 1937. The years which followed were extremely hard for its inhabitants. In 1941 the young priest Jose Maria Arizmendi-arietta, Arizmendi for short, was sent there with instructions to give special attention to the young and to social problems. Arizmendi was familiar with the Catholic Church's social teaching; he was also influenced by the thinking and work of Cardijn and Mounier, and he was aware of the achievements of the Rochdale Pioneers. The first need, he perceived, was for technical education. In 1943 he opened a small school which was funded entirely by local people. He also arranged for those who progressed beyond this school to study part-time and take examinations at the school of technical engineering at Zaragoza. The first students passed their examinations there in 1952. They then mostly took jobs at a large local firm of conventional capitalist structure, which made a range of metal products. Under the influence of Arizmendi, however, they soon decided to set up their own 'new model' enterprise structured to be more in line with his moral teaching. They achieved this in 1955, 14 years, it will be noticed, after Arizmendi arrived in Mondragon. One factor which accounts for the success of the Mondragon co-operatives is the patience and planning which preceded them. We have seen that lack of preparation can be blamed for many failures in the nineteenth century.

The first Mondragon co-operative was ULGOR, which now makes a wide range of domestic appliances. Others followed, many in metal manufacture which is traditional in the area. Along with the production co-operatives, there is a range of other institutions owned partly by those who work in them and partly by the production co-operatives themselves. These include the Polytechnic, Lagun Aro, which provides insurance since members of co-operatives, being self-employed, fall partly outside the Spanish State insurance system, and the bank, the Caja Laboral Popular (CLP). It is unlikely that Arizmendi ever examined the files of *L'Européen* for 1831–2. The constitutional arrangements at Mondragon, however, are a natural development of those drafted by Buchez. Perhaps what chiefly differentiates Mondragon is a combination of its insistence on a significant capital contribution from all worker members and its emphasis on and provision for good management. Buchez, while making the General Meeting ultimate sovereign, reposed the management in an annually elected board. At Mondragon there is an elected board of directors between the General Assembly and the management proper. This hires managerial expertise, not necessarily from within the Mondragon federation. Moreover the CLP has a special section which prepares new ventures with those who want to initiate them, and provides a full consultative service once they are started.

The Mondragon co-operatives have been almost unbelievably successful. At the latest count they were giving employment to 19,000 persons, and providing social security for 50,000. Moreover they have managed to sustain this employment and even to increase it slightly during the recession of the 1980s, when Spanish and Basque regional unemployment has been growing to record levels. Mondragon is a flourishing community the economic basis of which is mainly co-operative industrial production. Visitors are struck not only by the solidarity of the community but by its overall high morale. Mondragon has found a satisfactory solution to the problems generated by the Industrial Revolution.

CHAPTER NINE

Is There A Christian Tradition?

We have now seen how Christians actually responded to the Industrial Revolution. We have also seen some political and social factors which help to explain why the Church, in a phrase of Tawney's, 'was not more effective in giving inspiration and guidance' in the early stages. But it is necessary to consider if there may not be a deeper explanation. Does Christianity in fact dispose of any theory or set of principles which could have been applied to the situation which arose? Christians are, of course, called upon to care in general for others, to help the poor and weak, to be socially responsible. But is there anything in the Christian tradition to provide a basis for a specific socio-economic programme?

Any philosophy which purports to be Christian must have roots in the Old Testament. Ancient Jewish law, as is well known, forbids the charging of interest on loans (Exodus 22.24–5). In addition Leviticus 25 provides for a remission of debts every seven years, and for a restitution of land to its original owners every fiftieth or jubilee year. The ground for this latter provision is that the land itself belongs to God, and men can alienate at most the usufruct of it. It is extremely doubtful whether any restitution of land was ever carried out, but there is evidence for redistributions of land in Mesopotamia at the beginning of the second millennium BC, and it is possible that attempts were made in Israel to put this part of the law into practice before the Babylonian captivity; at any rate it remained in the books (Deuteronomy 11 as well as Leviticus) as an ideal.

The Prophets consistently champion the poor against the rich and condemn the pursuit of wealth. Isaiah denounces those who grind the faces of the poor (3.15) and add house to house and field to field (5.8). Amos inveighs against the dishonest business practices of the rich (8.4–6). Israel of the

Old Testament was well supplied with what we call 'social conscience'.

Max Weber says that Calvinists of the sixteenth and seventeenth centuries concentrated on the Psalms and Proverbs. Proverbs in particular contains strictures on idleness (6.6–10, 24.30–4), and passages which could be used to glorify hard work (22.29, 31.16). These, however, are commonplaces of traditional wisdom; they no more express what Weber calls the spirit of capitalism than Hesiod's *Works and Days*.

It is generally acknowledged that the New Testament contains no formal socio-economic teaching. According to Luke (3.10–14), John the Baptist was asked for guidance by tax-collectors and soldiers, and told the former to exact only what was legally due, and the latter to respect the civilian population and be content with their pay. The implication is that these questionable professions are not evil in themselves. Christ equally refrains from condemning any specific contemporary institution (such as slavery) or way of earning a living. Francesco Nitti says that Christ held all wealth to be sinful, and poverty to be a necessary condition of entering the Kingdom of Heaven,[1] but the passages he cites do not justify this extreme interpretation. The famous dictum that it is easier for a camel to get through the eye of a needle than for a rich man to enter the Kingdom (Mt 19.23–6) is a warning that riches make salvation difficult, not impossible; when Christ tells the rich young man to sell what he has and give it to the poor (Mt 19.21), this is not a command but a counsel of perfection. Even the severe words of James (5.1–6) do not imply that the Christian is under an absolute obligation to renounce wealth. On the other hand in the Sermon on the Mount (Mt 6.19, 25–34) and elsewhere Christ says very explicitly that we should not store up treasures on earth or take thought for the morrow, but concentrate on saving our souls and serving God. It is a point to which we shall return that Christ demands a radical conversion (*metanoia*) of the whole man, intellectual and emotional: he calls for an inversion of existing values, and a change from resentment, vengefulness and ambition to humility and unlimited forgivingness.

Christ's verbal teaching, as presented in the New Testament, remains strictly on the level of ethics. He either ignores or explicitly disavows an interest in questions of politics and economics. On the other hand he does not appear merely as a teacher and theorist. Christians have disagreed strongly about how far he set up an institutional, visible Church, but it is hardly controversial that his disciples were organised (Jn 6.5–7, 12.4–8) for works of poor relief.

For our present purposes, fortunately, we need not enter into the question of the historical truth of the New Testament, since the events reported there form part of the Christian tradition whether they occurred or not. From Acts (6.1–6) we hear that in the earliest Christian community in Jerusalem there was a daily distribution of supplies to widows, and that seven persons were given the office of seeing to this. In 2.44–6 and 4.32–5.11 the faithful are said to have everything in common. It has been debated how far we should conceive them as living together in genuine Communism like monks or Shakers. Although in 1.13 the close personal followers of Christ are apparently lodging together, this does not seem to have been the position of the 3,000 converts after Pentecost (2.46), and on a natural reading of 4.32 ff., people merely sold houses and land which they could spare. In any case it is clear from 5.3–4 that there is no obligation on Christians either to sell their possessions or to pool the whole of the proceeds.

The pastoral letters of the New Testament are notably uninflammatory: revolution in the political and social spheres is the last thing they breathe. 1 Peter (2.12–15) enjoins submission to every kind of human authority or establishment (*ktisis*), and 1 Timothy (6.1) tells slaves to be respectful and conscientious. In both cases the declared objective is to disarm criticism by non-believers; Christians should try to obtain freedom to pursue their own way of life among themselves by showing they had no designs on the existing social order. 2 Thessalonians (3.10) contains one further precept which has often been quoted: 'If a man is not willing to work, let him not eat'; in other words (*cf.* 1 Tim. 5.11) the funds available for charity should not be used to maintain able-bodied people in idleness.

Of early Christian writers Tertullian (160–225) is some-times mentioned for saying: 'We have all things in common but our wives' (Apology 39). It is clear, however, that this is just a rhetorical flourish. The early Christians did have some property in common (Eusebius X.v.11), but Tertullian implies that they did not have literal and total community of goods when he goes on to speak of monthly collections for the poor, orphans, the old, etc.

In 'Who is the rich man that will be saved?' Clement of Alexandria (*circa* 150–212) points out that Zacchaeus is not ordered to divest himself of all his riches, and that even the Rich Young Man is not told simply to abandon them. What is important, says Clement, is to abandon attachment to riches. Wealth in itself is neither good nor bad, and there is positive good in using it to benefit others. Nitti considers this a fatal compromising of the primitive Christian doctrine, and calls it 'a specimen of perfect sophistry, such as could only be conceived in the mind of an Alexandrian writer'. As we have seen, however, Nitti's primitive Christian embargo on private property is an illusion, and to most readers Clement's essay will appear both sensible and sincere.

Communism first appears only in the fourth century, and it then comes in two forms. In the first place, round about 300 individuals started to lead solitary religious lives in the Egyptian Thebaid. Other individuals settled near them, and collective arrangements came to be made for provisioning. In about 320 Pachomius (*circa* 290–346), a disciple of the hermit Palemon, started the first so-called cenobitic community – cenobites differing from groups of hermits in that they lived and ate together. In Egypt there was traditionally more sexual equality than elsewhere round the Eastern Mediterranean, and Pachomius was soon called to set up communities for women. The cenobitic movement developed fast. Sozomen[2] reports that by the end of his life Pachomius had 7,000 followers distributed through a number of communities, the largest, Tabennisi, with 1,300 monks. Monasteries of this size had extensive buildings surrounding them, including cattle sheds, bakeries and workshops for a considerable range of trades. Monks and nuns seem to have been divided up by trades into small groups of about 20 persons, each with its own immediate superior.

From Egypt monasticism spread first to Syria. By the end of the fourth century it had reached Gaul, and the idea of a religious community was influencing bishops. Eustathius in Armenia went too far, condemning marriage altogether and getting involved in scandals; nevertheless the respectable Greek monasticism of St Basil (329–79) appears to be indebted to him. Augustine of Hippo (354–430), we learn from his *Sermons* 355–6,[3] instituted a kind of communal life for his clergy and forbade them to own private property. It is natural to suppose that this development of religious communities has some connection with the appearance of communistic ideas in more theoretical thinking at about the same time.

Ambrose of Milan (337–97) says:

> Our Lord God wished this earth to be the common possession of all men, and its produce to supply the needs of all. But avarice has assigned private rights of possession. It is just, therefore, if you have anything of your own, which belongs in common to the human race, or rather to all living things, at least to give something from it to the poor; in order that you may not deny nourishment to those to whom you owe partnership in your right.[4]

He also remarks[5] 'nature, then, generated the common right, and usurpation the private one'.

Augustine takes the same view. It is by human law only that we possess what we possess: 'by divine law the earth and its fulness are God's'.[6] And that this way of thinking is not confined to Western Christendom can be seen from a sermon by John Chrysostom (347–407), on 1 Tim 12:[7] 'To grow rich without injustice', Chrysostom declares, 'is impossible.' A particular individual may inherit his wealth, but 'the root and origin of it must have been injustice. Why? Because God in the beginning did not make one man rich and another poorer; nor did he afterwards take one and show him treasures of gold, and deny to the other the right of searching for them, but he left the earth free to all alike.' Granted that the heir is not responsible for the crimes of his ancestors, he still has a duty to distribute his riches. It is an evil 'that you alone have the Lord's property, that you alone should enjoy what is common . . . If our possessions belong to one common Lord, they belong also to our fellow-servants.' Chrysostom goes on to advocate Communism as more in accordance with nature than private ownership: earth, air, water and light were created common by God, and the things made by men which are common, like bath-houses and market-places, never give rise to disputes. On the other hand in his Homily 11 on the Acts[8] he recognises that true Communism, as practised by monks, is an ambitious project, and advises his hearers to start with something more modest, like giving up swearing.

This teaching of the Fathers, both Greek and Latin, is powerfully summarised by Gregory the Great (*circa* 540–604):

> The land is common to all men, and therefore brings forth nourishment for all men. Those people, then, are wrong to think themselves guiltless when they claim what God has given to men in common as their private property; who because they do not distribute what they have received, proceed to the slaughter of their neighbours, since they kill each day as many of the dying poor as could have been saved by what they keep to themselves. For when we give necessities to people in need, we are returning to them what is theirs, not being generous with what is ours; we are rather paying a debt of justice than performing a work of charity.[9]

With this theory of property went a theory of natural law. In an influential passage[10] Isidore of Seville (*circa* 560–636) distinguishes natural law, which is 'known to men by natural instinct, not by human institutions' from the *ius gentium*, the laws which are common to 'nearly all peoples'. The former, he says, includes '*communis omnium possessio*'. Later writers interpreted this to mean 'the common possession of all things', though R. W. and A. J. Carlyle are probably right that Isidore himself meant only 'the possession of things by all men in common', the 'things' so possessed being air, daylight and the like. The notion of natural law is Stoic rather than Biblical, and the idea that appropriation is unnatural also owes much to Stoicism. From the time of Hesiod the Greeks and Romans had myths of a golden age in which there was no strife and the earth produced abundance for all of its own accord. The Stoics, however, rationalised these myths into a picture of an ideal state of nature in which all men were equal and there was no coercion.[11] The Fathers identified this primitive state with the state of mankind before the Fall. Where the Stoics had no clear explanation of the discrepancy between the ideal and the actual, Christian thinkers could put it down to sin. It was common to ascribe to sin the institutions of slavery and administrative coercion,[12] and later writers added private property.[13]

A number of writers, including Troeltsch and A. J. Penty, have thought that these ideas induced political defeatism and conservatism: if inequality, slavery and the like are due to the Fall, it is a waste of time to try to eliminate them. There is probably some truth in this, and also in Penty's suggestion that Roman law imparted to Christian thinking the irresponsible conception of ownership as the right to use and abuse.

The history of Christian social thought between the fifth and the twelfth centuries is very badly documented; or the documents, if they exist, have received very little attention from historians. In the 860s Photius initiated the split between the East and the West which was to become final in 1052. Social conditions were, of course, completely different in the two divisions of Christendom. The Byzantine empire had universities and trained doctors and lawyers throughout its duration; government was centralised and bureaucratic; and at least in the centre there were many of the institutions of the Welfare State. Down the twelfth century the West was deprived of the advantages, such as they may be, of university education; government was not centralised; and administrative functions which in the East were performed by imperial officials, in the West were often discharged by bishops or abbots.

From the twelfth century on, Christian critics of the existing order are not lacking in the West, but the most radical are heretics. The Waldenses of Italy and Southern France, some Lollards and Hussites, and the Moravian Brethren, were agreed in wishing to do away, peacefully or in some cases by violence, with accumulations of riches and revolutionise society conformably to New Testament ideals as they understood them. Both on this account and because of doctrines of a more purely theological kind, they all came into conflict with the institutional Church. Orthodox Christians mostly accepted the existing social framework, and concentrated their thinking on specific problems, especially those of usury and a just price.

In *Summa Theologiae*[14] Aquinas (1226–74) declares that it is not in general legitimate to sell something for more than it is worth; though the price may be raised if both the vendor and the buyer have special need of the thing – not, Aquinas insists, if the need is restricted to the buyer. At the same time he allows[15] that the vendor may sell goods for more than he gave for them, provided the profit is moderate and sought for a good purpose. Aquinas distinguishes in this passage between necessities and luxuries, and seems to think that providing necessities should be the responsibility of persons other than businessmen seeking profits. The question of necessities apart, Aquinas's treatment of the ethics of buying and selling or 'commutative justice' cannot be applied until criteria are found for determining just what the true value of a thing is.

Aquinas argues[16] against usury, the word (*'usuria'*) here being employed not in the broad sense in which medieval writers often used it for any kind of commercial sharp practice or profiteering, but in the strict sense for taking interest on loans of money. Aquinas's reasoning is as follows. In some cases we can separate the use of a thing from the thing itself, while in others we cannot. There is a distinction between the use of a house and the house, since you can use a house for years, that is, live in it, and the house may be just as good at the end. That being so, if I lend you my house, I can ask you not only to return it to me, but also to pay the rent for the use of it. But in other cases to have the use is the same as to have the thing. To use wine is to drink it. You can use it only once, and in using it you consume it. It follows that if I lend you a litre of wine, and then ask you to pay me for the use of it as well as letting me have a litre back, I am asking to be compensated for the same thing twice over; and that is unjust. Now interest is payment for the use of money, as the word 'usury' implies. But money cannot be separated from its use any more than wine: using it is spending it, and therefore consuming it. Hence to ask for interest as well as a return of the principal is unjust. To the modern reader it should be clear where this argument can best be attacked; but to the thirteenth century it looked pretty cogent, and a practice essential to modern economic life therefore seemed immoral.

Aquinas held that value is determined by utility,[17] but this opinion is not elaborated into a theory in his surviving works. The first medieval writer to produce what deserves to be called a theory of value is Pierre de Jean Olivi (1248–98). Olivi's personal reputation was tarnished by suspicions of heresy, and his work remains unpublished to the present day, but it was studied by Bernardino of Siena (1380–1444) and is embodied in his treatise *On Commerce and Usury*.[18]

According to Bernardino, the just price is that which is 'in accordance with the estimation of the current market, according to what the thing which is being sold commonly fetches in that place at that time'.[19] Value, therefore, is proximately determined by market forces in a competitive situation, though Bernardino and other scholastics speak favourably of having prices fixed by the civil authorities for the common good; what they disapprove of is arbitrary pricing by individual vendors and purchasers. But what determines price in the open market? Following Olivi, Bernardino distinguishes three factors, 'virtuosity', 'complacability' and rarity. Virtuosity is utility measured by objective criteria, such as the strength of a horse, the nutritional value of food; complacability is utility as determined by individual taste and subjective caprice, according to which one might like one horse or one ornament better than another which objectively was equally serviceable.[20] Colours and sensory qualities generally pertain to complacability, whereas virtuosity depends partly on durability and partly on whether a thing is material for something else or more of a finished product.[21] But although value is determined partly by these various kinds of utility, the theory does not exclude labour as a determinant altogether. Rarity itself seems to be viewed as contributing to complacability: people wonder at what is rare;[22] but Olivi and Bernardino insist that the cost of both goods and services depends on the labour, danger and skill (*'industria'*) needed to provide them, and they explain in this way why doctors and architects are paid more than diggers.

The argument against usury turns on the supposition that the only use of money is spending and thereby consuming it. The authority for this view is not the Old Testament –

biblical authors never give reasons for their injunctions and prohibitions – but Aristotle, who in a much quoted passage from the *Politics* (1258^b2–8) says that money was introduced for the sake of exchange, and that breeding more money from it by charging interest is contrary to nature. From these observations even so perceptive a writer as Nicholas Oresme (1320–82), author of the first treatise on currency, derived the idea that money is naturally sterile. Olivi's words, then, quoted by Bernardino,[23] are highly significant:

> That which, in the firm intention of its owner, is destined to some probable profit, does not have the nature simply of money or goods, but beyond that has a certain seminal, profit-yielding nature, which we commonly call 'capital' [*quam communiter capitale vocamus*].

The embargo on straightforward interest-charging remained throughout the Middle Ages. Olivi, however, states a principle which largely undermines the moral argument against usury:

> The entitlement to and actual possession of a thing which is present are more valuable, other things being equal, than the mere entitlement to a thing not yet in existence or not immediately delivered.[24]

As time passed, various ways round the usury prohibition were approved. Archbishop Antonino of Florence (1389–1459) allowed money-lenders to charge for '*lucrum cessans*', profit foregone.[25] He also allowed bankers to pay interest on deposits provided that depositors regarded this as a piece of free generosity on their part, a slightly unrealistic proviso. During the fifteenth century interest on government debt gradually became accepted as licit, and a good deal of financing was done legally if inconveniently by means of foreign exchange transactions.

As Raymond de Roover points out in his monograph *San Bernardino and Sant Antonino*,[26] medieval writers have little to say about wages. Aquinas describes wages as 'a sort of price for work and labour', and Antonino, though well acquainted with conditions in the silk and wool industries, treats the just wage as a special case of the just price: it is to be determined

by market forces, not, apparently, by the needs of the
workers.

Since Bernardino and Antonino were both canonized, the
former in 1450 and the latter in 1523, we must suppose that
their work had the official approval of the pre-Reformation
Church. Their approach is very different from that of the
laissez-faire economists in that they see economics as a moral
science, not as a mechanistic one; they take it that events are
determined, in the long run, by human choices, not the other
way round. It will be seen, however, that their practical
conclusions are not inimical to industrial capitalism. They
favour competition and the free play of market forces; they
view labour as a commodity; they do not condemn either
high finance or the capitalistic organisation of the textile
industry. Antonio was last reprinted in Verona in 1740–41.
One factor, though hardly a major one, which inhibited
Catholic criticism of developments in the Industrial Revolution may be that this accommodating attitude is one of the
strands that goes to make up the Christian tradition.

The work of Bernardino and Antonino is marked by
realism and attention to practical problems. There has
always, however, been a strand of Utopian thinking in the
Christian tradition. It appears in Italy with Filarete's *Sforzinda*
within a few years of Antonino's death, but the paradigmatic
expression of it must be More's *Utopia* itself, published in
1516.

The feature of *Utopia* most important from our point of
view is its emphasis on there being no private property. At
the end of Book I the narrator says explicitly that as long as
there are private property and money, a State cannot be
either just or happy. More refers to Plato, but it appears to
have been only the rulers of Plato's Ideal State who had
community of goods, and More makes it clear that he derives
his idea of Communism from the New Testament. The
Utopians welcome Christianity because they think it Communistic, whereas Europeans 'refrain from pressing most of
the things Christ taught us'.

Of the details of life in Utopia, some, like communal
meals, are probably derived from Plato and Plutarch, whose
Life of Lycurgus has always been an encouragement to
amateurs of radical change, and some from More's own

imagination. Communism of goods is to be conjoined with monogamy. Magistrates elected annually ensure that everyone works, though people are not required to work more than six hours a day. In towns family dwellings are reallocated by lot every ten years. Perhaps the most interesting provision is that agriculture is carried on by households of 40 persons, of whom half are replaced from the towns every two years. In this way everyone gains a knowledge of agriculture, and at the same time everyone has a non-agricultural trade.

The sixteenth and seventeenth centuries produced a fair crop of political fantasies, but it is enough to mention one other, *The City of the Sun* by Thomas Campanella (1568–1639). Campanella is at one with More and with the Protestant Utopians Andreae and Vairasse d'Allais in advocating Communism, but unlike them he belonged to a religious order, and his ideas probably owe something to his experience of religious life. He argues that people will always want private property so long as they have private families, and therefore recommends community of wives and children, exactly anticipating J. H. Noyes of Oneida.

While in Europe men were working out ideal States on paper, in America there were attempts to bring them to birth in reality. We consider these attempts here rather than in Chapter Eight because they antedate the Industrial Revolution. They are not solutions, then, to the problems it generated, but they were available as models to anyone looking for help with those problems in the Christian tradition.

In the same year in which More published *Utopia*, Bartolemé de la Casas handed to Cardinal Ximinez, at that time Regent of Spain, a plan for the American Indians. Casas's motive was hostility to the *encomienda* system by which settlers (on this account called *encomenderos*) were allocated natives whom they could force to work for them; he blamed this system for the fact that, in less than one generation, some of the newly discovered populations had been almost completely wiped out. He proposed that the Indians should be removed from their *encomenderos* and settled in villages of about 1,000 persons grouped round, but at a distance from, Spanish towns. Where populations had already fallen below the level of viability, as in Hispaniola, peasants were to be sent out from Spain to teach the Indians to live like Spaniards (everyone concerned with the West Indies took this to be the ideal), and eventually to form a mixed population with them. Local Spaniards, on the other hand, were to have no direct contact with the Indians: Casas perceived at this early date that it was essential to any plan for the Indians to protect them from Europeans who had already formed habits of exploitation.

The Spanish government made several serious attempts to set up pilot schemes in line with the recommendations of Casas. In 1519 Rodrigo de Figuera was sent to Hispaniola, and founded or tried to found three villages of free Indians. In 1520 Casas was authorised to recruit Spanish peasants and set up a mixed Indian and Spanish colony in Venezuela. In 1526 there was an attempt to establish a community of free Indians in Cuba. These experiments all failed through the opposition of local officials and the impossibility of keeping out local adventurers, but in 1537 Casas got permission to try a peaceful conversion of part of Guatemala, together with a guarantee that no Spaniard should enter the area for five years. Although this project too succumbed in the end, initially it went well: the Indians welcomed the missionaries and agreed to being concentrated in towns.

It was while the Guatemalan experiment was still proceeding that the first Jesuits appeared in America. The order was founded in 1540. In 1549 Manuel da Nobrega and five companions arrived in Brazil. Within a couple of generations there were Jesuit missions throughout Latin America. The Jesuits followed Casas in trying to concentrate Indians in villages and exclude Europeans, and these goals they achieved. Their settlements, known as *aldeias* in Portuguese territory and 'reductions' in Spanish, each held between 1,000 and 8,000 inhabitants, directed by two priests. When the Spanish and Portuguese governments expelled them from their American dominions in the second half of the eighteenth century, about 700,000 Indians were living under their regime.

The most famous of these settlements were the thirty odd reductions beside the River Parana in what was then Paraguay. For more than 150 years, from 1610 until 1767, they constituted a small theocratic state, nominally subject to Spain but in practice almost completely separate from the rest of the world, which caught the imaginations of a long series of European thinkers beginning with Voltaire. Certainly the establishing of these reductions in a district in which they could not easily be reached by slave-hunters called for feats of leadership comparable with those of Xenophon and Cortes. It is clear also that the Indians were better off under the Jesuits than they would have been under ordinary Spanish or Portuguese administration. Whether the Jesuits really made the best possible use of their opportunity, and what the real character was of their arrangements, are questions on which there is less agreement.

The Paraguayan reductions have traditionally been regarded as an attempt at Communism, successful according to Godwin and Charles Hall, unsuccessful according to Lamennais and Proudhon. In *Daily Life in Paraguay under the Jesuits*,[27] Maxime Haubert argues that the communistic elements in the regime were forced on the Jesuits by the Indians' resistance to the spirit of capitalism: the Jesuits were constantly urging them to work and accumulate wealth, but neither prospect appealed to them. Certainly it seems likelier that the institutions of the reductions were worked out pragmatically in response to local conditions, than that they were the result of a theoretical hostility to private property.

Of the land belonging to a reduction, part was set aside for the Church, and the rest was entrusted to the chiefs to allocate for cultivation among their people. The Jesuits preserved the traditional Indian organisation under chiefs while importing the Spanish system of appointed mayors and elected councillors. Agricultural produce belonged to the producer, but because of the Indians' reluctance to plan ahead the Jesuits found it necessary to supervise storage. Individuals owned their own tools but were reluctant to take responsibility for beasts of burden or means of transportation, which were therefore maintained by the commune. Cattle, sheep and horses, which formed a large part of the economy, were managed in common. Building was planned and executed communally, and homes, which generally consisted of a single room, were allocated to couples when they married but remained inalienable. Reductions had a wide enough range of trades to meet most of their needs and enable them to trade with the external world. They had printing presses, could make elaborate clocks, and exported textiles. These trades were under the control of the Church rather than the commune. One consequence was that craftsmen also had land which they took time off to cultivate; another was that the Jesuits were able to determine what was produced. They seem to have used this ability to prevent luxury and even idiosyncrasy in life-styles.

The main criticism of the Jesuits in Paraguay is that they were excessively paternalistic: they treated the Indians as children and never permitted them, much less taught them, to assume responsibility for themselves. It is hard to decide how just this criticism is. Some of the evidence points to a quite intolerable regimentation of the Indians' lives, but there must be limits to how far it is possible for two people to regiment upwards of 8,000 and allowance must be made for the facts that the Indians were taught to read and that the men received extensive military training. The impression which remains, however, of a great deal of praying combined with rigid separation of the sexes outside marriage, suggests that the reductions may have had something of the atmosphere of religious communities like the early twinned male and female monasteries, or the American non-celibate communities of Amana, Zoar and Ephrata.

Comparable with the Jesuit missions in size, if not in duration, was the Quaker State in Pennsylvania. In 1681 William Penn (1644–1718) obtained from Charles II a grant of land which was thereupon called Pennsylvania. Not only did he acquire the ownership of 47 million acres;[28] the patent gave the Proprietor and his heirs 'free, full and absolute power . . . to ordain, make, enact and under his and their seals to publish any laws whatsoever . . . by and with the advice, assent and approbation of the freemen of the said country'. Penn was given this not inconsiderable kingdom in satisfaction of debts of £16,000 which the king owed his family, and he and his heirs never ceased to consider it as a financial speculation; at the same time Penn resolved to use it, in his own words, 'that an example may be set up to the nations; there may be room there, though not here [in America if not in England] for such an holy experiment'.

The example Penn hoped to give was of a political rather than an economic order. He wanted a State in which there were religious freedom, mild laws and a perfect republican constitution. For the last he may have drawn on James Harrington's constitutional proposals addressed to Cromwell under the title *The Commonwealth of Oceana* in 1656. While he followed Harrington, however, in seeking a balance between the governor, a senate or Council and a more general Assembly, and in having limited terms and rotation in office and a good deal of balloting, he rejected what Harrington had made the foundation of his ideal commonwealth, equality in land-tenure. From the start he sold off land in very unequal parcels, and larger agricultural holdings entitled settlers to larger shares of urban property in the new city of Philadelphia.

Penn's ideal State cannot really be said to have lasted beyond 1701. In that year a new constitution removed his checks and balances and gave absolute power to the Assembly, which by that time had become small and oligarchic. After reluctantly agreeing to this constitution Penn returned to England and during the remainder of his life was trying to sell his political powers back to the Crown. The experiment had been successful in part, since the death penalty was restricted to murder and treason, and both Catholics and Protestant sectaries from Europe found in Pennsylvania the religious freedom they had lacked at home. From the beginning, however, the richer settlers had resisted Penn's constitutional ideas. From 1684 black slaves were being bought in Philadelphia, and in 1700 slavery was legally recognised, a development hard to reconcile with Quaker egalitarian ideals. It is interesting to observe that like the Jesuits Penn wished to concentrate the agricultural population in villages, and here too he failed. Those settlers especially who had been sold large farms preferred to live by themselves. These failures can be ascribed partly to the economic inequality which Penn did nothing to guard against or control, partly to the fact that he himself was not on the spot: from 1684 to 1699 he lived in England and governed through deputies.

While these Utopian ventures were going on at the Western frontiers of civilisation, in Europe there was proceeding that separation of Church and State which was noted in Chapter Two. With the passing of authority from ecclesiastical into lay hands, though mostly a generation or two behind it, went a change in men's moral thinking in the political and economic sphere. It is possible to exaggerate the solidarity and organic character of medieval society, but wealth and rank were in general conceived to carry responsibility, while the concentration of wealth in a diminishing number of hands was viewed with unease. In the middle of the sixteenth century it was still possible for Edward VI's government to prescribe a sobering prayer for landlords:

> We humbly pray thee to send thy holy spirit into the hearts of them that possess the grounds, pastures and dwelling places of this earth that they, remembering themselves to be thy tenants, may not rack and stretch out of their houses and lands, nor yet take unreasonable fines and incomes after the manner of covetous worldlings.[29]

As late as in the 1630s Archbishop Laud, with the backing of Charles I, was taking bitterly resented measures to check enclosures. But people came more and more to see the rights of property as absolute, and to accept the existence of a population that had to depend for survival either on charity or by selling its labour in a competitive market.

It would not be profitable to try to connect this shift in moral thinking in any systematic way with the divisions and strife which have weakened Christianity since the end of the Middle Ages; it was, in fact resisted by Christians of all denominations. What we can say more usefully is that it was not a natural development of the tradition we have been surveying, but runs counter to it.

CHAPTER TEN

Is There a Christian Programme?

At the end of his massive and influential work *The Social Teachings of the Christian Churches* (1911), Ernst Troeltsch declares that Christianity has produced only two responses to social problems, both of which are inadequate. On the one hand there is 'the social philosophy of medieval Catholicism, which is based on the family, guild and class'; the trouble with this is that 'it is almost a sheer impossibility to realise its aims at the present day' – we cannot put back the clock. We have also 'the social philosophy of ascetic Protestantism, which developed out of that kind of Calvinism which was tinged with a Free Church, pietistic outlook . . . with diligence in one's calling and a glorification of work for its own sake, with political democracy and liberalism, with the freedom of the individual and the all dominating idea of the social group'. This 'finds to its dismay that the results of its theory have long ago slipped away from its control, and that they have cast aside as useless all the original restrictions and landmarks, whether religious, intellectual or metaphysical'.

Troeltsch's book was published more than 70 years ago and it is to be hoped that the preceding chapters have shown that his account is too simple. It is too simple to divide Christian social philosophies in this denominational way between Catholics and Protestants. Troeltsch's view of Catholicism is influenced – naturally, but as it has turned out, excessively – by the corporativist Catholic writers of Germany and other European countries in the nineteenth century. On the Protestant side he ignores the tradition of English Christian socialism; and in the present century the division of Christian social thinkers along confessional lines has become anachronistic. More important, it is now quite wrong to say that a patriarchal corporativism and an ascetic individualism are the only serious philosophies in the field.

In Chapter One we listed a number of fundamental questions which a social philosophy ought to answer. Although different Christian thinkers have differed in emphasis, and we have seen some disagreements which extend beyond emphasis to substance, a broad consensus should have emerged.

In the first place, property rights are not absolute. They must depend, as Charles Gore concluded in *Property*, on their social effects. The world was created for the benefit of all men (or even, as Ambrose says, for all living things). Everyone, then, has a natural right of access to nature to obtain a living. To deprive anyone of that access without providing an alternative source of livelihood is a frustration of God's purpose and a grave injustice. Despite the prudential considerations of Malthus, this seems to be a principle on which Christianity cannot waver. That it is respected is a limiting condition which must be satisfied by all specific laws about the acquisition and use of property.

Questions about how property may rightly be appropriated lack the urgency they had in the past. As was pointed out in Chapter Two, those who raised them imagined intelligent individuals who belonged as yet to no political society going out and pegging claims to more or less uninhabited territory. Study of surviving primitive societies reveals something very different: territory owned collectively by tribes or groups of families which individuals may have the right, at best, to use in approved ways. Since the rights to abuse and to alienate are mostly acquired either by violence or at a very late stage in political development, it is slightly unrealistic to ask whether the right to appropriate is natural, as Leo XIII argued, or created by human laws. On the whole, however, the Christian tradition favours the latter view, though it does not challenge Leo's liberal premises that the individual is prior to the family and the family to the State. It could be argued that these premises need to be brought into harmony with the idea that the world belongs to living things in common, and with those parts of Christian theology in which God is represented as dealing with the human race as a unity.

The Christian idea of the common ownership of the earth can clearly provide support for Henry George's proposals.

For pre-industrial societies it can also be linked to Christian views about what would be called in the 1980s the 'right to work'. We cannot emphasise too strongly the persistence of these views in the Christian tradition or the fact that they have been voiced at least as strongly in industrial as in pre-industrial societies. They have also provided the motive for Christian job creation initiatives which go back at least to the seventeenth century. About the evils of unemployment there seems in fact to be a remarkable consensus: through time, between Christian and non-Christian and across almost the whole length of the political spectrum. For, on the issue of unemployment, there is nothing new about the social conservatism preached by people like the Earl of Stockton and Mr Edward Heath in the 1980s. Carlyle had the same message more than a century ago:

> A man willing to work and unable to find work is perhaps the saddest sight that fortune's inequality exhibits under this sun.[1]

In the nineteenth century Christians tended to say that capital and labour are mutually dependent. Over the years, however, there has been a move away from the idea that wages are paid out of capital, and towards the idea that workers are entitled at least to the larger part of the produce of their labour. The assertion that they are entitled to the whole, simplistically interpreted, is hard to sustain. All Christians, however, would agree that labour's share of the produce ought not to diminish as technology advances; some, like William Temple, while permitting interest on loans for productive purposes, have wished to limit dividends of the kind associated with equity stock; and there can be few Christians who would demur at the principle of profit sharing.

There has also been a movement away from a patriarchal conception of an entrepreneur and in favour of some kind of industrial democracy or participation by workers in management. There is disagreement about how this should be effected, and in particular, whether worker representatives should be elected by the workers as individuals or appointed by trade unions. The general proposition, however, that workers should share both in the profits and in the policy-making of businesses, though it is not conspicuous in either of Troeltsch's philosophies, is now fairly central to Christian thinking.

In cases where the work contract is not modified by any kind of partnership, we have seen how Christians formulated criteria for a just wage. We have also seen how they came to accept the right of workers to combine and strike for better wages and working conditions.

Initially there was disagreement about the ideal form for workers' associations. Today exclusively confessional unions are strong only in Belgium, where they are connected with the provision of all kinds of services, many of them quite unconnected with work. The discharge by religious groups of functions discharged elsewhere by the State is in accordance with the Principle of Subsidiarity. The Belgian system may have roots reaching back to the medieval social order which Troeltsch describes; but it is differentiated from that order by its modern democratic character. On the other hand even if it were ideal, which is open to question, it could not be applied in a society in which religious groups were non-existent or numerically weak. Mixed unions comprising both employers and employees which were much favoured in Continental Europe in the nineteenth century, in the twentieth have been supported only in those countries, notably Austria, Salazar's Portugal and Franco's Spain, which tried to set up corporative states. Their attempts, for the time being at least, have discredited the whole idea of corporativism. But it should be kept in mind that the corporative ideal can be applied at different levels. When persons appointed by trade unions sit on boards of management or direction as they do in Germany in the coal and steel industries, a step has been taken towards corporativism. Equally a partnership can be seen as a form of corporativism on the scale of the enterprise.

A feature of Christian thinking which has particularly impressed the present writers and which we have tried to document, is the growing conviction that some middle way must be found between unrestricted individualistic competition on the one hand and State socialism on the other. The prophecies of Christians and anarchists alike that State socialism would prove bureaucratic and tyrannical have been disturbingly well fulfilled by events since 1917. Disenchantment with individualism is not due primarily to its failure to deliver the goods. Give it time enough and it results, as Mandeville says, in the poor living better than they did before. The damaging considerations are concerned with personal fulfilment and justice. Among the latter we may mention a change (initiated, perhaps, by thinkers outside the Christian community like Proudhon) in Christians' views of the relative contribution to the creation of wealth of individuals and societies. We are more conscious than we were of our interdependence. We take the point that the power of an organised group of people, whether they are trying to move a large stone or to design a spaceship, is incomparably greater than the sum of the powers of the individuals in it.

It is Marxist doctrine that through competition and mergers, capitalist enterprises grow without limit. At least until recently, experience seemed to bear this out. In recent years, however, the feeling has been spreading among Christians that small is beautiful. There are those also who while acknowledging that a large concern can be a source of pride to those who work in it, nevertheless fear that modern multinational companies are too large to be controlled by law or even to function properly.[2] At the other end of the scale, the commitment of Christians to the family has obliged them to plead for the retention of the small family business and still more the family farm. Among Christians renunciation of private property altogether has always been confined to those who also renounce marriage and opt for the religious life. Although, therefore, many Christians might gib at Pius XI's austere formulation of it, the Principle of Subsidiarity does more or less correspond to Christian thinking about the optimum size of economic enterprises.

But perhaps the point which has been most stressed by twentieth-century Christians who have thought deeply about the question of scale is the need for balance. A close reading of Simone Weil and of Fritz Schumacher will show that they both sought to combine, through linking small businesses together in federal groupings, the virtues of large and small. And it is no accident that this had been precisely the policy adopted by the Mondragon co-operatives in this respect.

The desire to prevent enterprises from becoming too large does not go with a parochial outlook; on the contrary, those who share it tend to be notable for concern about societies other than their own. This concern can be expressed in various ways. We saw that the Church of England and some of the churches in America try as shareholders to influence the policy of multinational companies in developing countries. Individuals have felt obliged to contribute anything from small sums of money to years of their lives to helping the poorer nations. Although it has to be said that the vast majority of Christians do extremely little in this direction, Church leaders since 1945 have taught with hardly a dissenting voice that the richer nations have a serious moral responsibility for suffering and injustice elsewhere.

Our last question in Chapter One concerned the place of work in human life. No Christian can well reject the general Aristotelian doctrine that the good for man is the realisation of his distinctively human capacities. Doubtless there are still those (especially in the Roman Catholic Church) who think that the most perfect realisation of these capacities is contemplative prayer. Nevertheless for general consumption most Christians would settle for something nearer to what we find in Marx's Paris Manuscripts: free and intelligent productive work, or use for the benefit of all men of the natural world God has created for the benefit of all. That, at least, seems to be the conclusion of so prominent a Roman Catholic as John Paul II in his *Laborem Exercens*. It also helps to explain the overriding Christian concern for the 'right to work' which we have just highlighted.

All this philosophy reinforces the need to seek a middle way between State socialism and laissez-faire individualism. Where there is less agreement is on the exact form of social and economic arrangements to which the middle way will lead. It would be absurd to suppose that there must be some single system which is best for every nation and every productive or commercial undertaking. In the preceding chapters we have seen a range of opinions on several distinct issues. There are those who favour co-operative production in which enterprises are owned and directly or indirectly managed by the totality of persons working in them. These co-operatives may be seen (though they do not have to be) as functioning in an economic environment of free competition with minimal planning from above, and in a political environment of the liberal democratic kind which exists in developed Western countries. Some thinkers, however, whether for A. J. Penty's or for other reasons, are doubtful about how large a proportion of economic activity can be organised in this way. But if individualistic capitalism is retained, it will not be enough to have laws protecting employees from exploitation. There will have to be institutions between the individual employees or their companies and the State. The Christian tradition suggests two kinds of intermediate institution: trade unions which are co-ordinated with other intermediate bodies providing welfare and similar services; and regulative as distinct from productive guilds or corporations. The increasing adoption of voluntary 'codes of practice' by a range of service and other industries can clearly be seen as a form of self-regulation.

We do not claim that there is anything like a unanimous endorsement in the Christian tradition for a system of production co-operatives operating in the environment of a basically competitive market. Nevertheless, especially if we think of such a system as embodying a kind of 'voluntary socialism', it is entirely consistent with two of the key values in the tradition we have examined: those of individual freedom and personal responsibility on the one hand, and those of social and neighbourly concern on the other. Moreover if such a system can result, as it unquestionably has done in the case of the Mondragon group, in a wide distribution of real ownership and wealth, then this Christian tradition is fully behind it on that ground as well. And if it can also, as again it unquestionably has at Mondragon, be markedly successful both in creating new jobs and in securing existing ones during a recession, then on this ground too the Christian tradition speaks up loud and clear in its favour. We think, therefore, that in the economic sphere the systems which have been developed by the Mondragon co-operatives come close, and certainly closer than anything else we know about, to what the Christian tradition has pointed to.

The feasibility of this solution has been argued at length by one of the present writers elsewhere (Robert Oakeshott: *The Case for Workers' Co-ops*) and will not be reargued here. But supposing it is feasible in itself, how can producers' co-operatives be brought into being? To the question how Christian social aims generally are to be achieved, the tradition gives an unambiguous answer: not by imposition from above, but by education at the base of society. Education is what Kingsley called for in 1856; it was only, as we saw, after 14 years of preparation that Arizmendi's pupils launched the first co-operative at Mondragon.

What kind of education? Coady's way of making working people 'masters of their own destiny' was by study groups and courses at the Extension Department of the Antigonish university.[3] That has been the regular Christian strategy. It goes back, in Catholic countries, at least to the Oeuvre des Cercles; we have seen that the Methodist system of 'classes' provided, perhaps unintentionally, something comparable in England. But it may be questioned whether this kind of adult education by itself will ever effect any change in the overall social and economic order. Those who receive it are a tiny minority, and they are already, it may be said, awakened. What is needed is to reach a younger age-group.

It has always been recognised by religious leaders that religious education must start when children are very young. The same goes for education for personal relationships and for economic life. If workers generally are to take control of their economic lives, if they are to divide up the work to be done in such a way that no one is without some opportunity to work, they must look forward to responsibility and learn to act together from their earliest years. It is this moral education which is most important, though there is room for improvement in the form and content of academic teaching, perhaps along Kropotkin's lines.

To the question of this chapter, then, 'Is There a Christian Programme?', we suggest that the answer is 'Yes'. There is a wide measure of agreement about the social ends towards which Christians should work, about the kind of society, avoiding the opposed vices of individualism and collectivism, they should try to create. The Christian tradition offers several means for achieving these ends, of which the most promising, at least for the majority of modern societies, seems to us to be co-operatives functioning in a free economy. The difficulties in getting this means adopted are to be overcome by education. To this we may add that the

Christian churches are well placed to influence education particularly at the crucial early stages.

In many countries the churches have long established systems of schools. Churches like the Catholic Church and the Church of England which have a centralised governmental structure could perfectly well initiate economic education, once thought had been given to the forms it might take. Such an innovation might have little chance of success if it were not understood and approved by parents. The task of selling it to the parents would fall naturally on the clergy. One of the more surprising lessons of the period we have been studying is that the clergy have a role to play in the economic sphere. If they can overcome initial mistrust, working people will combine and act together under their leadership more willingly than under the leadership of one of themselves. We have seen that throughout the nineteenth and early twentieth centuries clergy in many European countries, Protestant as well as Catholic, were active political leaders, and it is extremely doubtful how wise the Catholic Church is being at present in trying to stop political and social activity by priests in Latin America.

The main thrust of a Christian programme should therefore, we think, be educational. But we would not wish to exclude more specific initiatives. There is no reason why more Christian businessmen should not choose to follow those who have restructured their undertakings as partnerships or co-operative ventures. There is no reason why Christian trade unionists should not advocate such solutions when appropriate opportunities arise: for example when faced with government acts of privatisation. And there is no reason why Christian clergymen should not seek to follow the example of Jose Maria Arizmendiarietta.

Notes

CHAPTER ONE   *The Social Problem*

1. M. Weber, *The Protestant Ethic and the Spirit of Capitalism* (1904–5), (tr.) T. Parsons, London 1930.
2. So J. Gilchrist, *The Church and Economic Activity in the Middle Ages*, London 1969.
3. G. Woodcock, *The Anarchist Reader*, Hassocks 1977, p. 88.
4. J. Necker, *The Importance of Religious Opinions*, (tr.) M. Wollstonecraft, London 1788.
5. *Ibid.*, p. 31.
6. Ketteler is here quoted by C. D. Plater, *Catholic Social Work in Germany*, p. 11.
7. *cf.* C. H. Hopkins, *Rise of the Social Gospel in American Protestantism 1865–1915*, New Haven, Conn., 1940.
8. J. Bateman, *The Great Landowners of Great Britain and Ireland*, New York 1971.

CHAPTER TWO   *The Eighteenth-Century Church and Laissez-Faire*

1. A. Smith, *The Wealth of Nations* (1776), (ed.) E. Cannan, London 1961.
2. H. R. Wagner with H. R. Parish, *Life and Writings of Bartolemé de Las Casas*, Albuquerque, New M., 1967.
3. D. Hume, 'Dialogues concerning Natural Religion' (1779) in *On Religion*, London 1963.
4. J. J. Rousseau, *Social Contract* (1762), (tr.) G. D. H. Cole, London 1913, II.3.
5. D. Hume, 'On Refinement in the Arts' (1742/3), in *Essays*, London 1963.
6. *Ibid.*
7. *Ibid.*
8. B. Mandeville, *The Fable of the Bees* (1714), Oxford 1924.
9. A. Smith, *Theory of Moral Sentiments* (1759), Oxford 1976, IV.1.10.
10. Smith, *Wealth*, V.1.3.Art.iii.

11. J. Bentham, *Manual of Political Economy, Works*, Vol. III, (ed.) J. Bowring, New York 1962.
12. J. B. Say, *Treatise on Political Economy*, (tr.) C. R. Princep, London 1821, Ch. 14.
13. J. C. L. Simonde de Sismondi, *New Principles of Political Economy* (1819), Paris 1827.
14. *Ibid.*, VII.7.
15. *Ibid.*, II.3.
16. *Ibid.*, VI.2.
17. F. Bastiat, *Economic Harmonies*, (tr.) P. J. Sterling, London 1860, Ch. 8.
18. H. Spencer, *Principles of Ethics*, Vol. II, London 1893.
19. T. Malthus, *Essay on the Principle of Population* (1798), London 1890.
20. W. Godwin, *Enquiry concerning Political Justice* (1793), Toronto 1946.
21. Malthus, *Essay*, III.2.
22. *Ibid.*, IV.3.
23. *Ibid.*
24. A. R. J. Turgot, *Reflections on the Origin and Distribution of Riches* (1766), London 1914.
25. Smith, *Wealth*, I.8.
26. J. S. Mill, *Principles of Political Economy* (1848, 1849, 1852), London 1885, II.xii.2.
27. H. George, *Progress and Poverty* (1879, 1881). Condensed edition, London 1966.
28. C. S. Devas, *Groundwork of Economics*, London 1883.
29. H. Spencer, *Principles of Sociology*, Vol. III, London 1896, Pt. VIII, Ch. xviii.
30. H. Spencer, *Social Statics* (1850), London 1868, Ch. xxv.
31. Spencer, *Ethics*, Vol. II, Pt. VI, Ch. vii.
32. *cf.* R. Hofstadter, *Social Darwinism in American Thought*, New York, N.Y., 1965.
33. J. Locke, *Second Treatise of Civil Government* (1690), Oxford 1948, sections 27, 28, 85.
34. Mill, *Economy*, II.i.2.
35. Locke, *Second Treatise*, Ch. 5.
36. D. Hume, *Treatise of Human Nature*, II.iii.3.
37. Smith, *Moral Sentiments*, VII.iii.Intro.
38. Hume, *Treatise*, II.iii.3.
39. G. Ryle, *Dilemmas*, Ch. IV.
40. Malthus, *Essay*, III.2.
41. F. Hirsh, *The Social Limits of Growth*, London 1978.
42. T. Paine, *The Rights of Man* (1792), London 1958.
43. J. S. Mill, *On Liberty* (1859), Oxford 1948.

CHAPTER THREE *Britain Before 1855*

1. E. P. Thompson, *The Making of the English Working Class*, London, 1963. Subsequent quotations are from the revised edition, London 1968.
2. A. Smith, *The Wealth of Nations* (1776), (ed.) E. Cannan, London 1961, p. 412.
3. S. Cripps, *Towards Christian Democracy*, London 1945, p. 57.
4. W. Paley, *Principles of Moral and Political Philosophy* (1785). Quotations are from M. L. Clarke, *Paley: Evidences for the Man*, London 1974.
5. Clarke, *op. cit.*, p. 42.
6. *Ibid.*, p. 42.
7. R. Wallace, *A Dissertation on the Numbers of Mankind*, Edinburgh 1753, p. 90, *cf.* p. 168.
8. G. Battiscombe, *Shaftesbury: A Biography of the Seventh Earl*, London 1974, p. 334.
9. *Ibid.*, p. 248 (quoted by Battiscombe).
10. *Ibid.*, p. 102.
11. C. Raven, *Christian Socialism 1848–54*, London 1920, p. 106.
12. *Ibid.*, p. 48.
13. *Ibid.*, p. 48. (Southey quoted by Raven).
14. *Ibid.*, p. 32. (Quoted by Raven from *Past and Present*).
15. T. Carlyle, 'Chartism' in *Selected Writings*, (ed.) A. Shelston, London 1971.
16. P. N. Backstrom, *Christiam Socialism and Co-operation in Victorian England. Edward Vansittart Neale and the Co-operative Movement*, London 1974, p. 31. (Editor italics added.)
17. Raven, *Christian Socialism*, pp. 130–1.
18. Quoted by Benjamin Jones, *Co-operative Production*, Oxford 1894, Vol. I, p. 121.
19. Raven, *Christian Socialism*, p. 336.
20. *Ibid.*, p. 337.
21. Kingsley, *Letters to the Chartists* (1848). Quoted by Backstrom, *op. cit.*, p. 29.
22. C. Hill, *Reformation to Industrial Revolution*, London 1967, p. 137.
23. A. C. Underwood, *A History of the English Baptists*, London 1947, p. 116.
24. *Ibid.*, p. 117.
25. *Ibid.*
26. W. T. Whitley, *A History of British Baptists*, London 1932, p. 365.
27. Underwood, *Baptists*, pp. 149 ff.
28. E. Halevy, *History of the English People in 1815*, London 1924.

29. *Ibid.*, p. 359.
30. *Ibid.*, p. 361.
31. Thompson, *English Working Class*, p. 412.
32. *Ibid.*, p. 419.
33. R. Wearmouth, *Methodism and the Working Class Movements of England 1800–1850*, London 1937, pp. 16–17.
34. K. S. Inglis, *Churches and the Working Classes in Victorian England*, London 1963, pp. 9 ff.
35. W. Jessop, *An Account of Methodism in Rossendale and the Neighbourhood*, Manchester and London 1880.
36. Halevy, *op. cit.*
37. R. Wearmouth, *Methodism and the Common People of the Eighteenth Century*, London 1945, p. 260.
38. Inglis, *Churches and the Working Classes*, p. 252.
39. Halevy, *History*, Vol. III, p. 166.
40. *Ibid.*, Vol. I, p. 394.
41. G. E. Milburn, 'Piety, Profit and Paternalism'. Proceedings of the Wesley Historical Society 1983.
42. Fox is here quoted by W. C. Braithwaite, *The Second Period of Quakerism*, London 1919, p. 555.
43. *Ibid.*, pp. 561–5.
44. *Ibid.*, p. 588.
45. A. Raistrick, *Quakers in Science and Industry*, London 1950, p. 82.
46. Braithwaite, *The Second Period of Quakerism*, p. 588.
47. *Ibid.*, p. 578. (Quoted by Braithwaite).
48. *Ibid.*, p. 582.
49. *Ibid.*, p. 587.
50. *Ibid.*, p. 588.
51. Raistrick, *Quakers*, pp. 143–4.
52. *Ibid.*, p. 319.
53. *Dictionary of National Biography*. (Editor italics added.)
54. Fielden is here quoted by R. V. Holt, *The Unitarian Contribution to Social Progress in England*, London 1952, p. 185.
55. *Ibid.*, p. 184.
56. *Ibid.*, p. 185.
57. J. H. Noyes, *History of American Socialism*, Philadelphia, Pa., 1870, p. 594.

CHAPTER FOUR   *Britain After 1855*

1. G. K. Clark, *Churchmen and the Condition of England 1832–1885*, London 1973.

2. J. Ruskin, *Works*, Vol. XVII, (eds.) E. T. Cook and A. Wedderburn, London 1905.

3. H. Pelling, *A Short History of the Labour Party*, London 1961.

4. H. George, *Progress and Poverty*, Middleton and New York 1879.

5. C. Gore (ed.), *Property, its Duties and Rights*, London 1913.

6. *Ibid.*, p. xv. (Editor italics added.)

7. R. H. Tawney, *Religion and the Rise of Capitalism*, London 1926.

8. Hughes is here quoted by K. S. Inglis, *Churches and the Working Classes in Victorian England*, London 1963, p. 288.

9. *Ibid.*, p. 289.

10. *Ibid.*, p. 289. (Inglis is here quoting M. L. Edwards, *Methodism and England*.)

11. *Ibid.*, p. 292.

12. *Ibid.*, p. 292.

13. Clifford's pamphlet appeared with others in *Fabian Socialist Series*, No. 1, pp. 32–3. The Fabian Society later published the series as *Socialism and Christianity*, London 1908.

14. R. Holt, *The Unitarian Contribution to Social Progress in England*, London 1952, p. 232.

15. P. Wicksteed, *The Common Sense of Political Economy* (1910), London 1933.

16. *Ibid.*, Vol. II, p. 701.

17. Wicksteed is here quoted by Inglis, *Churches and the Working Classes*, p. 218, 219.

18. H. V. Faulkener, *Chartism and the Churches*, New York, N.Y., 1916, p. 44.

19. H. Pelling, *Origins of the Labour Party, 1830–1890*, London 1954, p. 152.

20. W. H. G. Armytage, *Heavens Below*, London 1961, pp. 337, 357–8.

21. Booth is here quoted by Inglis, *Churches and the Working Classes*, p. 195.

22. R. Wearmouth, *Social and Political Influence of Methodism in the Twentieth Century*, London 1957.

23. A. Henderson, *Labor Speaks for Itself on Religion*, (ed.) J. Davis, New York, N.Y., 1929, pp. 144–5.

24. R. Wearmouth, *Methodism and the Trade Unions*, London 1959, p. 38.

25. Wearmouth, *Social and Political*, p. 81.

26. *Dictionary of National Biography*.

27. R. Moore, *Pit-men, Preachers and Politics: the effects of Methodism in a Durham Mining Community*,

28. W. Temple, *Christianity and Social Order*, London 1942, p. 19. (Editor italics added.)

29. R. Preston, *Religion and the Persistence of Capitalism*, London 1979, p. 86.
30. Temple, *Christianity*, p. 75.
31. *Ibid.*, p. 76.
32. *Ibid.*, p. 77
33. *Ibid.*, p. 82.
34. *Ibid.*, p. 79.
35. *Ibid.*, p. 83.
36. *Ibid.*, p. 49.
37. *Ibid.*, p. 78. (Editor italics added.)
38. *Ibid.*, p. 78.
39. *Ibid.*, p. 11.
40. *Ibid.*
41. *Men Without Work*. A report prepared for the Pilgrim Trust, Cambridge 1938 with an Introduction by William Temple. Those responsible for producing the report were the late Prof. A. D. K. Owen, Dr Hans Singer and Walter (now Sir Walter) Oakeshott.
42. R. H. Tawney, *The Attack and Other Papers*, London 1953. The passage here is quoted by Preston, *op. cit.*, p. 103.
43. R. H. Tawney, *The Acquisitive Society* (1921), London 1982, p. 82.
44. *Ibid.*, p. 57.
45. *Ibid.*, pp. 82–3.
46. R. H. Tawney, *Equality* (1931).
47. Temple, *Christianity*, p. 46.
48. E. Norman, *Church and Society in England, 1770–1970*, Oxford 1976.
49. D. Sheppard, *Bias to the Poor*, London 1983.
50. *Ibid.*, p. 56.
51. *Ibid.*, p. 151.
52. *Ibid.*, p. 156.
53. *Ibid.*, p. 137.
54. *Ibid.*, p. 133.
55. Source: *A Basic Manual for Industrial Chaplains*. The Churches' consortium on Industrial Mission(s), 1982, p. 3.
56. See Wickham's contribution in D. L. Edwards (ed.), *Priests and Workers, An Anglo-French Discussion*, London 1960–61.
57. E. R. Wickham, *Church and People in an Industrial City*, London 1957.
58. A. W. Benn, *Arguments for Socialism* (1979), Harmondsworth 1980, pp. 28–9.
59. Temple, *Christianity*, p. 42.
60. W. G. McClelland, *And a New Earth*, London 1976.
61. *Ibid.*, p. 32.

62. *Ibid.*, p. 32–3.
63. *Ibid.*, p. 33. (Editor italics added.)
64. *Ibid.*, pp. 31–2.

CHAPTER FIVE   *Catholic Thinking Before 1891*

1. J. M. Roberts (ed.), *French Revolution Documents*, Vol. I, Oxford 1966, p. 173.
2. J. de Maistre, *Considerations on France* (1796), (tr.) R. A. Lebrun, McGill 1974, Ch. 4, p. 73.
3. Denzinger 2980.
4. A. de Villeneuve-Bargemont, *Traité d'économie politique chrétienne*, Vol. I, Paris 1834, p. 83.
5. *Ibid.*, Vol. III, pp. 151, 171.
6. *Ibid.*, Vol. III, pp. 154–89.
7. *Ibid.*, Vol. I, pp. 187–8.
8. F. le Play, *Réforme sociale* (1864), Vol. III, Bk. vii.
9. O. von Gierke, *Natural Law and Theory of Society, 1500–1800*, (tr.) E. Barker, Cambridge 1934.
10. J. Althusius, *Politica Methodice Digesta* (1603), Cambridge, Mass., 1932.
11. *Ibid.*, II. 36.
12. J. G. Fichte, *Sammtliche Werke*, Vol. III, Berlin 1834–46.
13. *Ibid.*, p. 418, (tr.) I. Hellen.
14. A. Müller, *Die Elemente der Staatskunst* (1809), Vol. II, p. 126. In *Herdflamme Sammlung*, (ed.) Othmar Spann, Jena 1922.
15. *Ibid.*, Vol. I, p. 48, *cf.* p. 37.
16. *Ibid.*, Vol. I, pp. 29, 31.
17. *Herdflamme Sammlung*, (ed.) Othmar Spann, Vol. XIV, Jena 1925, p. 325.
18. *Ibid.*, p. 329.
19. W. von Ketteler, *Schriften*, (ed.) J. Mumbauer, Munich 1924, Vol. II, p. 210.
20. W. von Ketteler, *Die Arbeiterfrage und das Christenthum*, Mainz 1864, Ch. 3.
21. *Ibid.*, Ch. 6.
22. *Ibid.*, Ch. 7.
23. W. von. Ketteler, *Die Katholiken im Deutschen Reiche*, Mainz 1873, Article XII.
24. [J. J. Laux] 'G. Metlake', *Christian Social Reform*, Philadelphia, Pa., 1912, p. 210.
25. R. Aubert, *History of the Church*, Vol. VII, p. 267.
26. E. Ducpétiaux, *Mission de l'etat*, p. 16.
27. V. M. Crawford, *Catholic Social Doctrine*, London 1933. (cf.

R. Rezsohazy, *Origines et formation du catholicisme sociale en Belgique 1842–1909*, Louvain 1958.

28. J. Dauby, *Des grèves ouvrières*, Brussels 1879, pp. 70–1.
29. J. Dauby, *Livre de L'ouvrier*, Brussels 1857.
30. H. J. Browne, *The Catholic Church and the Knights of Labor*, Washington, D.C., 1949.
31. T. Powderly, *Thirty Years of Labor*, Ohio 1889.
32. C. H. R. (de) La Tour du Pin, *Vers un ordre social chrétien*, 1907, 1910, 1919, p. 29.

CHAPTER SIX   *Official Catholic Teaching and Action After 1891*

1. Bishop Galván is here quoted by C. E. Castēnada in *Church and Society*, (ed.) J. N. Moody, New York, N.Y., 1953, p. 771.
2. John Stuart Mill, *On Liberty*, Ch. V.
3. Statements which are quoted in later documents occur in the allocutions of 1 September 1944 (*Acta Apostolicae Sedis* XXXVI.254) and 8 October 1956 (*Acta Apostolicae Sedis* XLVIII.798–800).
4. H. Perrin, *Journal d'un prêtre ouvrier en Allemagne*, Paris 1945.
5. H. Godin and Y. Daniel, *France, pays de mission?*, Paris 1943.
6. *Quadragesimo Anno*, section 105.
7. *Mater et Magistra*, sections 32, 75–7, 84–103, 113–5, 142–6.
8. 1 September 1944.
9. Encyclical *Gaudium et Spes*, is quoted in the Catholic Truth Society translation by W. Purdy.
10. Roman Catholic Bishops of England and Wales, *The Easter People*, London 1980, section 164.
11. Encyclical *Populorum Progressio*, section 59.
12. Source: *Annuarium Statisticum Ecclesiae*, containing figures to 31 December 1982.

CHAPTER SEVEN   *Non-Christians*

1. J. Bentham, 'Pauper Management', *Works*, Vol. VIII, (ed.) J. Bowring, New York, N.Y., 1962.
2. P. Schwarz, *The New Political Economy of J. S. Mill*, London 1972.
3. J. S. Mill, *Principles of Political Economy*, London 1885, IV.viii.
4. J. S. Mill, *Autobiography* (1873), Oxford 1924, Ch. VII.
5. H. Feugueray, *L'Association Ouvrière*, Paris 1851. Mill, *Principles*, IV.vii.6–7.
6. E. Halevy, *History of the English People in 1815*, Vol. I, London 1912, pp. 510–11.
7. Mill, *Autobiography*, Ch. VII.
8. Mill, *Principles*, IV.vii.1.

9. W. Godwin, *Enquiry concerning Political Justice* (1793), Toronto 1946, VIII.2.
10. *Ibid.*, VI.8.
11. R. Owen, *New View of Society* (1813), London 1927. Essays 1 and 2.
12. C. Fourier, *Nouveau monde industriel et sociétaire* (1829), (ed.) M. Butor, Paris 1973.
13. Mill, *Principles*, II.i.4.
14. E. Ducpétiaux, *De la condition physique et morale des jeunes ouvriers et des moyens de l'améliorer*, Brussels 1843, Vol. II, pp. 6–7; J. B. Duroselle, *Debuts du catholicisme sociale en France 1822–70*, Paris 1951.
15. P. J. Proudhon, *What is Property?* (1840), (tr.) B. J. Tucker, London 1898, V.ii.
16. J. J. Rousseau, *Social Contract* (1762), (tr.) G. D. H. Cole, London 1913, I.8.
17. Proudhon, *Property?*, III.5.
18. *Ibid.*, V.ii.
19. P. J. Proudhon, *General Idea*, Third Study.
20. F. le Play, *Les Ouvriers Européens*, Vol. I, Paris 1855, p. 423.
21. R. B. Rose, *Gracchus Babeuf*, Stanford, Ca., 1978, p. 390.
22. *Ibid.*, p. 263.
23. F. Engels, *Feuerbach and the End of Classical German Philosophy* in K. Marx and F. Engels, *On Religion*, Moscow 1975, p. 195.
24. G. W. F. Hegel, *Philosophy of Right* (1821), (tr.) T. M. Knox, Oxford 1965, section 258.
25. *Ibid.*, section 308.
26. *Ibid.*, sections 252, 288.
27. *Ibid.*, section 202.
28. A. Schäffle, *Theory and Policy of Labour Protection*, (tr.) A. C. Morant, London 1893, Ch. xiv.
29. Pages 378–411.
30. *Deutsch-franzozische Jahrbücher*, 1844. *On Religion*, p. 29.
31. A. Kelly, *Mikhail Bakunin*, Oxford 1982.
32. P. Kropotkin, *Mutual Aid* (1890–6), London 1972, Ch. 8.
33. P. Kropotkin, *Fields, Factories and Workshops* (1888–90), London 1912, Ch. IX.
34. *Ibid.*, Ch. VIII.

CHAPTER EIGHT *Applications and Individuals*

1. J. M. Kirschbaum, *Co-operative Movements in Eastern Europe*, (ed.) A. Balawyder, London 1980, on Jugoslavia (p. 31); E. A. Pratt, *The Organisation of Agriculture*, London 1904, on Belgium (pp. 93–6); Italy (pp. 118–20); Holland (p. 139);

Hungary (pp. 145, 153); Switzerland (p. 172); and (ed.) R. Schou, *L'Agriculture en Danemark*, Paris 1900, on Denmark (p. 237).

2. A. Briggs, *Social Thought and Social Action: A Study of the Work of Seebohm Rowntree*, London 1961, p. 215.

3. *Ibid.*, p. 237.

4. *Ibid.*, p. 143.

5. *Ibid.*, p. 144.

6. *Ibid.*, pp. 334–5.

7. *Ibid.*, p. 321.

8. H. Rollet, *L'Action sociale des catholiques en France, 1871–1914*, Vol. II, Paris 1947, p. 202.

9. *Ibid.*, Vol. II, pp. 24–5.

10. Cardijn is here quoted by M. de la Bedoyere, *The Cardijn Story*, p. 173.

11. A. Sheehan, *Peter Maurin*, New York, N.Y., 1959, Ch. 1.

12. E. Mounier, *A Personalist Manifesto* (1936). Translated by the monks of St John's Abbey. London 1938, Ch. XII.

13. Mounier's statement is quoted by J. Duquesne, *Les catholiques Français sous l'occupation* (1966), pp. 375–6 in R. W. Rauch, *Politics and Belief in Comtemporary France: Emmanuel Mounier and Christian Democracy, 1932–50*, The Hague 1972, p. 249.

14. Mounier, *Manifesto*, Ch. XVI.

15. A. J. Penty, *Towards a Christian Sociology*, New York, N.Y., 1922, Ch. XV.

16. A. J. Penty, *Distributism: A Manifesto*, London 1937, p. 8.

17. *Ibid.*, p. 7.

18. *Ibid.*, p. 25.

19. S. Pétrement, *Simone Weil*, (tr.) R. Rosenthal, London 1976.

20. S. Weil, *The Need for Roots* (1943), (tr.) A. Willis, London 1952, p. 41.

21. *Ibid.*, p. 70.

22. *Ibid.*, p. 209.

23. *Ibid.*, p. 85.

24. E. F. Schumacher, *Small is Beautiful*, London 1973, p. 245.

25. *Ibid.*, pp. 248–9.

26. *Ibid.*, p. 259.

27. Coady speaking in Winnipeg in 1945.

28. M. M. Coady, *The Maritime Co-operator*, 1951.

CHAPTER NINE   *Is There a Christian Tradition?*

1. F. S. Nitti, *Catholic Socialism* (1891), (tr.) M. Mackintosh, London 1911, Ch. III.

2. P. J. Migne (ed.), *Patrologiae Cursus Completus* (1855), series Graeca (PG) and series Latina (PL). PG 67, 1067 ff.

3. Migne, PL 39.

4. Migne, PL 16.67. Exposition on Ps. CXVIII 8.22.

5. Migne, PL 16.67. De officiis ministrorum I.28.

6. Migne, PL 38. Tract. vi in Johannis Epistulam, section 25.

7. Migne, PG 62.

8. Migne, PG 60.

9. Migne, PL 70. Book of Pastoral Rule II.21.

10. Migne, PL 82. *Etymol.* V.4.

11. *cf.* Seneca, Letter 90.

12. Migne, PG 7. *Irenaeus Adv. Haer.* V 24.

13. Migne, PL 187. Gratian, *Decret.* xii.i.2.

14. *Summa Theologiae*, II^{a}II^{ae}77.1.

15. *Ibid.*, 77.4.

16. *Ibid.*, 78.1.

17. *Ibid.*, 77.2 ad 3.

18. St Bernardino of Siena, *Opera Omnia*, Vol. IV, Florence 1950, 1956, 1963, pp. 117–416.

19. *Ibid.*, pp. 157–8.

20. *Ibid.*, p. 191.

21. *Ibid.*, p. 197.

22. *Ibid.*

23. *Ibid.*, p. 170.

24. *Ibid.*, p. 167.

25. *Summa Theologiae*, II. tit.i. cap.7, s.15; see also sections 14 and 18 for 'damnum emergens' (losses arising).

26. R. de Roover, *San Bernardino and Sant' Antonino*, Boston 1967.

27. M. Haubert, *La vie quotidienne au Paraguay sous les Jésuites*, Paris 1967.

28. This figure is taken from J. E. Illick, *Colonial Pennsylvania*, New York, N.Y., 1976.

29. Quoted by R. H. Tawney, *Religion and the Rise of Capitalism*, London 1926, p. 150.

CHAPTER TEN   *Is There a Christian Programme?*

1. T. Carlyle, 'Chartism' in *Selected Writings*, (ed.) A. Shelston, London 1971, p. 168.

2. *cf.* J. Pestieau, *Essai contre le défaitisme politique*, Montreal 1973, Chs. V–VI.

3. M. M. Coady, *Masters of Their Own Destiny* (1939), Antigonish 1980.

Index